CARPENTRY AND JOINERY

(Wood Trades Part 2)

A. B. Emary
F.B.I.C.C.

**MACMILLAN
EDUCATION**

First published 1976
Reprinted 1979, 1982, 1984, 1986, 1987

Published by
MACMILLAN EDUCATION LTD
Houndmills, Basingstoke, Hampshire RG21 2XS
and London
Companies and representatives
throughout the world

Printed in Hong Kong

ISBN 0-333-18822-5

Contents

Preface

This book—the second in the series—is designed to cover the craft of carpentry and joinery, as laid down in the Wood Trades Part 2 syllabuses of the City and Guilds of London Institute.

Owing to the space restrictions and the large content of the syllabuses, in many of the chapters only the bare essentials have been covered — a fact which, it is hoped, will again motivate the student to go beyond the point where these chapters end and find out for himself many of those things which continually crop up in the classroom: by asking his teacher, joining in class discussions and visiting the college library. A few problems have been included at the end of each chapter which may be the subject of class discussions to bring out some of those unanswered questions.

The teacher will find it difficult to cover all subjects in the time he has available, especially with the shortened length of apprenticeship and the consequent demand from employers and college authorities for students to reach craft certificate level in two years instead of the three that have been available up to now. The book, for this purpose alone, may be able to help the teacher by encouraging his students to do some of the work in their spare time, thus providing 'breathing space' during the two years to allow for revision, internal examinations and — dare I mention? — one or two visits to sites and factories.

Since the publication of the first volume in this series, the Woodworking Machines Regulations have been revised, and instead of including those revised sections in this volume it was decided that the entire regulations as they now stand should be printed. The main reason for this is that the City and Guilds of London Institute have recently announced that advanced syllabuses for carpentry and joinery have been published in which it is noted that other more advanced machines will be included.

I would like to express my thanks to Stanley—Bridges Ltd, Wolf Tools Ltd, Hilti Ltd and Trend Machinery Ltd, for the very useful photographs and information on their portable electric tools.

1976   A.B.E.

1. TIMBER

GROSS FEATURES OF COMMON HARDWOODS AND SOFTWOODS

Seen with the naked eye, a piece of timber, whether it be a piece of hardwood or a piece of softwood, appears to be just a solid block with lines of different colour on all its surfaces. Seen through a microscope, however, an entirely different picture is obtained.

A piece of timber can be cut in three different directions, as figure 1.1 shows. A is the end grain surface of the timber and is called the transverse section; B is a vertical surface, cut across all the growth rings and in the direction towards the centre of the log — this is called the radial section — and C, which is cut approximately at right angles to section B, is called the tangential section because the surface is tangential to the growth rings.

Now let us get some idea of what the various sections would look like for a common softwood timber. Figures 1.2a, b and c show transverse, radial and tangential sections respectively, through a piece of pine. The transverse section (end grain) shows the difference between the springwood growth and the summerwood growth, both running across from left to right, with the parenchyma cells (rays) running from top to bottom of the drawing. The parenchyma cells would not be seen with the naked eye but when viewed through a microscope they appear as thin lines of cells, running across the timber at right angles to the growth rings.

The main constituents of softwoods are tracheids — which form the largest part of the bulk — and rays which are parenchyma cells and which store food. The growth rings are formed by the tracheids; those made by the tree in spring are thin walled to allow the sap to rise easily to the leaves, while those made in the summer are thick walled (because of the lower amount of sap needing to be conveyed to the leaves) which help to give strength to the tree. The tracheids are like long tubes stacked very closely together and lying in the vertical direction in the living tree. The sap rises upwards through these tubes passing through pits from one tracheid to another until it arrives at its destination — the leaves — where it is turned into the sugar and starches on which the tree lives, see figure 1.3.

The main constituents of hardwoods are vessels — thin-walled hollow tubes — which convey the sap upwards to the leaves, as do the tracheids in softwoods. The vessels may appear on the transverse (end grain) section as concentric rings, in which case they come from ring porous hardwood trees; or they may appear evenly or unevenly distributed across each growth ring, in which case they come from diffuse porous hardwoods. One example of each of these is oak (ring porous) and birch (diffuse porous). The other main constituent of hardwoods is fibres, which make up the bulk of the timber. These are often thick walled and give strength to the timbers, see figure 1.4. Hardwood rays are usually much larger than softwood rays.

SELECTION OF TIMBER

The correct selection of timber for a particular job is probably as important as the work itself. Choosing good-grade timber for a rough job would be economically unwise because of the enormous cost of joinery-quality wood. A strong timber must be used for work that demands strength, and a timber that has a reputation for withstanding attacks by fungi or beetles should always be used where these dangers are present. There are many other things to consider where correct selection is concerned: species, colour, matching qualities, weight, strength, durability, ability to be glued or nailed, workability, etc.

EFFECTS OF MOISTURE ON TIMBER

When timber absorbs moisture it increases in size, and when moisture is removed from the timber it decreases in size. This all sounds very simple, but the 'movement' in timber can be the cause of a vast amount of trouble in the woodworking

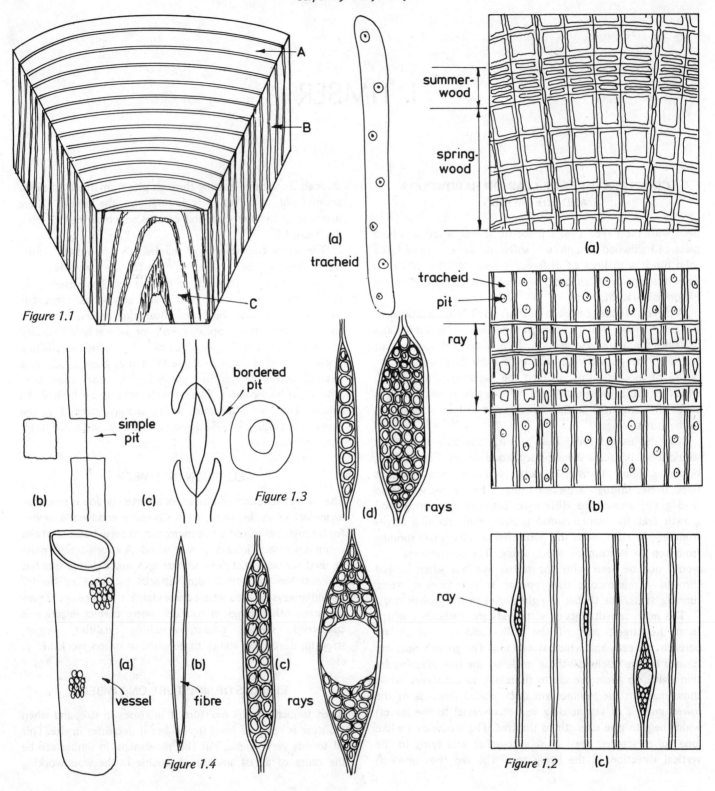

Figure 1.1

Figure 1.2

Figure 1.3

Figure 1.4

(a) tracheid

bordered pit

simple pit

(a) vessel

(b) fibre

(c) rays

(d) rays

summer-wood

spring-wood

(a)

tracheid

pit

ray

(b)

ray

(c)

industries. For instance, if timber is allowed to dry quickly, it dries unevenly and stresses are set up that will cause the timber to split. The more splits that appear in timber the less chance there is of being able to use the timber economically. Doors and windows that are allowed to absorb moisture become stuck in their rebates; floorboards have been known to bow upwards away from the joists; wide gaps can appear between skirting boards and flooring; mitres between wide architraves may open; etc. All these degrades (defects) in workmanship have occurred either because of moisture being absorbed by the timber or because of the material giving off moisture. In more severe cases of timber absorbing moisture, if certain other conditons are present, it is quite possible for the timber to be attacked by a fungus such as dry rot.

What can be done to prevent these degrades occurring? Timber used for joinery purposes must, in the first instance, have its moisture content reduced to a level equal to the surrounding atmosphere at the point where it is to be fixed. Having reduced the moisture to this level the material must be sealed either with a paint, varnish, French polish, or some other recognised sealer; this should keep the moisture at the correct level. Total prevention is difficult even when the timber is treated with a sealer but movement will be reduced to a minimum.

Other timbers, especially those used for external purposes, will require more moisture in their cell walls than those used for internal work. Even so, the rule that it must be sealed when the correct moisture content is reached still applies.

Timbers used for carpentry work, which are exposed to dangers such as dry rot, are not sealed but they must be rendered safe from fungal attack. This involves using a preservative which poisons the food, within the wood cells, on which the fungus would feed.

There are items of joinery where some movement cannot be avoided — things like wide solid table-tops and panels — and provision must be made in the design of the joinery to allow this movement to take place without any adverse effect on the work.

Natural and artificial methods used for achieving correct moisture-content

The seasoning of timber to bring it down to the required moisture content is most important. Wet timber is prone to decay, is often weaker than dry timber and may warp and split, rendering it less valuable as a joinery timber.

Timber shrinks when moisture is removed from it. This movement is greatest in the direction of the growth rings; this is why joinery timbers should, where possible, be quarter sawn, with the growth rings running through their thickness rather than their width. Unequal shrinkage caused by haphazard drying results in stresses being set up in the timber and if these are not released (by sawing into small pieces) splitting and checking occurs.

End splitting of large planks may be caused by moisture leaving the timber through the end grain. This can be prevented by sealing the ends of boards if they are going to be in store for any length of time.

The amount of moisture in a piece of timber is expressed as a percentage of its dry weight. If a piece of wet timber is weighed very carefully and accurately and then dried so that no moisture remains within its cells and cavities, the difference between the weights would equal the amount of water removed. The percentage moisture-content, m.c., may be found by use of the following formula

$$\text{m.c.} = \frac{\text{initial weight (wet)} - \text{dry weight}}{\text{dry weight}} \times 100$$

Supposing the wet timber sample is 25 g and its dry weight is 20 g, then the percentage m.c. would be

$$\frac{25 - 20}{20} \times 100 = 25\% \text{ m.c.}$$

The drying of timber by stacking it in an open shed (air drying) has been explained in volume 1 of this series and the reason why it is seldom considered to be a satisfactory method was also explained. To be able to bring down the m.c. of timber to any required level demands a drying kiln and a skilled person capable of working the kiln efficiently. Drying schedules are used for each type of timber, and if these are strictly followed the result should be a stack of timber with no degrades, other than natural ones, capable of being safely used in the conditions for which it is needed.

Kiln drying

A kiln is a compartment, usually of brickwork, into which a stack of timber can be placed. The temperature of the kiln may be raised or lowered, as may its humidity (moisture in the air). The kiln also has fans that are capable of blowing the air round the compartment in either direction, thus the warm or cold air and the humidified or dried air can reach all the surfaces of the stacked boards.

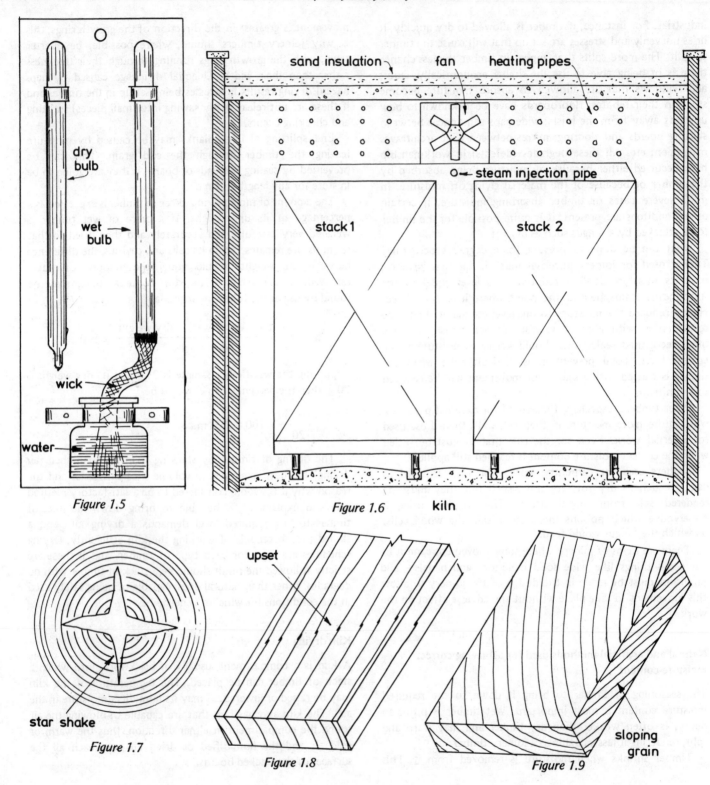

Figure 1.5

Figure 1.6   kiln

Figure 1.7

Figure 1.8

Figure 1.9

It is necessary to stop the moisture around the surfaces of the boards drying out too quickly, resulting in splitting owing to the stresses built up in the timbers. So when the drying process begins the operator will keep the temperature down and the humidity fairly high (according to the species); as drying progresses the temperature is gradually raised and the humidity lowered. This will result in the even drying of all the boards in the stack.

Some timbers are more difficult to dry than others, which means that raising the temperature and lowering the humidity will have to be carried out over a longer period, but if the schedule for that particular timber is strictly followed, the timber can be brought down to any required m.c. without degrades appearing. The temperature and humidity are checked at intervals by the operator, by taking readings from wet- and dry-bulb thermometers (see figure 1.5) that are placed at points around the kiln. The dry-bulb thermometer shows the temperature and the wet bulb measures the humidity. A typical drying kiln is shown in figure 1.6.

DEFECTS

Boards in store should be stacked correctly so that degrades do not appear. The stacking of timber has been dealt with in volume 1 of this series as have knots, splits and shakes.

Defects can be caused by reasons other than faulty seasoning. They can be caused in the tree during its growth, for example, beetle damage; cup shakes are said to be caused by the swaying of trunks during heavy winds; over-maturity before felling causes the trunk to start decaying from the centre outwards; star shakes (figure 1.7), thunder shakes and upsets (figure 1.8) are all said to be caused during the tree's lifetime. Pieces of metal, such as staples for fixing barbed wire fencing to the trees, and other foreign bodies such as bullets and shot are also classed as defects because of staining and localised damage. Other defects may be caused during the felling operation, such as splits caused by the tree crashing to the ground.

When the tree has been felled other defects can be caused by bad log-conversion — such as sloping grain, (figure 1.9) — making the timbers unfit for certain structural work, and others can be brought about by bad use of the timber. Blue stain, for instance, is a staining caused by a fungus that does not damage the timber but just consumes the food it requires in the timber cells. Since no damage is done to the wood it can be used for all purposes so long as there is no objection to the staining. Placing timber in certain conditions can be the cause of the more serious degrades such as dry rot and insect attack — these will be considered later.

Attacks by some microscopic creatures can cause defects that enhance the value of the timber; for example, the attack of a certain fungus on maple giving it the bird's eye effect (bird's eye maple) which is used by furniture manufacturers. Burrs are defects in the growth of trees that have had their brances lopped off continuously around one level over a long period. The effort the tree makes to recover from these prunings will produce bulbous growths around the cut areas. These growths, when cut through will show the complicated growth pattern that is often used for veneer work in furniture, panelling, etc. Crotch is another sought-after type of pattern and is obtained from timber taken from a fork in the tree as shown in figure 1.10.

Grain and figure are used for decorative purposes, some timbers being more suitable with the former and others with the latter. Usually the difference in colour between springwood and summerwood growths will determine whether the grain can be used as a decorative feature; timbers that are often used for this purpose are pitch pine, elm, walnut and rosewood. Others such as European oak, Australian silky oak, etc., are used for the figure that can be produced by quarter sawing the logs. Interlocked grain can also be used to advantage — when these logs are cut in a radial direction (quarter sawn) a contrasting colour stripe pattern is obtained; this stripe pattern is caused by what is called spiral grain, where one layer of fibres will grow in a spiral direction and then another layer will grow spirally in the opposite direction, see figures 1.11a and b.

Colour is also used for decorative purposes: teak is a yellowish brown colour, sycamore is almost white, mahogany is reddish brown. All these and many others are chosen because of their colour. Some timbers change colour when they are cut into boards and exposed to light or air. Teak is often green when cut and rapidly changes to its well-known yellow-brown colour. Cedar changes from a reddish brown to a silvery grey. Often steam is used for changing the colour of certain timbers such as beech and sycamore.

Another characteristic in certain timbers is their resistance to decay and this must be taken into consideration when choosing a timber for a purpose that will expose it to adverse conditions. Teak, iroko and oak are excellent timbers for use in wet conditions. Western red cedar, although a soft timber, is excellent if used for cladding purposes. Greenheart, which is very heavy and expensive, is commonly used for underwater work such as piers, lock gates, etc. When used correctly timber can be beautiful to look at and can last for many generations.

Durability is due to the amount of certain chemicals contained in the various timbers. Tannin in oak is the reason why this timber is useful in damp conditions. Resin and oils in other timbers give them a resistance to attack from fungi and insects.

TEXTURE

The texture of timbers usually depends on the size of the vessels or tracheids. Coarse timbers, such as English oak, are said to have a coarse texture because the vessels are large and as they break through the surfaces of the boards they create a rough surface. Birch, which has small vessels distributed evenly through the growth rings (diffuse porous), has a smooth surface to the touch and so is termed a fine-textured timber. Douglas fir, a hard softwood, has very thick summerwood tracheids and soft springwood growth and should be termed a coarse-textured softwood; other softwoods that have smallish thin-walled tracheids throughout the growth rings, for example cedar, should be classed as fine-textured timbers.

ATTACKS BY FUNGI

Dry timber will not be attacked by a wood-destroying fungus. To be free from this danger, the amount of moisture in the timber must be below 20 per cent of its dry weight. But it must be remembered that the spores of fungi are always around and on the surfaces of timber whether it is dry or not. If dry timber is allowed to become wet, then the spores on its surface will germinate and an attack will take place. Some fungi attack the living tree and these usually die when the tree is felled. Other fungi, especially that commonly known as dry rot, attack the timber in its semi-seasoned state. When the attack has fully developed, the timber becomes brown in colour and is soft and powdery with cracks across the width of the boards as well as along their lengths. This splitting is called 'cubing'.

The treatment of timber attacked by dry rot has been explained in volume 1, but prevention is much more important than a cure. Good construction, plenty of ventilation and, if necessary, preservation, are the points to be kept in mind at all times where timber is placed in suspect positions.

INSECT ATTACK

Most of this damage is caused by certain beetles which lay their eggs on the timber. These eggs hatch and the larvae bore their way into the timber, feeding on the wood as they travel; they then pupate near to the surface where, as adult beetles, they bore their way out. The holes they make in emerging from the timber are called exit holes. (Many people think, wrongly, that these holes are made by the beetles boring *into* the wood.) When the adult beetles come out of the timber, they are able to fly off and lay their eggs on other timber and so the cycle is repeated.

Perhaps the most common of the beetles that attack timber in the United Kingdom is the *furniture beetle (Anobium punctatum)*, so called because it was once thought that it confined its attack to furniture. This is not strictly true since it is now commonly found in the structural timbers of buildings; the cost of the damage this beetle does in the course of a year is estimated to be many millions of pounds. It attacks roofing and flooring timbers, floorboards, skirtings, picture frames, and all kinds of furniture. The adult beetle emerges from timber between June and August and lays its eggs. The exit holes are about 2 mm diameter. The larvae bore their way into the wood for between one to two years. Since the beetle usually attacks the sapwood of hardwoods and softwoods, the obvious way to avoid an attack is to avoid using the sapwood. This is not usually a very practical step, so preservation seems to be the most economical way to avoid attacks by the furniture beetle.

Powder post beetle (Lyctidae) — this attacks the sapwood of certain hardwood timbers, usually when stored as boards in merchants' yards. Softwoods are seldom attacked because of their particular structure. Exit holes are in the region of 2 mm diameter.

House longhorn beetle (Cerambycidae) — this usually attacks living trees but several attacks on structural timbers in buildings have been known in the United Kingdom. When structural timbers are affected, there is usually no sign of the attack until there is a collapse of the structure. The severity of the attack is observed when a portion of the affected timber is seen to be completely consumed on the inside, leaving only a thin shell, the original outer surface of the wood. The exit holes are large, usually 3–20 mm in diameter, the frass is coarse pellets.

Death watch beetle (Xestobium rufovillosum) — this beetle usually attacks large hardwood timbers in old buildings such as churches. (One of the most well-known attacks by this beetle is the one that affected the large hammer-beam roof trusses in Westminster Hall, which is part of the Palace of Westminster and on the same site as the Houses of Parliament.) The remedy for such an attack is the removal of all the affected parts, replacing with new preserved timbers and preserving as much as possible of the original timbers in the structure. This preservation treatment should be repeated several times over the following two or three years.

There are many other insects that attack timber, for example, pinhole borers attack the living tree but when the tree is felled, converted and seasoned, the insects die. Wood wasps, too, attack the living tree and often emerge from the timber after it has been put into use. They leave rather large round holes.

If it is thought that an attack has already taken place, it is best to treat the affected timber with a preservative either by brushing or spraying and this, if repeated several times over the following years, will kill the beetles as they prepare to emerge and thus prevent further attacks.

Preservation has been covered in volume 1 but a few notes on the subject will not be out of place here. There are three types of preservative: the tar-oil, the water-soluble and the oil-solvent types. All these will poison the food in the timber required by the fungi and insects, but the type of preservative chosen for a particular job will be decided by several factors:

(1) Will any smell that may come from the preservative prevent it from being used?

(2) Will it be possible for it to taint food?

(3) If the wood is to be fixed on to plastered surfaces, will the preservative in the wood stain the surrounding plasterwork?

(4) Is the timber to be painted?

(5) If the timber is to be fixed outside, will the preservative be washed out?

All these points, and possibly others as well, must be considered before the preservative is chosen. Creosote, a tar-oil preservative, must not be used where food is to be stored, must not be put in contact with plasterwork, and must never be used if the timber is to be decorated. Water-soluble types should not be used in damp positions because of the possibility of leaching.

The method of application must also be considered. Some timbers are easy to preserve, in other words, they absorb the liquid readily and a deep penetration is possible. Among these are European redwood and beech, while others, such as oak, are extremely resistant to absorption. Sometimes timbers such as those last mentioned are placed in an incising machine (figure 1.12) which makes regular incisions (cuts) into the surface of the timber to allow the preservative to be absorbed more easily.

Seasoning has been covered in volume 1 but additional notes on kiln seasoning are also necessary at this stage. With the correct equipment it is possible to ascertain the percentage moisture content of a stack of timber at any stage during the drying process. Suppose a stack of timber is to be dried to a certain m.c. without the use of drying schedules. When constructing the stack on trolleys prior to transportation into the kiln, notched piling sticks (figure 1.13) should be included so that the boards in various positions in the stack (figure 1.14) can be removed for testing purposes. The board seen in figure 1.15 can easily be removed for testing for m.c.

A laboratory oven is required for the testing, (figure 1.16) and some fine balances for weighing the samples (figure 1.17). Samples are taken from all the boards chosen for testing purposes. The samples are cut some distance away from the end of each board (figure 1.18) since an inaccurate reading would be obtained at the end because of the end grain giving off moisture more readily than wood nearer the centre. Each of these samples is carefully weighed to ensure that the m.c.s in each board are equal. These weights are carefully noted. The boards are then replaced in their original positions in the stack. To obtain the percentage moisture content of the samples they must all be placed in the oven and reweighed periodically until they appear to be losing no more moisture. They are then said to be completely dry. The formula on p. 3 is then used to find the m.c. of each piece at the time it was taken from the stack.

When the drying process has been in operation for some time, a sample is taken from one of the sample boards near the middle of the stack (these may not be giving up their moisture so readily as those on the outside). The board is then returned to the stack. The sample is weighed carefully and the weight noted. It is then put through the oven-drying procedure until it loses no more weight and its dry weight is noted. The same formula is applied, the result being assumed (because the sample came from the centre) to be the moisture content of the whole stack, at the time of testing. However, the outside boards may be slightly drier than those near the centre. To prove whether this is correct or not, other samples can be taken from the other boards at various points throughout the stack. If, when they have all gone through the same process as the first sample, it is found that their m.c.s are the same, then it can be said that all the boards in the stack are equal in moisture content.

The above procedure is followed until the resulting weights of the samples show that the m.c. of the whole stack is at the required level. The stack is then removed from the kiln and placed in a store where the m.c. can be maintained.

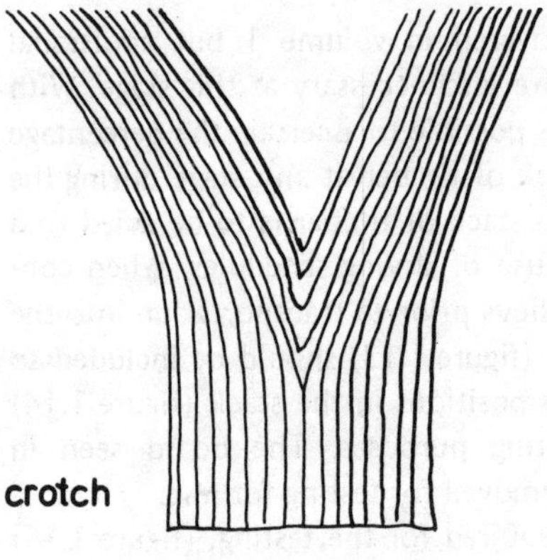

crotch

Figure 1.10

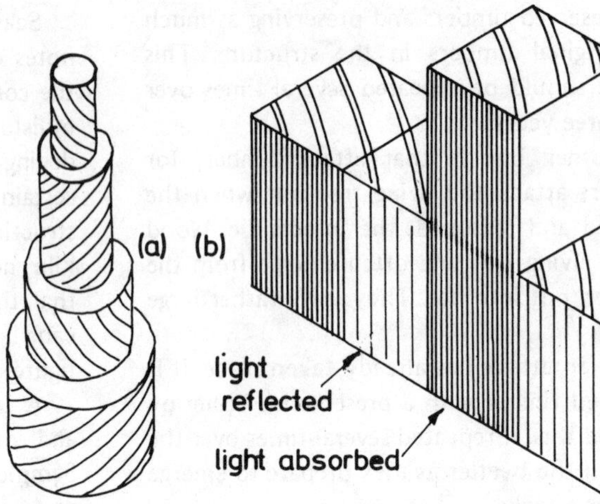

(a) (b)

light reflected

light absorbed

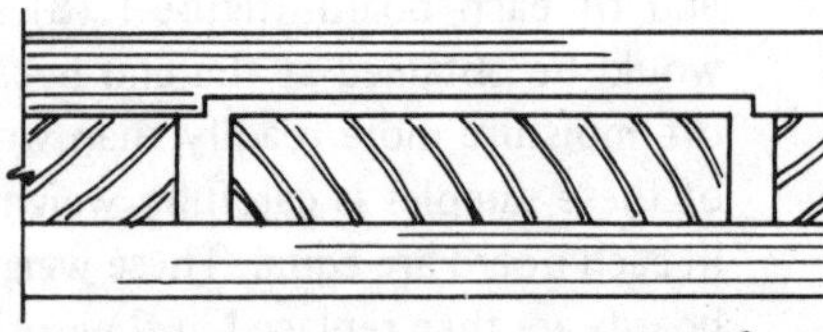

Figure 1.11   stripe

A   B

C

D

E   F

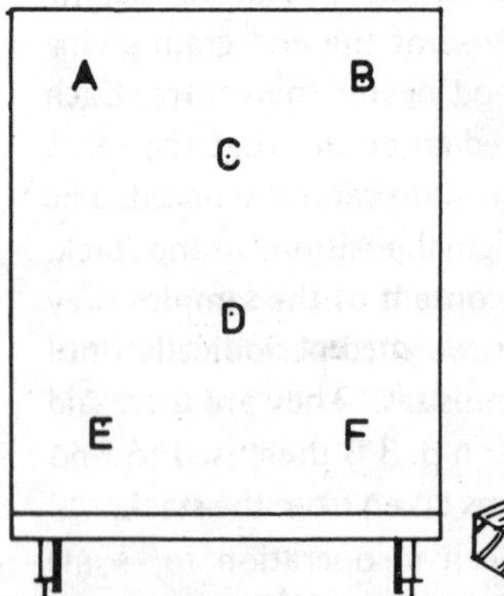

Figure 1.14

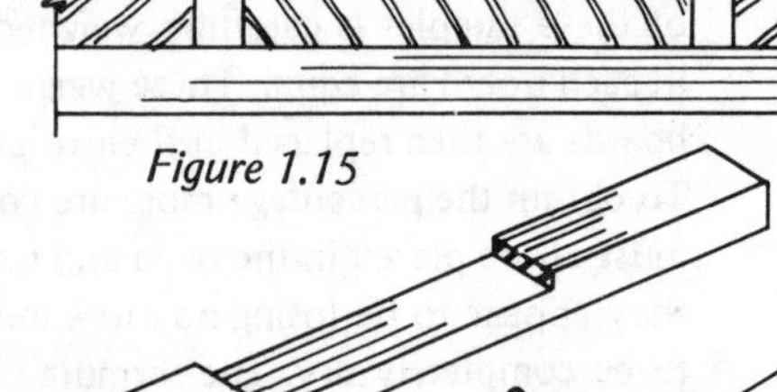

Figure 1.15

Figure 1.13

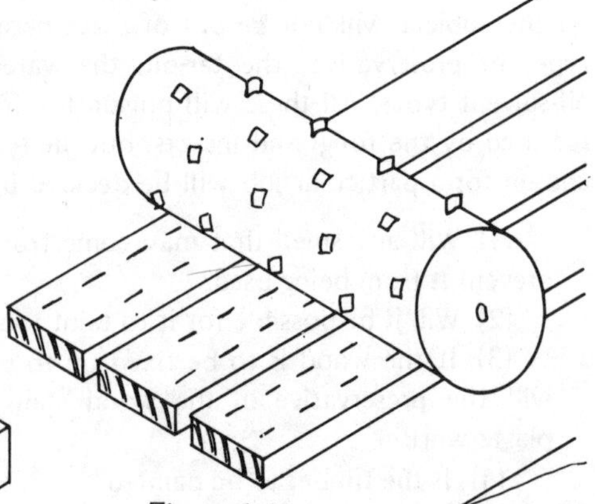

12

225

sample

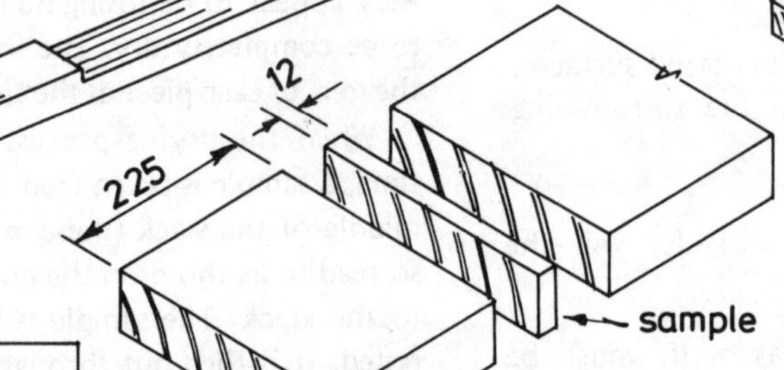

Figure 1.18

0

Figure 1.12

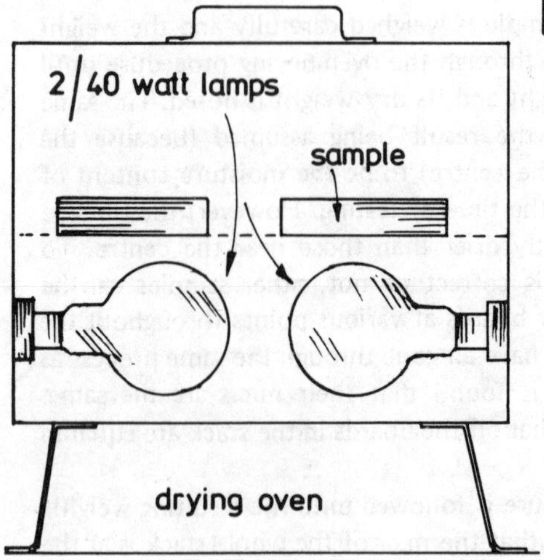

2/40 watt lamps

sample

drying oven

Figure 1.16

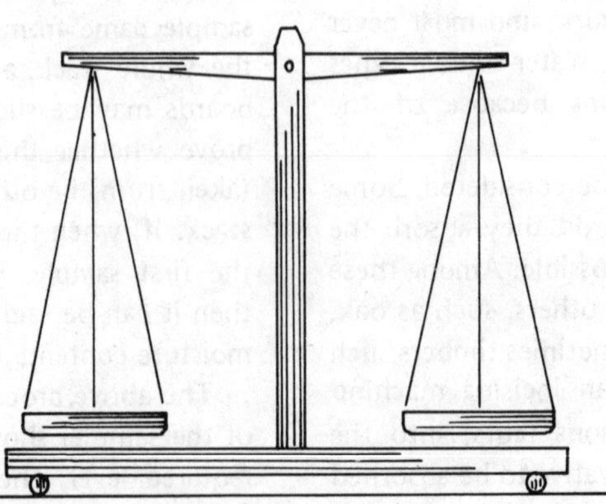

Figure 1.17

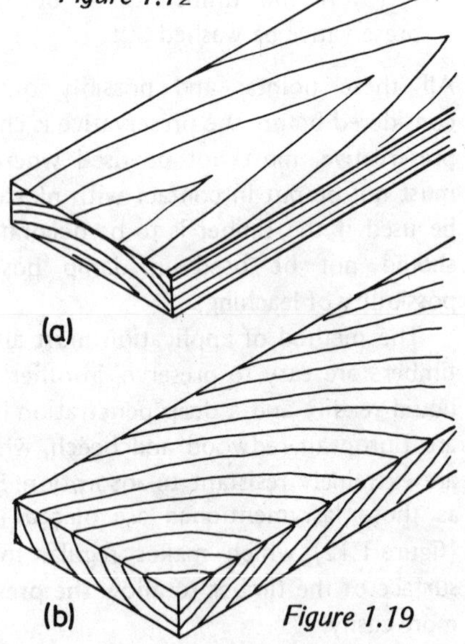

(a)

(b)

Figure 1.19

CORROSION AND ITS EFFECT ON TIMBERS

Under certain conditions wood can accelerate the corrosion of metals. Very serious corrosion of this type is only likely to occur when timbers such as oak are in contact with metal. Western red cedar, (sweet) chestnut, jarrah and Douglas fir are other timbers that can be put into the class of timber that will affect metals (especially ferrous metals) in a serious way.

These timbers (in common with almost all others) contain some amount of acids and it is these acids that will accelerate the corrosion, especially under moist conditions. It must be remembered, of course, that all timbers contain moisture, so this, combined with the acids in the timbers, will aid the corrosion of the metals.

The amount of acidity (pH) of a timber can easily be measured with a meter but a list of levels for various timbers is available from the Forest Products Research Laboratory. The usual method for finding the acidity level of timber is to prepare a suspension of timber sawdust in distilled water in the proportion of one part of wood to five parts distilled water and measure the pH with the meter. The higher the pH value, the less chance there will be of corrosion.

It must be pointed out that if timber in contact with ironmongery items has a moisture content below 18 per cent and is kept in a dry atmosphere, corrosion should not take place. Most of us know what happens to the timber when, say, oak is placed in contact with steel; for example, when an oak gate is fitted with steel hinges an unsightly staining of the oak results. If these two materials must be in contact with one another, corrosion and staining will have to be avoided. This can be done by treating each of the materials before they are placed together. The hinges (and other fitments) can be given one or two coats of red lead paint and the fixing screws should be galvanised or treated in some other way. Bolts, if used, should be treated in the same way as screws or hinges. The timber should be given at least two coats of a good external-grade varnish or some other clear coating of a preserving nature.

STRENGTH OF TIMBER

Some timbers are strong and will resist bending when subjected to loads. Others are weak; some will bend easily, yet resist breaking, while others will break when the fibres are subjected to overloading. Some resist compressive forces which tend to compact the fibres, while others will be crushed under the same kind of force.

It may be said that the heavier the timber the stronger it is, but this must be qualified by stating that two pieces of the same timber can differ in strength because the way they have been cut from the log will affect their strength. For instance, a straight-grained piece of European oak may be very strong but another piece of the same log of exactly the same size could prove weak if the conversion from the log resulted in that piece being short grained, see figures 1.19a and b. A piece of timber could be strong because it has no knots or weak because it contains knots, see figure 1.20.

Rate of growth may also affect strength. A piece of softwood, which relies mainly on the summerwood tracheids for its strength, is, when slow grown, much stronger than a piece which is fast grown, see figures 1.21a and b. The opposite is true for hardwoods: slow-grown hardwoods, especially the ring-porous variety, are weak compared with fast-grown because they rely on the fibres for their strength, see figures 1.22a and b.

Moisture content affects strength: dry timber is stronger than green timber. When a piece of timber is supported at each end — such as in a floor joist — and is subjected to loading, it will tend to bend. If the joists in a floor are too small they show either excessive bending or they may even break, see figure 1.23.

Sometimes, even when joists are the correct size, they may become weakened by cutting out sections for water-supply pipes or heating circuits to pass beneath the floorboards, if those sections are removed without giving the matter considerable thought. Figure 1.23 shows the elevation of a piece of timber supported at each end with a weight placed at its centre. The broken line shows that it tends to bend under the weight. No doubt students will be taught simple mechanics in their course and will remember that, when a joist such as the one shown in figure 1.24 bends under loading, the timber above the neutral axis will be in compression — in other words the fibres are being forced into one another — and the timber below the neutral axis will be in tension — the fibres are tending to be torn apart. We can now see that to cut a notch for a pipe out of the part of the joist that is in tension would considerably weaken it; thus it will be necessary to make the notch on the top edge, preferably near the walls because here weakening will not be so pronounced. To cut the notch from the top edge near the centre of the span would tend to lessen the effective depth of the joist, therefore we must keep as near to each top end of the joist as possible. (Students familiar with simple mechanics will see that the shaded portion of figure 1.25 is a diagram of the bending moment of the joist and notches should be taken from the unshaded portion.)

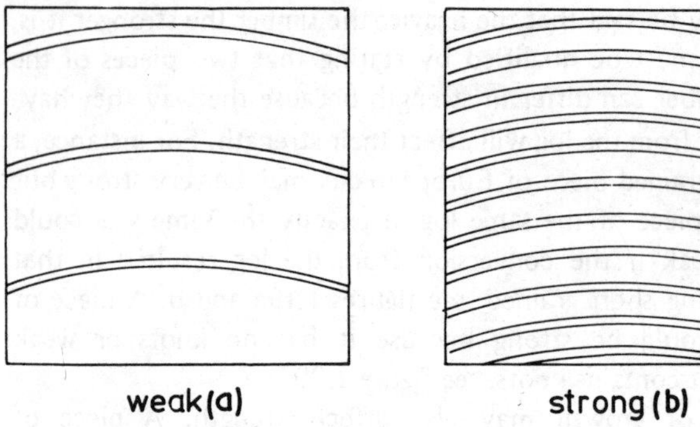

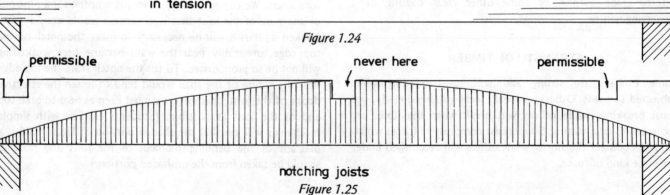

weak(a)   strong(b)   strong(a)   weak(b)

Figure 1.21 softwoods 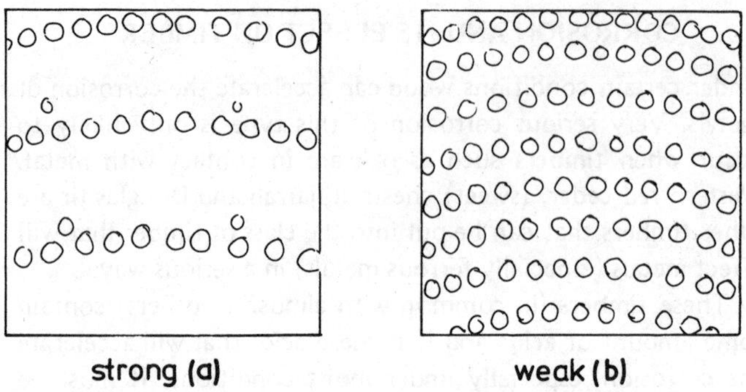   *Figure 1.22* hardwoods

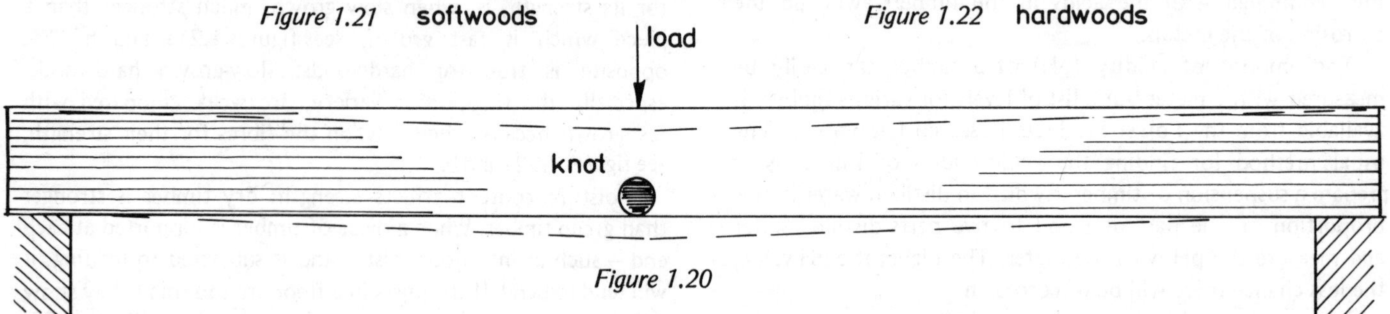

load

knot

Figure 1.20

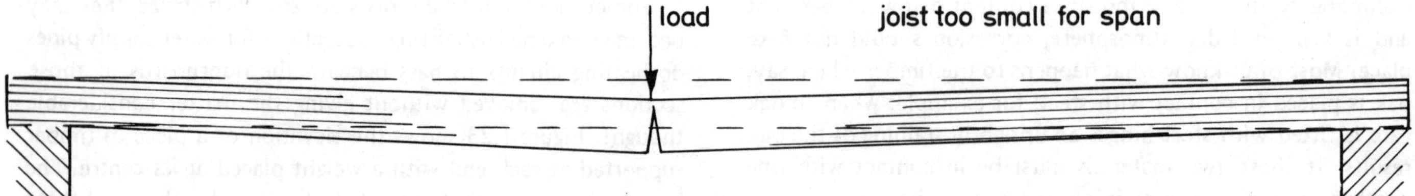

load   joist too small for span

Figure 1.23

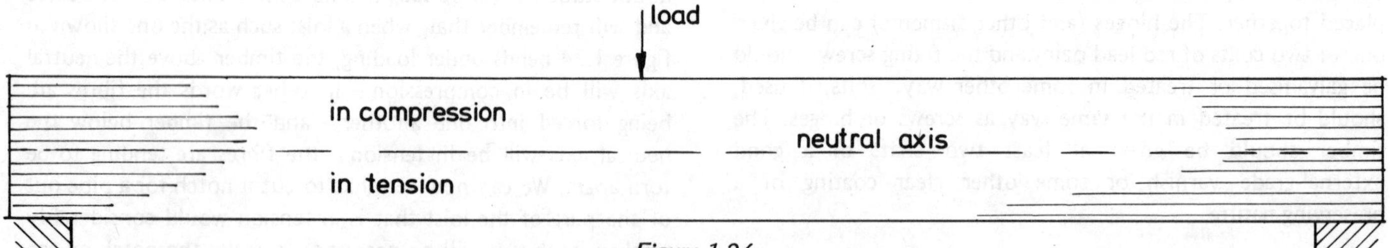

load

in compression

neutral axis

in tension

Figure 1.24

permissible   never here   permissible

notching joists

Figure 1.25

TIMBER AS A CLADDING MATERIAL

Timber in its natural state, and also as manufactured sheet materials, is often used for cladding purposes, that is, for forming horizontal and vertical surfaces. This form of work is used for both internal and external purposes. Perhaps the most common form of cladding is what is known as weatherboarding; this can be in the form of feather-edged boarding, matchboarding and shiplap boarding, etc. Some forms of cladding board are more suitable for vertical use, for example, matchboarding; others such as feather-edge boarding and shiplap boarding are best fixed horizontally; further details are given in chapter 12.

One very important thing to remember is that when fixing cladding boards horizontally or vertically, they must be fixed so that movement in the timber can take place. This is very easily accomplished by fixing at one edge only. Each board should be fixed with only one row of nails and that row of nails should not pass through any other board. Adequate overlap should be given when feather-edge boarding is used, typically 25 mm. This also applies to shiplap boarding, and as added precautions a good bituminous building paper should be used immediately behind the boards and the fixing nails should be galvanised. Fixing battens or studs should be no more than 600 mm centres apart. Vertical boarding should also be fixed with single lines of nails, if possible, secretly. Horizontal fixing timbers must be provided, such as nogging pieces in stud partitions, and these should be around 600 mm centres throughout the length.

PROPERTIES AND THEIR EFFECT ON CUTTING TOOLS

Many timbers in commercial use have little or no apparent effect on the cutting edges of tools and these timbers can be run through planing machines and sawing machines for a great length of time before the cutters and saws need sharpening. Other timbers, however, are either very hard or contain foreign matter that has been absorbed by the roots in liquid form, so that blunting of cutters takes place fairly rapidly. Timber impregnated with certain salts also tends to blunt cutters in the same way. Although little can be done to avoid blunting where timbers with natural deposits in their grain are involved, it should be noted that the preparation of the timber should be carried out before the impregnation process.

FIRE-RESISTANCE TREATMENT OF TIMBER

When timber is exposed to great heat and its temperature is raised to approximately 250—300 °C, inflammable gases are given off and it is the ignition of these which causes the wood to burn. Generally speaking the heavier the wood the more difficult it is to ignite and the longer it takes to burn. The object of treating timber to be fire resistant, is to increase its resistance to ignition and spread of flame. There are generally two methods used to increase a timber's resistance to fire — impregnation and surface coating. As has already been mentioned, salts used for fire resistance can affect the working qualities of timber, so it is essential that the timber be prepared before the salt treatment takes place. This also avoids cutting into the treated areas.

The impregnation treatment can be carried out in a similar manner to that used for preservation, namely, pressure impregnation, hot and cold soaking and brushing and spraying (these have been explained in volume 1). The first two methods are the most effective. Brushing special paints over the surfaces of the timber is done with the object of forming a fire-resistant skin over all its surfaces. This method is less expensive than impregnation and it can also be carried out on timber in its final position; however, this method is less effective than impregnation.

(1) Does a softwood come from a broad-leafed tree or one that produces cones in its growing season?

....

....

(2) What does the term deciduous mean?

....

....

(3) What is a wet- and dry-bulb thermometer used for?

....

(4) What do the letters m.c. mean?

....

(5) What is the following formula used for

$$\frac{\text{initial weight} - \text{dry weight}}{\text{dry weight}} \times 100$$

....

....

....

....

(6) What characteristics can lead to the identification of a timber?

....

....

(7) What does the term 'texture' mean when applied to timber?

....

....

(8) What type of texture would you say birch would be included in?

....

(9) What can be done to timber to make it fire resistant?

....

....

(10) Name the various methods used for the preservation of timber.

....

....

....

....

....

(11) Is a softwood stronger if it is fast grown or is it a weaker timber?

....

(12) Which timbers are known for their corrosive effect on metal fittings?

....

....

....

2. HOARDINGS AND BOUNDARY FENCES

It is sometimes necessary, for various reasons, to hide from public view wasteland areas, allotments and even building sites. The word 'hoarding' can be interpreted as a screen and a pictorial view of the rear of a hoarding is seen in figure 2.1. The drawing shows that sheets of external-grade plywood have been secured to a timber framework which is supported by raking timbers, extending from the top of the screen down to ground level, where they are fixed to timbers that have been concreted into the ground. If the hoarding is to be semi-permanent — which means that it is to be in position for a fairly long period of time — the pieces of timber in the ground would be replaced by concrete posts or even metal angles. Similarly the vertical posts of the framing to the screen could also be secured to concrete posts or metal angles.

Figure 2.2 shows a vertical cross-section through a hoarding and includes a temporary walkway to be removed at the same time as the hoarding, when the work in the area beyond has been completed. The walkway consists of 150 x 50 bearers, bolted to the uprights to the screen at one end and supported on sleepers or concrete blocks at the other. These bearers support 100 x 50 joists to which is fixed 12 mm thick external-grade plywood. Safety rails will have to be provided and the posts to these can be secured to the bearers and outside joist by bolts. Two 100 x 38 timber rails may be screwed to the inside surfaces of the posts to form a guard.

Often viewing panels are provided in hoardings, so that interested members of the public can see what is going on on the building site without having to wander on to the site. If only a small number of people pass along the roadway the viewing panel can be provided on the main run of the hoarding but if there is any danger of congestion being caused by large numbers stopping on the walkway to view, then it would be sensible to break the main run of the hoarding and provide a recess, so that the viewers would be out of the way of passers-by. A plan of a viewing area is seen in figure 2.3. One section of the hoarding has been set back (say, 1 m) and an opening has been prepared in the set-back section to allow viewing to take place. The bearers to the walkway in this section can be extended to support an additional joist, which will, in turn, support the extra piece of plywood required for the walkway surface.

Figure 2.4 shows details of the arrangement at each end of the temporary pathway for pedestrians. It shows that a ramp has to be formed to give pedestrians easy access to the pathway. Small strips of wood should be nailed across the surface of each ramp to avoid accidents by slipping.

CONSTRUCTION OF BOUNDARY FENCES

Nothing will cause the rotting of untreated timber faster than placing it on, or burying it in, the ground. This is very evident when one sees fence posts leaning over at an angle when they have been placed in the ground only a short time before. Of course the rotting can be delayed by using certain timbers, such as European oak, but even these if untreated will gradually disintegrate over a number of years.

If it is to be buried in the ground timber must be treated — preferably with creosote, figure 2.5 — but not by brushing on, which is hardly any better than the untreated timber, rather by a process which will bring about fairly deep if not full penetration. This means either the hot-and-cold method or long steeping (see volume 1); the former is preferable, assuming that a pressure process is out of the question.

To avoid sinking fence posts into the ground, concrete spurs may be concreted in, protruding above the surface sufficiently to be able to bolt them to the shortened post (figure 2.6).

There are numerous ways of constructing boundary fences, three of which are shown in figures 2.8, 2.10 and 2.13. In figures 2.7 and 2.8, are shown a part elevation and a vertical section through a fence with open boarding. The boards are screwed to the outside and inside surfaces of the posts alternately, with a slight overlap so that no one can see

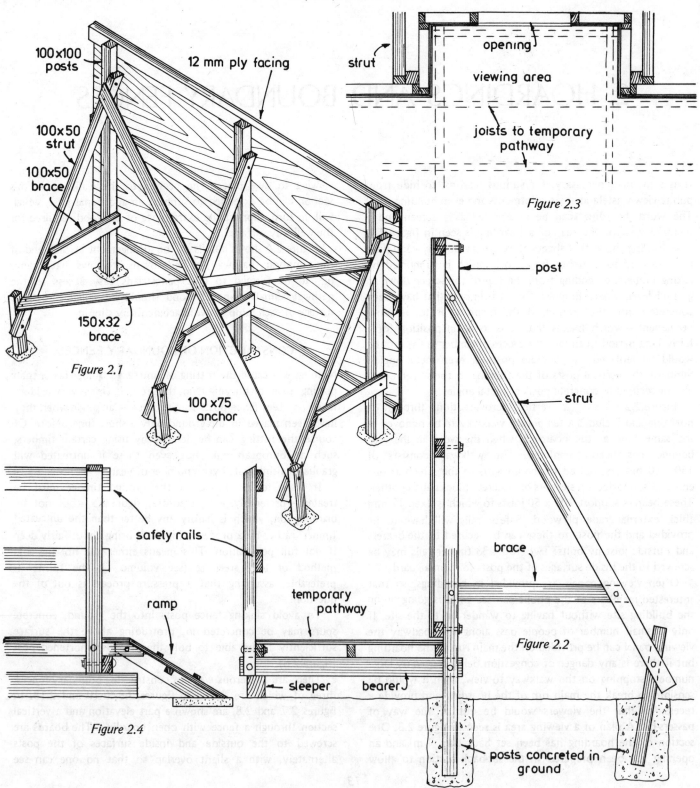

100×100
posts

12 mm ply facing

100×50
strut

100×50
brace

150×32
brace

Figure 2.1

100×75
anchor

safety rails

ramp

Figure 2.4

temporary
pathway

sleeper   bearer

strut

opening

viewing area

joists to temporary
pathway

Figure 2.3

post

strut

brace

Figure 2.2

posts concreted in
ground

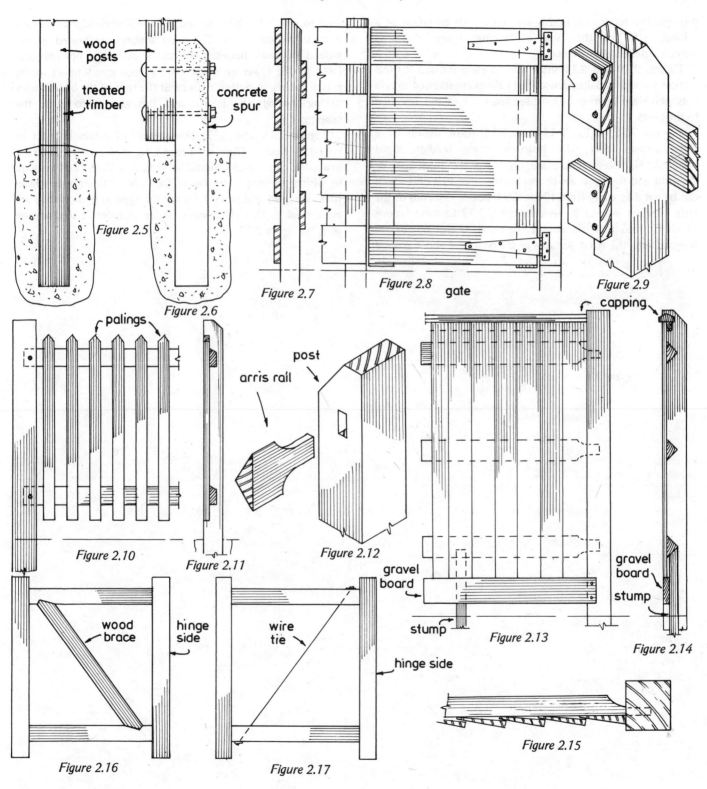

wood posts

treated timber

concrete spur

Figure 2.5

Figure 2.6

Figure 2.7

Figure 2.8

gate

Figure 2.9

palings

Figure 2.10

Figure 2.11

arris rail

post

Figure 2.12

capping

Figure 2.13

gravel board

stump

gravel board

stump

Figure 2.14

wood brace

hinge side

wire tie

hinge side

Figure 2.16

Figure 2.17

Figure 2.15

through the fence. Figure 2.8 also shows the elevation of a suitable gate for this type of fencing; figure 2.9 shows isometric details of the fence.

Figures 2.10 and 2.11 show a front elevation and vertical section through a paling fence. The palings are screwed to two rails which are themselves mortised and tenoned and dowelled to the posts.

Figures 2.12, 2.13, 2.14 and 2.15 show details of a close-boarded fence, the boarding being feather edged (figure 2.15). These fences are usually made from oak or chestnut and the posts are connected by three arris rails which can be cut diagonally from 100 x 100 timbers. The ends of the arris rails are shaped as seen in figure 2.12 to form tenons which fit into mortises cut in the posts. Gravel boards are recessed into the front surfaces of the posts just above ground level to which the bottom ends of the feather-edge boards are butted. Well-creosoted (75 x 75) timbers are buried in the ground half-way between the posts, extending upwards and fixed to the lower arris rail. The stumps give support to the gravel boards. A batten is fixed at the tops of the boarding by nailing through the boards and this gives a fixing to the capping.

Figures 2.16 and 2.17 show details of braces in gates to boundary fences. The first, figure 2.16, shows a wooden brace in a gate; its lower end should be nearest to the side of the gate to which the hinges are to be fixed. Sometimes wire braces (ties) are used and since these are strongest in tension they are positioned so that their top ends are adjacent to the hanging stile, see figure 2.17.

3. SETTING OUT AND LEVELLING

Building lines

Building lines are often related to the centre or crown of the roadway running past the building plot, but they may also be related to

(1) adjoining buildings
(2) opposite buildings
(3) kerb to the pavement in front of the plot
(4) the face of a hedge or its centre.

SETTING OUT AND LEVELLING

It is seldom the work of a carpenter or joiner to set out a building. To set out a building, in this sense, means to mark the position of the building accurately in relation to the building line which is set by the Local Authority, and to provide and fix such accessories (pegs and profile boards) as are necessary to allow accurate digging of foundation trenches and building of walls. It is not unknown for carpenters or carpenter foremen to have to carry out this work, especially on small jobs.

Let us assume that a rectangular building has to be set out on a fairly level site. First, it will be necessary to ascertain the position of the building line, which is decided by the Local Authority. A block plan of the area usually shows this position but a visit by the local building inspector will clear up this point if there is any doubt. The building may come in front of this line only in very exceptional circumstances.

Two pegs, A and B, are driven into the ground (see figure 3.1) on the buiding line, sufficiently far apart to cover the width of the front of the building. They should protrude above the ground by about 100 mm. A nail is then driven into the tops of the pegs immediately over the building line and a strong thin cord stretched between the two pegs and secured to the nails (see figures 3.1 and 3.2).

Two more pegs, C and D, (figure 3.3) are knocked into the ground, protruding like the first two, after making certain

exactly where the two front corners of the building are to be. (This information may be obtained from the architect's drawings.) Nails are knocked into their top ends immediately adjacent to the cord denoting the building line (figures 3.3 and 3.4).

The next stage is to drive two more pegs into the ground (E and F in figure 3.3) so that angles ACE and BDF are right angles (assuming, of course, that the building is to be square or rectangular). There are several ways of constructing angles of 90° when setting out a building, three of which are

(1) a builder's square (figure 3.5)
(2) '3 : 4 : 5' by using a tape (figure 3.6)
(3) a site square (figure 3.7).

The two pegs G and H (figure 3.8) are driven into the ground, with a nail in the top end of each as before, to pin-point the rear corners of the building. A check is made by measuring the diagonals DG and CH. If these are equal in length and the sides CD, CG, DH and HG are all correct, then the setting out is as it should be.

Having completed this preliminary stage in setting out the building, profile boards must now be prepared and fixed to pegs in the ground. These will give the foundation-trench diggers the exact positions of the trenches and they will also give the bricklayer the positions of the walls of the building. Figure 3.9 shows the positions of profile boards required for a small rectangular building with no internal walls. If there are to be one or more internal walls, then profile boards would have to be provided for them (see broken lines in figure 3.9).

Figure 3.10 shows how profile boards are prepared and fixed to position the trenches and walls at a corner of a building. Four saw-cuts are made in each board, the two outer cuts showing the position of the trench in each case and the two inner cuts showing the position and thickness of the brick wall. It is always a good idea to paint the profile boards in a bright colour to make them clearly visible and thus stop them being damaged.

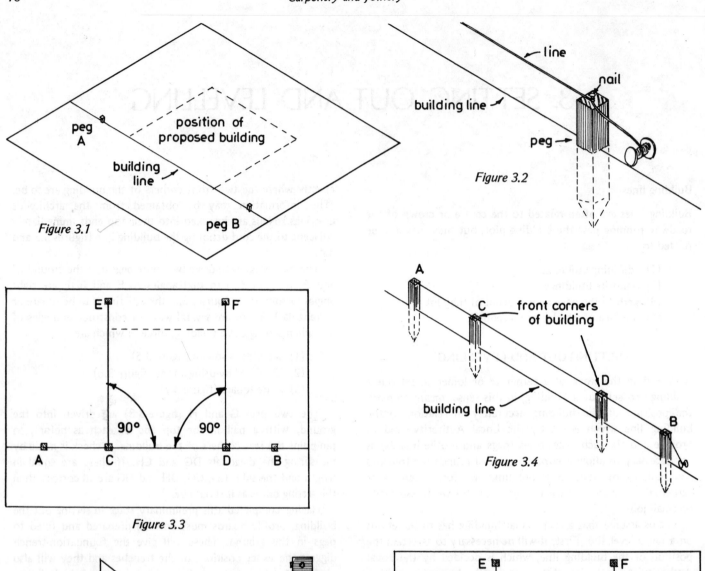

Figure 3.1

Figure 3.2

Figure 3.3

Figure 3.4

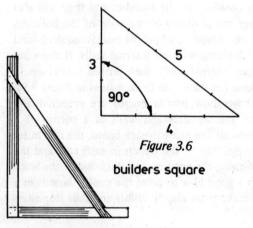

Figure 3.5

Figure 3.6

builders square

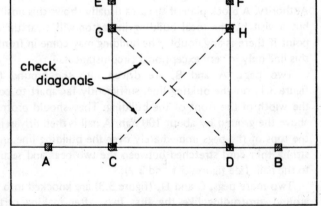

Figure 3.7

site square

Figure 3.8

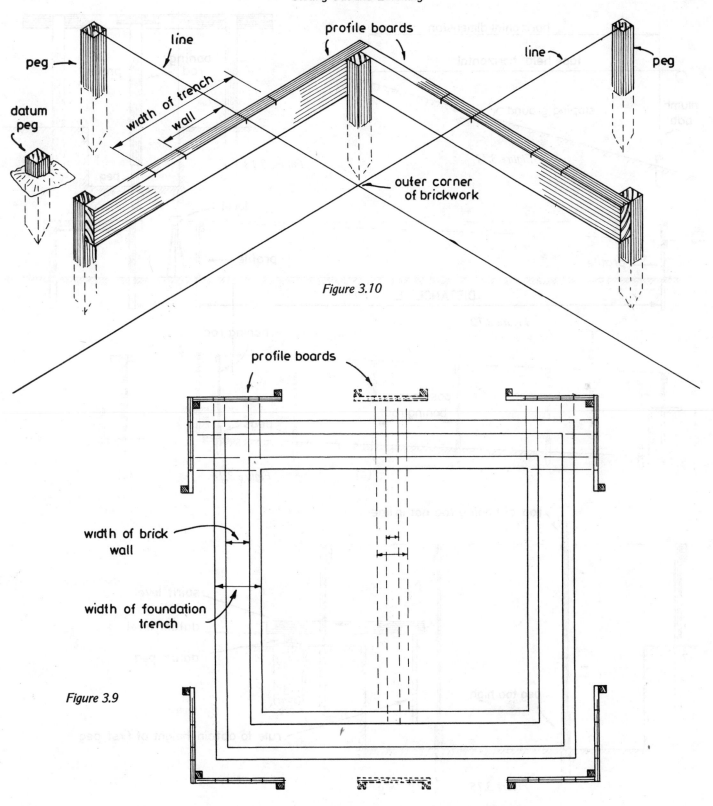

peg

line

profile boards

line

peg

datum
peg

width of trench

wall

outer corner
of brickwork

Figure 3.10

profile boards

width of brick
wall

width of foundation
trench

Figure 3.9

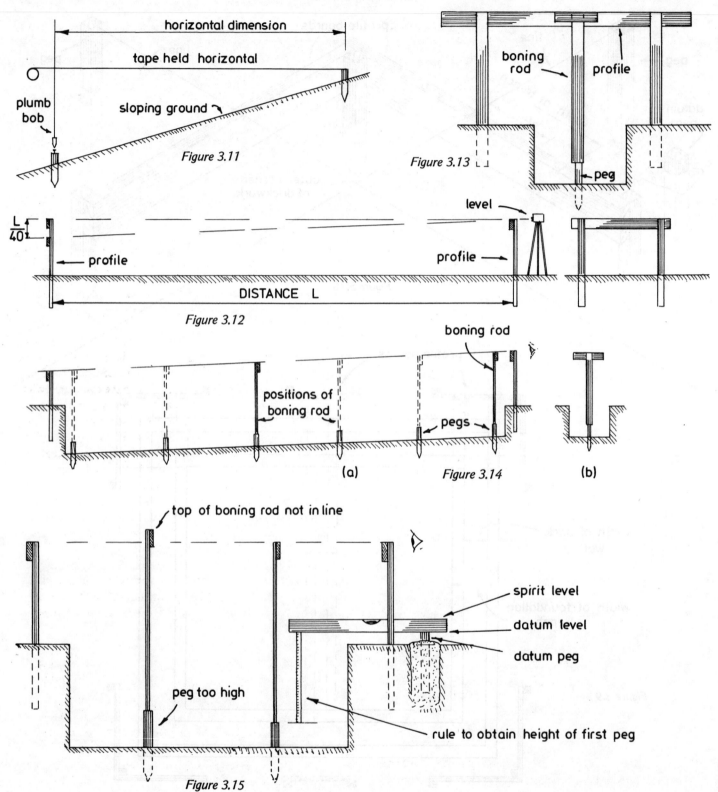

horizontal dimension

tape held horizontal

plumb
bob

sloping ground

Figure 3.11

boning
rod

profile

Figure 3.13

peg

$\frac{L}{40}$

level

profile

profile

DISTANCE L

Figure 3.12

boning rod

positions of
boning rod

pegs

(a)   *Figure 3.14*   (b)

top of boning rod not in line

spirit level

datum level

datum peg

peg too high

rule to obtain height of first peg

Figure 3.15

Where setting out has to be done on a sloping site the various distances must be measured by holding the tape horizontal and then pin-pointing the peg positions with the use of a plumb line, see figure 3.11.

Before positioning the saw cuts in the profile boards, check and recheck to ensure that the building corners are square; adjust if necessary.

It may be necessary for a carpenter not only to provide pegs and other accessories for the bricklayer and concreter but also — especially if he is responsible for the smooth running of the job — to assist in the positioning of those accessories. He may be required, for instance, to set the pegs in the bottom of a trench to give the top surface of the concrete for a run of drain. The drain would, of course, have to fall at some specified gradient, therefore the trench would have to slope downwards to the lower level of the drain, and the tops of the pegs driven in the bottom of the trench would also have to slope downwards at the correct gradient.

First it is necessary to set up some profile boards at each end of the run of drain. These, with the assistance of a Cowley or Dumpy level, can be fixed by driving the uprights into the ground at each end and fixing horizontal boards across them, so that the two boards are level. If a fall of, say, 1 in 40 is required for the drain, the distance between the profile boards should be measured and this dimension divided by 40. This figure should be deducted from the height of the profile at the lower end of the drain and the board fixed at the new height (see figure 3.12).

When the trench has been dug near enough to its correct depth, the first peg should be driven into the bottom with its top surface in the position of the top of the trench concrete at that point. Other pegs should also be driven into the trench bottom at regular intervals along its length and when all have been driven in, their tops should all be in line and at the correct gradient. To achieve this successfully a boning rod is required. This looks like a tee-square (figure 3.13) and is placed on each peg in turn; by sighting the top of the boning rod with the tops of the profile boards at each end, the top of each peg can be brought to its correct height. By sighting through the tops of the profile boards, (figure 3.14) it can be seen whether a peg is in its correct positon by placing the boning rod on the top of the peg. If it is correct, the tops of the profiles and the top of the boning rod will all be in line. Figure 3.15 shows what would happen if a peg were too high.

Datum

This is usually a level shown on a building site by a wooden peg set in concrete and often gives the level of the ground floor of the building being constructed; thus all other levels are related to the datum. The concreter will, of course, know how much below the datum level the top of his foundation concrete will be, so he will be sure to check that the tops of the pegs in the foundation trenches are that much below the datum level (figure 3.15). Other workers, such as the drain-layer, will also check to see that the levels related to their own trades are correct when compared to the datum level.

COWLEY AUTOMATIC LEVEL

The Cowley automatic level is used for levelling sites, foundations, setting out gradients, checking brickwork courses during erection and establishing levels in buildings for the fixing of joinery, wall tiling, plumbing, etc. It gives an automatic level line of sight which is accurate to 6 mm in 30 m and is extremely simple to use.

The instrument consists of a metal casing containing a dual system of mirrors and is mounted on to an aluminium-alloy tripod by slipping a vertical pin at the top of the tripod into a hole in the base of the instrument casing. The instrument can be revolved around the axis of this pin to point in the direction required. The last 5 mm of the insertion of the pin into the casing releases a pendulum inside the casing, allowing the pendulum to assume a vertical position even if the casing itself is not level. This pendulum has a mirror attached to it, and by its vertical position ensures that one half of the 'split' image is seen along a horizontal line. Having placed the instrument over the pin on the tripod, the level is ready for use; no further adjustment is necessary.

The level is used in conjunction with an aluminium-alloy staff with a target (a cross-piece that slides up and down the staff) that can be adjusted to give correct sight (see figures 3.16 and 3.17). The staff is marked in metric and Imperial units and has an indicator to enable the correct dimension to be read. When a correct sight is obtained the dimension indicated on the back of the staff is the measurement from the base of the staff to the horizontal line being viewed from the instrument.

Method of use

(1) Set up the tripod, place the instrument over the pin and, by eye, roughly, level the instrument.

(2) Sight the instrument on to the target; if the target is not on a level line you will see 'A', 'B' or 'C' (figure 3.16).

(3) Move the target up or down until a correct sight is obtained as 'D', 'E' or 'F'.

(4) The target is then level with the line of sight from the instrument and the height above the base of the staff can be read off the scales at the back of the staff.

It can now be seen that if several readings are taken the difference in ground levels can easily be obtained, see figure 3.17.

Datum lines around rooms for fixing of high-class joinery becomes a simple operation. The level is set up roughly in the centre of a room and the staff is placed at intervals along the walls and adjusted until a correct sight is seen in the instrument. The wall can then be marked directly off the staff scale or the measurement noted and then marked up the wall from the floor. These interval marks can then be connected up with a straight edge.

Gradients

To set out profiles for rise and fall gradients 'variable-slope attachments' are available. These attachments fit over the viewing aperture of the instrument and are clearly marked 'rise' and 'fall'. A dial is set to the gradient required and this alters the line of sight from horizontal along the required gradient. The method of use is as follows.

(1) Set up Cowley level.

(2) Attach the variable-slope attachment and set the gradient required.

(3) Sight through the level and fix the target at the correct height so that a correct sight is seen.

(4) Leave target at this position on the staff and use the staff as a 'traveller' on to the tops of pegs that are knocked down until a correct sight is seen at the level (see figure 3.18).

This method is adaptable to trench depths instead of peg tops.

A stand is available so that the level may be set up without using the tripod and can be used advantageously when checking brickwork courses. Two people are needed: one to view through the level and the other to hold, adjust and read the staff. It is essential that the level is always removed from the tripod/stand when being moved around. This ensures the protection of the mechanism inside the level, since the pendulum is locked when the level is removed from the pin on the tripod.

THE SITE SQUARE

The primary use of the site square (figure 3.19) is for setting out right angles on the site — as its name implies. It is a very accurate instrument and is very simple to use. The site square consists of

(a) A tripod with adjustable legs incorporating a datum rod containing a spike. The spike is reversible, one end has a point for use on marks, etc., and the other end is hollowed out to sit over a nail head. The spike slides up and down within the datum rod and can be fixed at any position by the spike screw.

(b) A cylindrical case in which two telescopes are accurately set at 90° to each other. Each of these telescopes can be moved independently in the vertical plane but are always at 90° to each other in plan.

The instrument is screwed to the tripod head and can then be turned in the horizontal plane, locked and slow motioned left or right on to targets. In the top of the instrument is a circular spirit bubble with an inner circle.

Method of use

(1) Mark out the front line of the building with 50 x 50 wood pegs with nails set in their tops so that the distances and angles can be measured accurately.

(2) Mount tripod directly on to the nail in one of the pegs. This is done by extending the spike (while the tripod legs are still closed) over the top of the nail and locking the spike screw. Release the legs, extending and locking them.

(3) Screw the site square to the tripod head by securing the locking nut and turning the instrument round until it locks. Release the locking screw and rotate the instrument until the lower telescope points roughly in the direction of the other peg, that is, along the front line of the building. Secure the locking screw.

(4) Position the instrument vertically over the nail using the circular bubble in the top of the instrument; this is done by releasing the tripod leg screws and, with the spike still sitting over the nail, moving the instrument about until the bubble is in the centre of the inner circle. Secure the tripod legs *and check the bubble.*

(5) Sight the bottom telescope on to the far peg by tilting the telescope up or down and using the fine-setting screw until a correct view is obtained (see figure 3.20).

(6) View the other telescope and position a peg and nail accurately for distance with a correct view so that the angle is at 90°. Repeat this by setting up over the far peg and setting out the other flank wall.

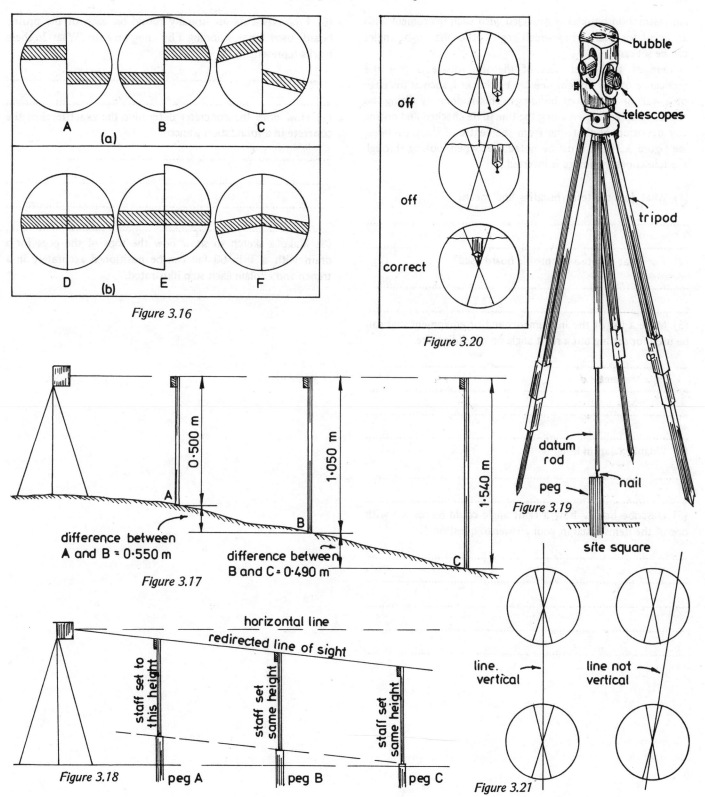

Figure 3.16

Figure 3.20

Figure 3.19

Figure 3.17

Figure 3.18

Figure 3.21

An instruction booklet is provided with each instrument with an angulator chart from which angles other than right angles can be set out.

One of the other uses of the site square is that the verticality of any upright line can be checked, such as the edge of a wall or corners of buildings. This is done by tilting the telescope up and down along the line to be checked and noting any deviation of that line from the centre of the cross-lines, see figure 3.21. (It must be noted that when looking through the telescopes the image is inverted.)

(1) What does the term 'building line' mean?

....

....

(2) For what purpose is a profile board used?

....

....

(3) Make a list of the instruments and/or equipment that can be used for setting out a right angle on a building site.

....

....

....

....

(4) What is a datum level?

....

....

(5) Describe briefly how a right angle could be set out with one of the items listed in your answer to question 3.

....

....

....

....

....

(6) Four saw-cuts are usually found on each of the profile boards used for positioning a building on a site. What do these marks represent?

....

....

(7) How does the concreter determine the exact level of the concrete in a foundation trench?

....

....

....

....

(8) Make a sketch to show how the tops of the pegs for a drain with a 1 in 60 fall can be positioned accurately in a trench and explain each step illustrated.

4. SCAFFOLDING

Many firms employ a skilled man to be responsible for the erection of scaffolding. These working platforms are subjected to superimposed loads (which include the people working on the scaffolding, the materials stacked on the platform, etc.), live loads, which can be quite substantial at times, include men walking along the platforms with loaded barrows, etc., and dead loads which are the weights of the various materials used in the structure. All these added together require a scaffolding to be erected to conform with good practice. The following are recommended for further reading, dealing with scaffolding and covering materials and good practice.

(1) BS 1139: 1964 Metal scaffolding
(2) BS CP 97: Part I: 1967 Common scaffolds in steel
(3) Construction Regulations S.I.94: 1966: Working
Places.

Although scaffolding is best erected by a skilled scaffolder, it may be necessary from time to time for craftsmen to erect their own scaffold, especially if it is to be one of up to two lifts. The selection of the materials for a scaffold is important. The tubes should be straight and rust free, the fittings used for connecting the various parts should be kept in good condition by periodic oiling. No couplers should be used if they appear to be bent or broken. Scaffold boards should be sound and free from splits and bound at their ends with hoop iron. Ladders should be carefully inspected to see that all the rungs are in position and sound and also that the strings are not broken.

There are two common types of scaffold: (1) putlog and (2) independent. Figure 4.1 is the elevation of a putlog scaffold. Figure 4.2 is an end view of a putlog scaffold. The standards must be perfectly vertical and the ledgers horizontal and fixed on the insides of the standards. The usual size for scaffold boards is 225 x 38; they are supported near to each end with at least one more support in between. Boards are usually butt jointed end to end and must never overlap their end supports by more than four times their thickness. The

supports to the boards are either putlogs or transoms (see figures 4.2 and 4.6).

A scaffold should only be erected on ground that is level. Plates, usually scaffold boards, are placed on the levelled ground and the scaffold erected over the plates (figure 4.3).

Figure 4.3 shows details of the foot of a standard and shows the end of a sole plate in position with a base plate resting on the sole plate ready to receive the lower end of the standard.

To prevent accidents to people below the platforms, timber toe-boards must be fixed along the outside edges of all platforms and at both ends. These are usually 150 x 32; they stop objects being accidentally kicked off the scaffolding. Also of importance is the fixing of a guard rail along the length and across the ends of a working platform, to protect those working on the scaffolding from accidentally stepping backwords and falling to the ground. If, for any reason at all, guard rails and/or toe boards are removed from the scaffolding, they must immediately be replaced, once the work for which they were removed has been completed. Failure to do this may result in an accident.

Figure 4.2 shows an end view of a putlog scaffold. It consists of boards supported on putlogs which are supported on ledgers at the ends furthest from the building, with their other ends resting on the brickwork. To enable the brickwork to be carried upwards above the putlogs, the ends that rest on the brickwork are flattened to approximately the thickness of a brickwork joint. They can be removed quite easily when the scaffolding is dismantled and the holes filled in. Care must be taken to ensure that the whole of the flattened portion of the putlogs rests on the brickwork, see figure 4.4.

Scaffolds should, wherever possible, be tied to the building. This means that short lengths of tube, fixed to the scaffolding, are made to pass through openings in the wall, windows, etc., with vertical tubes fixed to these inside the building; see figure 4.5. These ties will prevent any tendency for the scaffolding to fall away from the building. Pads of timber

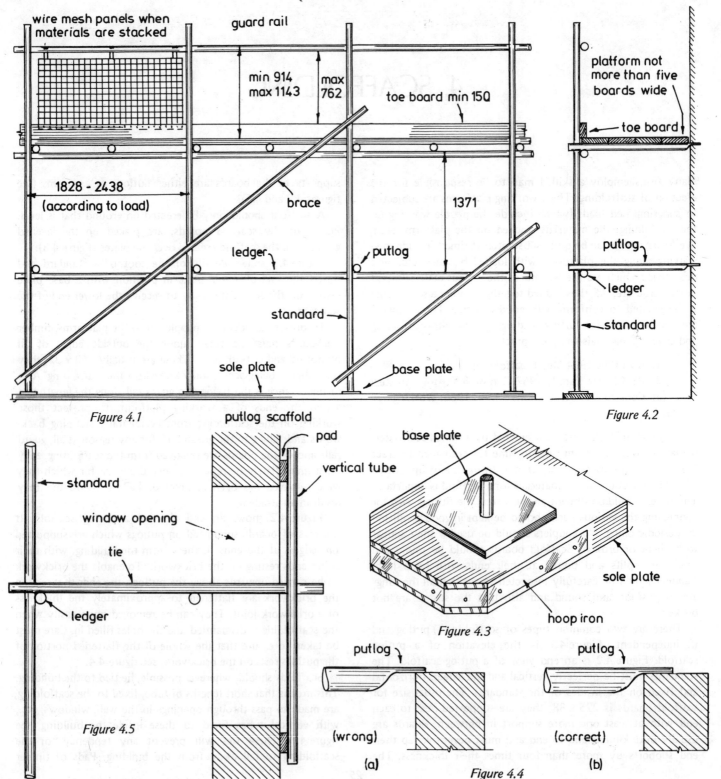

wire mesh panels when materials are stacked

guard rail

min 914
max 1143

max 762

toe board min 150

1828 - 2438
(according to load)

brace

ledger

putlog

1371

standard

sole plate

base plate

Figure 4.1 putlog scaffold

platform not more than five boards wide

toe board

putlog

ledger

standard

Figure 4.2

standard

window opening

tie

ledger

Figure 4.5

pad

vertical tube

base plate

sole plate

hoop iron

Figure 4.3

putlog

(wrong)

(a)

putlog

(correct)

(b)

Figure 4.4

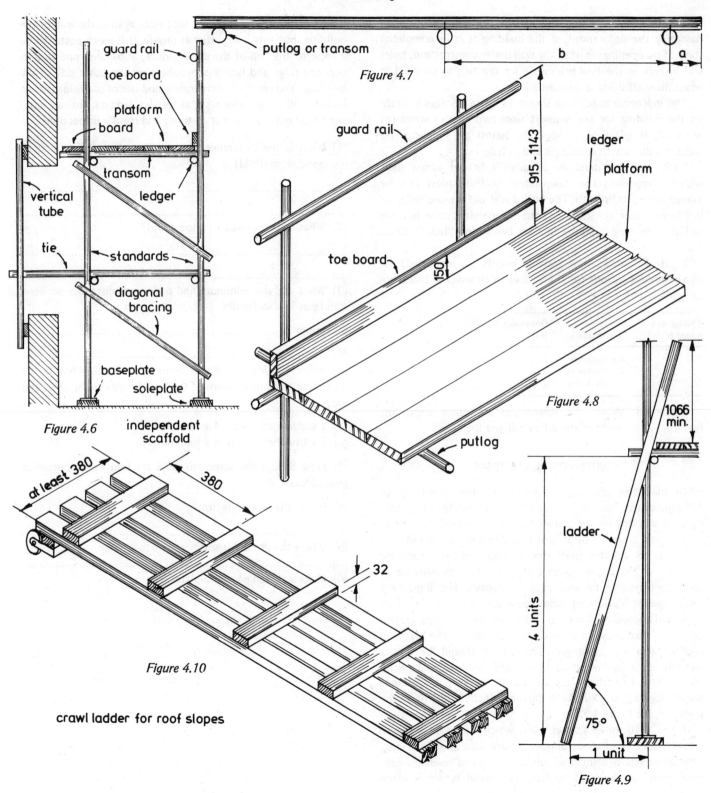

guard rail

toe board

platform
board

transom

vertical
tube

ledger

tie

standards

diagonal
bracing

baseplate

soleplate

Figure 4.6

independent
scaffold

putlog or transom

Figure 4.7

guard rail

ledger

platform

toe board

915 - 1143

150

Figure 4.8

putlog

b

a

at least 380

380

32

Figure 4.10

crawl ladder for roof slopes

ladder

1066
min.

4 units

75°

1 unit

Figure 4.9

should be placed behind the vertical tubes to stop them damaging the decorations, if the building is in its completed state. If no openings exist in the wall under construction, holes will be left in the new brickwork for the ties, to be filled in when the scaffolding is dismantled.

The independent scaffold shown in figure 4.6 does not rely on the building for any support since two lines of standards are used. In place of putlogs, the boards are supported on transoms that are fixed at each end to ledgers.

Both scaffolds must be adequately braced across their widest dimension; the independent scaffold must also be braced across its breadth. The putlog scaffold is more suited to buildings under construction; the independent type is more suited to existing buildings that are being renovated, repaired, etc.

Figure 4.7 shows how scaffold boards are supported; the maximum dimensions for the various thicknesses of board are as follows.

Thickness of board (mm)	Dimension a	Dimension b (m)
32	4 x thickness	1.0
38	4 x thickness	1.3
50	4 x thickness	2.5

Figure 4.8 shows the dimensions of other important features — the height of the safety rail and toe board.

WIDTH OF PLATFORMS

When platforms are used for access to other points, three 225 mm boards can be used as a minimum width, but where men are working on the platform and it is used for the storage of materials, it should be at least four 225 mm boards wide.

Access to working platforms on small jobs is usually by ladders. As has already been stated, the ladders must be in good condition or be sent back for repairs. The slope of a ladder against scaffolding should be around 1 in 4 or 75°. This slope will allow a workman to climb a ladder with comparative ease and also allow him to carry materials to the platform without too much danger. The ladder should be lashed securely at its top to the scaffolding and should extend a little more than 1 m above the platform to give a workman something to grip while he is stepping off the ladder on to the platform, see figure 4.9.

Figure 4.10 shows a crawl ladder which is used for access to a roof slope. The various dimensions are seen on the drawing. The ladder has two small wheels at its top end to enable easy movement up the roof surface. The crawl ladder is often

lashed to the top of a ladder that rests against the wall of the building, but this is regarded as unsafe. It is much better to tie a rope to the top of the crawl ladder, allow the rope to pass over the ridge and lash it somewhere on the other side of the building. The erection, dismantling and use of scaffolds (which includes all accessories such as trestles, ladders, fittings, etc.) need care and attention at all times and regular inspections.

(1) What is the difference between a putlog scaffold and an independent scaffold?

....

....

(2) What is the purpose of a toe board?

....

....

(3) What are the minimum and maximum distances between standards in a scaffold?

Maximum ....

Minimum ....

(4) When placing boards to form a platform, what is the maximum amount the ends of the board may overlap their end supports?

(a) 1 x thickness   (b) 4 x thickness
(c) 3 x thickness   (d) 6 x thickness

(5) How should the standards of a scaffold be supported at ground level?

(a) Where the ground is firm?

....

(b) Where the ground is soft?

....

(6) Make a sketch of a base plate.

(7) What are the maximum and minimum heights of a guard rail?

Maximum ....

Minimum ....

(8) Why must scaffolds be tied to buildings?

....

(9) Unskilled people should never be responsible for the erection of a scaffold. Why?

....

....

....

(10) What is the best timber for use as scaffold boards?

....

(11) How should a ladder be secured when being used for access to a scaffold platform?

....

....

....

....

(12) What should be done to make a ladder safe if the ground at its foot is sloping?

....

....

(13) How far should a ladder extend above the scaffold platform to which it is providing access?

....

....

(14) What should be done to preserve ladders?

....

(15) What is a crawl ladder?

....

....

(16) What defects are common in scaffold boards?

(a). ....

(b). ....

(c). ....

(d). ....

(17) What defects may be found in ladders?

(a). ....

(b). ....

(c). ....

(d). ....

(e). ....

(f). ....

(18) What defects may be found in wooden step-ladders?

(a). ....

(b). ....

(c). ....

(19) Various dimensions are given for putlog scaffolds in figure 4.1. You are advised to obtain a copy of *Construction Safety*, Section 2 and obtain the following information regarding independent scaffolds.

(a) Distance standards should be placed apart. ....

(b) Distance first row of ledgers should be placed above ground.

....

(c) At what intervals other rows of ledgers should be placed.

....

(d) Distance apart at which transoms should be situated.

....

(e) Where ties should be placed. ....

(f) Positions of bracing, longitudinal and diagonal........................

(g) Maximum height of scaffold. ....

5. ARCH CENTRES

In volume 1 various arch centres up to a span of 1 m were dealt with; we shall now cover simple centres up to a span of 3 m. Naturally as the span increases so do the timber sizes, but not necessarily in the same proportion. For instance, in two centres, one of 1 m span and the other of 2 m span, it would be found that the timbers of the largest centre would only be slightly larger than the others, provided each centre had been constructed correctly. Before going on to the larger type of centre, a centre for a pointed arch will be described.

Figure 5.1 shows the front elevation of a centre for an equilateral arch of 1 m span, with its supports and provision for adjustment and assistance in striking. The radius for this type of arch is equal to its span (see figure 5.2). Two separate frames, similar to those shown for the semi-circular arch in volume 1, should be built up in two thicknesses, as shown in figure 5.3. When setting out the shape of these frames, the thickness of the lagging around their outside edges must be allowed for; this would be, say 6 mm plywood. The curved parts of the ribs could be obtained from 100 x 25 material, as could the other components of these frames. The width of the lagging should be slighty narrower than the thickness of the wall in which the arch is to be constructed and the ribs should be positioned so that their outside edges are about 10 mm from the edges of the lagging, see figure 5.4. The lagging, which is nailed securely to the outside edge of the ribs and the battens fixed to the lower surfaces of the ribs, will complete the construction of the centre.

It may be thought necessary to nail two braces across the vertical strut and these are seen in the vertical section in figure 5.5. Two posts, extending down to plates at ground level, support the centre. To enable it to be raised to its correct height and to assist in the easy dismantling (striking) of the centre, two folding wedges are placed at the top or bottom of each post.

CENTRES OF LARGER SPAN

Figure 5.6 shows a method that can be used for the construction of a semi-circular centre of 3 m span. All the solid timbers in the work can be obtained from 150 x 38 material; the ribs are cut in sections, being cut on a bandsaw to the correct shape (obtained by preparing a templet of hardboard and using this to mark all the rib timbers, see figure 5.7). When marking the shape of the templet, remember that the thickness of the lagging must be allowed for. The lagging in this instance could be as much as 38 mm thick, so this amount must be subtracted from the radius when marking out the shape of the ribs.

If an outline of the frames (less the thickness of the lagging) is marked out on the workshop floor, the timbers can be placed on this to make sure the shape of the centre is correct. All the timbers are butt jointed and the joints covered on both sides with 12 mm plywood gusset plates and securely nailed. The strips of timber forming the lagging can then be nailed around the outside of the two frames and the three battens nailed on the bottom edges to complete the centre. Braces should be included in this job as shown in figures 5.6 and 5.8. Remember too that the length of the lagging pieces should be slightly shorter than the thickness of the wall and the frames kept within the laggings. Three posts may be necessary for the support of this centre and folding wedges as before should be provided for easing, striking and adjusting.

Occasionally centres have to be made for a job that involves projections such as the moulded bricks seen in figure 5.9. These bricks are usually found at springing-line level and can interfere with the centre. Also care must be taken so that the fixing and dismantling operations involved with the centre do not damage the moulded bricks. Obviously the woodwork must be kept well away from the bricks in question and details of

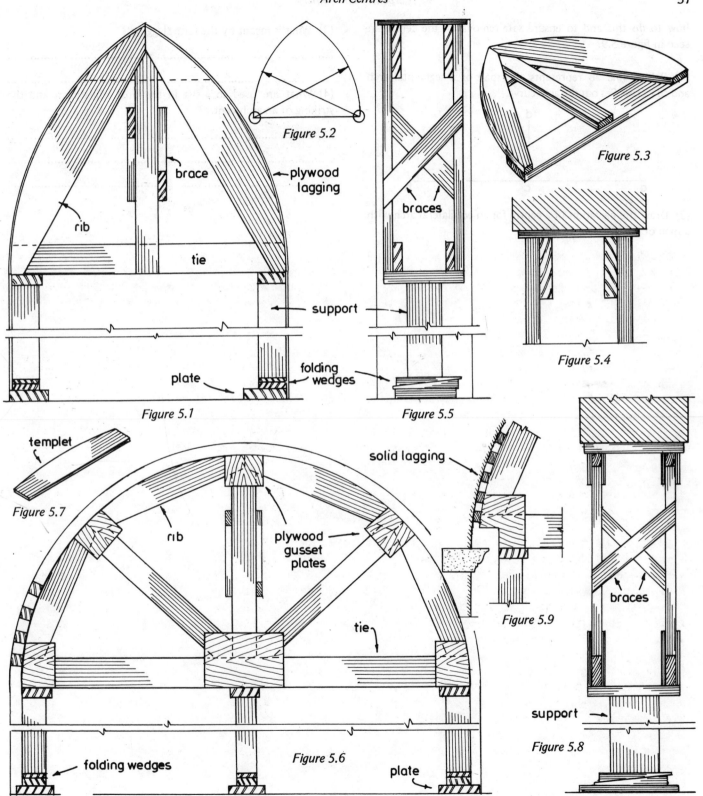

Figure 5.2

brace

plywood lagging

rib

tie

Figure 5.3

braces

support

folding wedges

plate

Figure 5.1

Figure 5.5

Figure 5.4

templet

Figure 5.7

rib

plywood gusset plates

solid lagging

tie

Figure 5.9

braces

folding wedges

Figure 5.6

plate

support

Figure 5.8

how to do this and to ensure safe removal of the centre are seen in figure 5.9.

(1) Below, line ab represents the span of a segmental arch and cd its rise. Set out the arch curve.

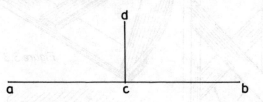

(2) Draw the elevation of a centre for an equilateral arch with a span of 1.5 m (scale 1 : 20).

(3) What is meant by the term 'lagging'?

....

....

(4) What are used to assist in the final adjustment and the striking of an arch centre?

....

....

....

6. FORMWORK FOR CONCRETE

As explained in volume 1 of this series, there are two methods of making concrete products, by the pre-cast method and by the *in situ* method. In the former the product is either made in a factory or on the ground on the site where the item is required. In the latter method the formwork is constructed in the position where the concrete item is actually needed. Let us take one or two examples of each.

Figure 6.1 shows details of a concrete sill and figure 6.2 shows a casting box that could be used for producing such an item. This method and the two that follow come under the heading of pre-cast work.

As can be seen in figure 6.2 the best way of producing the sill is to cast it in the upside-down position. This will allow the weathered surface and the drip groove to be formed quite easily. The drip groove can be formed by placing a short end of reinforcement rod across the grooves provided and it can be pressed into the newly poured concrete. The slope of the sill can be made by building up the inside of the box as shown. Figure 6.3 shows an isometric view of one end of the box and shows that the ends rest up against battens screwed to the longer sides, which are held together with bolts. For easy removal of the bolts, slots can be made in the side ends through which the bolts will slide. The sides of the box are prevented from bulging by distance pieces and folding wedges, one being screwed to the base. The other can be easily removed when the box is dismantled.

Figure 6.4 shows one end of a box for pre-casting beams. Yokes are placed around the box, distance pieces and bolts securing the box sides while the concrete is being placed in position. Figure 6.5 is a section through the formwork.

Figures 6.6 and 6.7 show details of a box suitable for casting concrete fence-posts two at a time. Holes are usually required in the posts and they can be made by placing, say, 9 mm mild steel rods through the boxes in the required positions, removing them after the initial set of the concrete has taken place. Triangular pieces of timber can be placed in

the top corners of the box to form the weathering on the tops of the posts.

The following examples all come under the heading of *in situ* work in concrete.

The first example is the sill that was considered for pre-cast work. In the case of *in situ* work the sill has to be cast in the position where it is needed to carry out its function as a sill. Figures 6.8 and 6.9 show how this can be accomplished. The front and back surface each have to be supported from the ground. Most of the formwork, except for the supports, can be of external-grade plywood. The slope of the sill can be formed quite easily if the concrete mix is correct. No supporting timber is required for the slope.

Figures 6.10–6.12 show details of the box required for forming a concrete lintel, say, over a garage doorway. The box is supported on what are called headtrees, which are posts with horizontal pieces at their tops, well braced to prevent distortion. Yokes similar to those in figures 6.4 and 6.5 support the sides of the box. The bottom of the box must be cut to fit in between the jambs of the brickwork but the sides must be longer to overlap the brickwork at each end.

Figures 6.13–6.15 show details of how a simple floor can be cast over, say, a corridor. Posts, spaced at around 3 m along the length of the corridor, support runners which in turn support joists spaced at approximately 600 mm centres. Over the tops of the joists are placed the sheets of plywood, which should be around 19 mm in thickness. Figure 6.13 shows a section through the width of the corridor, figure 6.14 a part of the formwork and support along its length and figure 6.15 an isometric view showing details from below. Remember that, in this and most other examples of a similar kind, folding wedges are required below each post to allow final adjustment and easing when the timber work is to be dismantled.

Figures 6.16–6.18 show details of the formwork required for a concrete floor with beams. The beam boxes are supported on headtrees (posts) which also support runners on

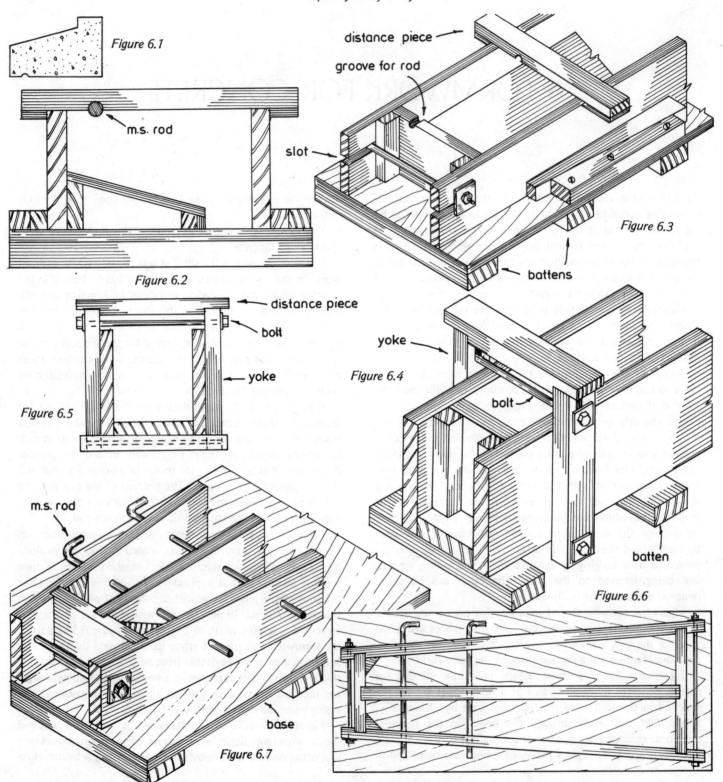

Figure 6.1

m.s. rod

Figure 6.2

distance piece

groove for rod

slot

Figure 6.3

battens

distance piece

bolt

yoke

Figure 6.5

yoke

Figure 6.4

bolt

batten

Figure 6.6

m.s. rod

base

Figure 6.7

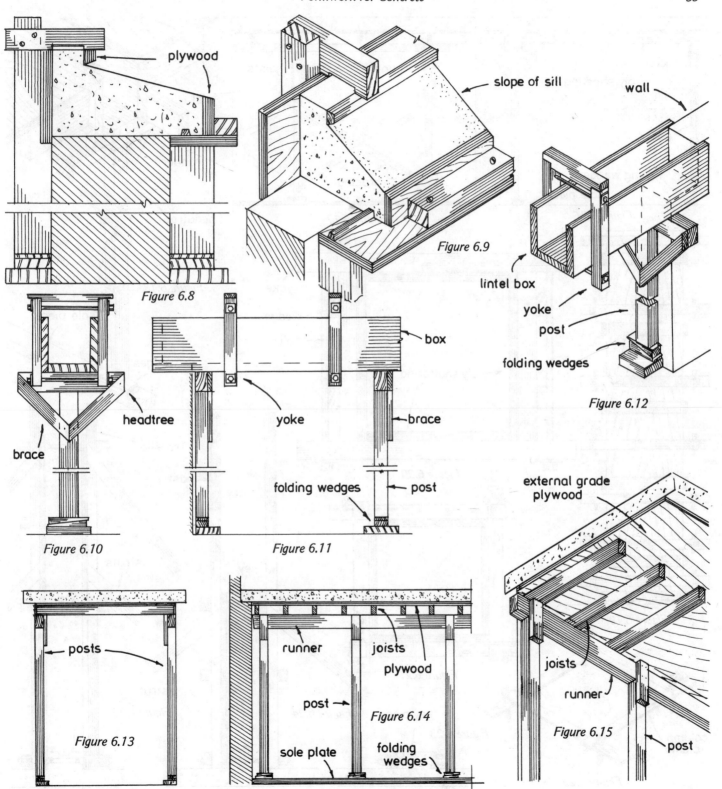

plywood

Figure 6.8

slope of sill

Figure 6.9

wall

lintel box

yoke

post

folding wedges

Figure 6.12

headtree

brace

yoke

box

brace

folding wedges

post

Figure 6.10

Figure 6.11

external grade plywood

posts

runner

joists

plywood

post →

Figure 6.14

sole plate

folding wedges

Figure 6.13

joists

runner

Figure 6.15

post

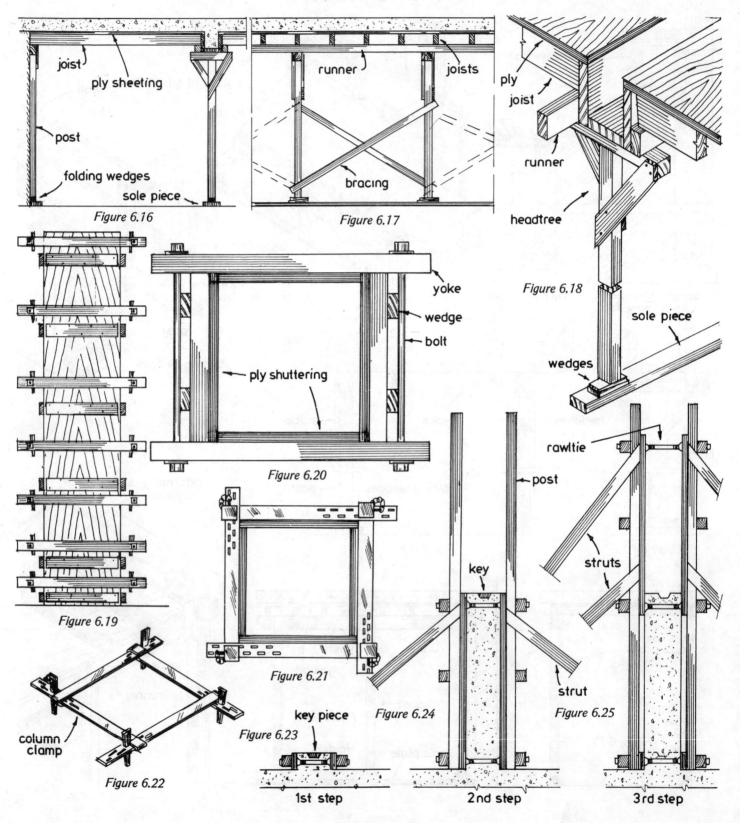

Figure 6.16

Figure 6.17

Figure 6.18

Figure 6.19

Figure 6.20

Figure 6.21

Figure 6.22

Figure 6.23

Figure 6.24

Figure 6.25

1st step

2nd step

3rd step

which the joists rest. The 19 mm plywood shuttering is placed over the tops of the joists which should be spaced at around 600 mm. The posts in such a case should be braced to prevent possible dislodging by barrows, etc., which may cause damage to the formwork or to the poured concrete. Posts should be spaced along the length of each beam at about 3 m centres and should be in the region of 100 x 75 or 100 x 100 in sectional dimensions. The depth of the joists should be in the region of 150 mm but this can be adjusted in either direction by spacing them at different intervals. The beam boxes can be of plywood (19 mm) or solid timber, when the sides could be 32 mm material and the bottom from 38 or 50 mm material.

Figures 6.19 and 6.20 show details of a box suitable for casting a concrete column. The box is made from four pieces of 19 mm external-grade plywood cut to the correct dimensions and supported around its sides by yokes. One of these yokes is seen in figure 6.20, consisting of four pieces of timber, say 75 x 50, held together with two bolts, with wedges placed between the bolts and yoke to keep the adjacent sides of the box tight up against the other two sides. The yolks can be easily removed by knocking out the wedges and loosening the bolts. It will be noticed that the yokes are placed much closer together near the bottom of the box than they are near the top. This is because the pressure of the newly poured concrete increases considerably from the top downwards.

Figures 6.21 and 6.22 show details of metal column-clamps that are now used extensively to take the place of timber yokes. Each set consists of four pieces of metal, each piece bent to form a hook at one end with a number of slots at the other end. Into one of these slots is placed a metal wedge and when four pieces are used together they form a support around the four sides of the column box.

Figures 6.23–6.25 show three stages in the construction of a concrete wall. In the first step a short upstanding portion is cast as shown in figure 6.23; the two shutters are held the correct distance apart by a Rawltie (see p. 169). A shaped piece of timber is placed in the top surface of the concrete at each stage to form a key between each pair of sections. Figure 6.24 shows how two shutters, say, 1 m high, are placed in position to form the second stage. Rawlties are again used at intervals along the top edge, the ties along the bottom of the wall being used again for the second stage. Runners and posts, suitably braced form the supporting timbers for the shuttering. The third stage is similar to the second, the original narrow shuttering for the first step being brought into use again for packing out and supporting the bottom of the posts; the shutters are raised up one stage to allow concrete to be poured into that section.

(1) What is the difference between the terms 'pre-cast' and '*in situ*'?

Pre-cast...

....

In situ..

....

(2) What is the weight of a cubic metre of newly mixed concrete?

....

....

(3) Calculate the weight of recently poured concrete in a square column box measuring 2.5 m x 400 mm x 400 mm.

....

(4) To stop the sides of a column box from bulging after it has just been filled with concrete, either column clamps or yokes are fitted around the box at various heights throughout its length. Make a sketch of a column clamp and a yoke and state which one in your opinion is best and give your reasons.

....
....
....
....
....
....
....

(5) What should be done to timber shuttering to stop it from damaging the concrete when the formwork is struck?

....

....

(6) What should be done to remove air pockets in freshly poured concrete? ....

....

(7) The drawings below show two methods of making a form box for the manufacture of a concrete lintel. Which do you think is the better method and why?

(a)   (b)

....

....

(8) Why are the sides of the form box in which a concrete lintel is to be cast *in situ* longer than the bottom of the box?

....

....

....

(9) Why are the yokes or column cramps placed nearer to each other at the lower end of the shuttering than they are at the top?

....

....

7. SUPPORTS TO BUILDINGS - SHORING

Sometimes it is necessary to support walls in buildings to prevent more damage when there are signs of collapse or to prevent any damage being done to a wall when alterations are being carried out in the building.

When the supporting timbers are inclined to the face of the wall they are supporting, and when their lower ends rest on the ground, the system of shoring is called raking shores. Figure 7.1 shows the elevation and side view of a single raking-shore. It is inclined with its top end resting against a timber wall-piece and its lower end resting on a number of timbers designed to spread any load that is transferred down the shore over a fairly large area. The positioning of the top of the raker against the wall piece is important and this depends on whether or not the wall to be supported is itself supporting the floors within the building. If the wall is supporting the floors, the centre line of the raker should, if carried upwards from the wall piece, eventually come to rest in the centre of the seating for the joists, see figure 7.2a. If the wall does not support the joists, the centre lines of the wall, floor and raker should all meet at a point, as shown in figure 7.2b.

Figure 7.3 shows the joints at the top of the raker. A hole, 100 x 75, is cut in the wall piece to coincide with the hole in the wall made by the removal of a half-brick, the position of which will be decided by the centre line of the raker. A needle passes through the hole in the wall piece — a piece of 100 x 75 timber long enough to pass into the wall to a depth of 100 mm and remain protruding from the wall piece to a distance of, say, 150 mm. Above the needle is a cleat, which should be recessed into the wall piece, as shown in the drawing. This cleat should also be cut from 100 x 75 timber. The raker is cut, as shown, to fit in the angle between the wall piece and the needle.

Figure 7.4 shows how the platform at ground level should be prepared, the foot of the raker resting on the centre piece, which will spread the load over to the other pieces. A cleat is placed behind the foot of the raker to stop it moving, and the platform should be so placed as to have its top surface slightly

less than 90° to the slope of the raker. The method of assembly should be as follows.

(1) Remove the half-brick from the wall when the position of the top of the raker has been decided.

(2) Prepare the wall piece, needle and cleat and assemble these as shown in figure 7.5.

(3) Put this assembly into position and fix with wall hooks (figure 7.6).

(4) Prepare the ground platform and raker, place in position and fix.

(5) Tighten up the raker by levering the foot over towards the building with a bar. Do not tighten too much or damage will be done to the wall.

(6) Fix the cleat behind the raker's foot and use metal dogs to secure the foot and head of the raker (figure 7.6).

(7) Fix stiffening boards.

(8) Inspect regularly and tighten timbers when necessary.

An isometric view of the top of the raker is shown in figure 7.7.

UNDERPINNING

This form of shoring gives support to a wall from below. A simple example of underpinning is shown in figure 7.8. Let us assume that a fairly large opening has to be made in the wall between two rooms in a dwelling; The wall above where the opening is to be made must be supported temporarily while a lintel is placed across the top of the opening and the brickwork made good above the lintel.

The first thing to do is to ascertain the direction of the joists in the floors above the two rooms. If it is found that they are supported in the wall in which the opening is to be made, they can be used to advantage, assisting in supporting the wall while the work is being carried out. A plate is placed on the ground floor a short distance away from the wall on each side, and posts placed on these plates to extend up to and

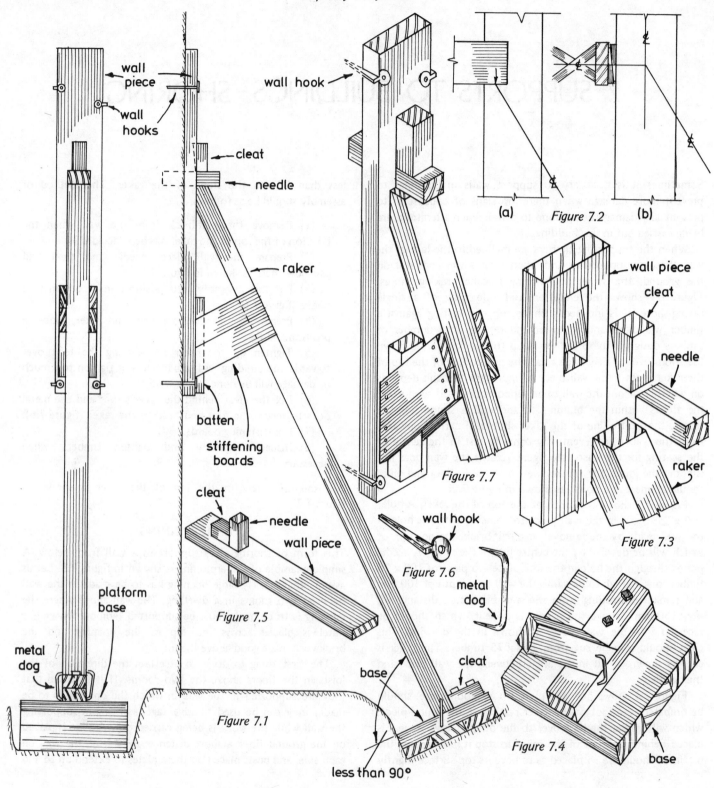

wall piece

wall hooks

cleat

needle

raker

batten

stiffening boards

cleat

needle

wall piece

Figure 7.5

platform base

metal dog

Figure 7.1

less than 90°

wall hook

Figure 7.2

(a)   (b)

wall piece

cleat

needle

raker

Figure 7.3

wall hook

Figure 7.6

metal dog

base

cleat

base

Figure 7.4

base

Figure 7.7

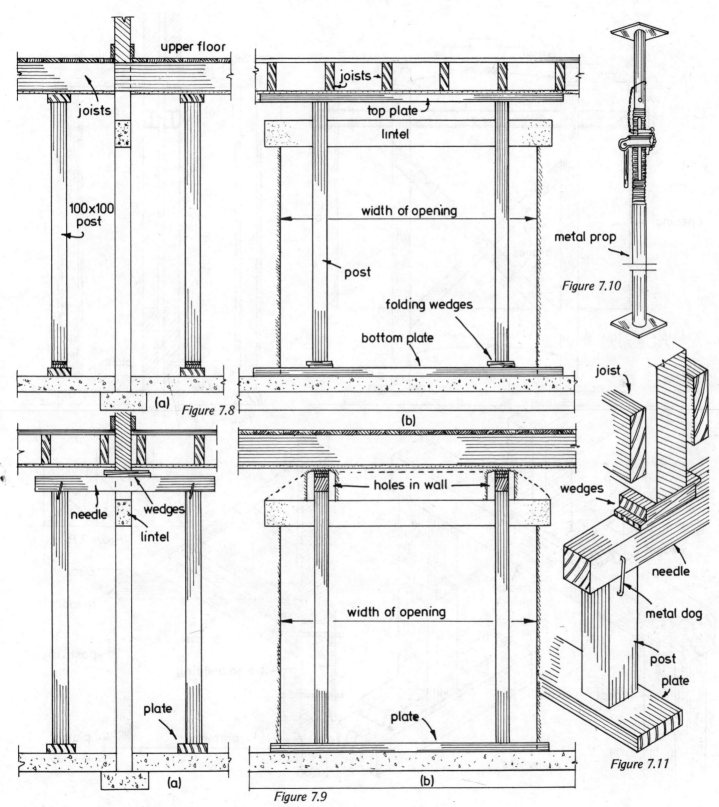

upper floor

joists

100x100 post

(a) *Figure 7.8*

joists

top plate

lintel

width of opening

post

folding wedges

bottom plate

(b)

needle

wedges

lintel

plate

(a)

holes in wall

width of opening

plate

(b)

Figure 7.9

metal prop

Figure 7.10

joist

wedges

needle

metal dog

post

plate

Figure 7.11

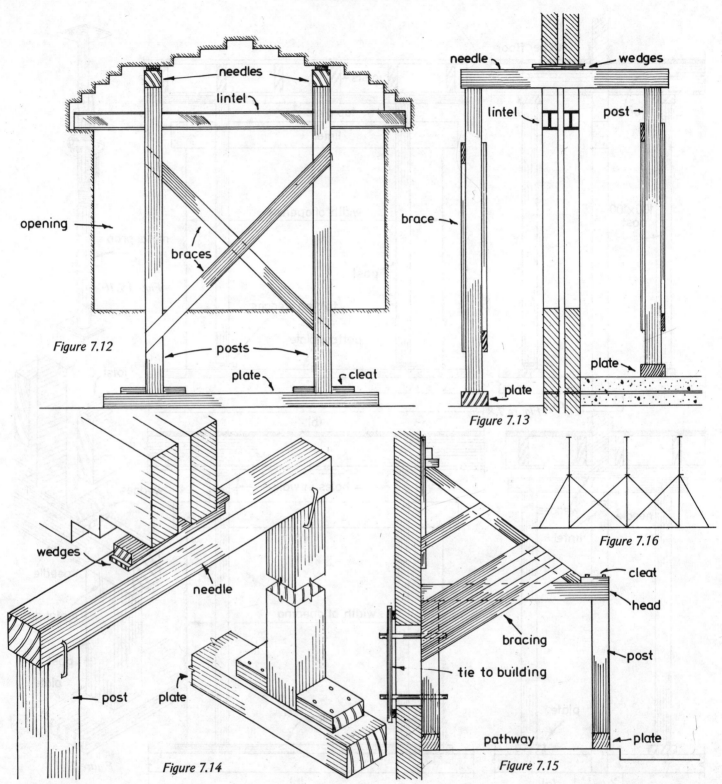

Figure 7.12

needles

lintel

opening

braces

posts

plate

cleat

Figure 7.13

needle

wedges

lintel

post

brace

plate

plate

Figure 7.14

wedges

needle

post

plate

Figure 7.16

Figure 7.15

cleat

head

bracing

tie to building

post

pathway

plate

support plates running across the ceiling. Folding wedges are placed between the posts and lower plates and tightened; this will have the effect of supporting the upper-floor joists which, in turn, will support the wall above the required opening (see figures 7.8a and b).

Figures 7.9a and b show what is done when the upper-floor joists run in the opposite direction and parallel to the wall. Holes (say, two) are cut in the wall and needles placed through to extend into both rooms, supported on each side of the wall by posts. The posts should rest on plates across the lower floor. Folding wedges for tightening up the work are placed between the needles and the brickwork as seen in figure 7.9a. The needles will support the brickwork while the opening is being formed and the lintel positioned. When this is done and the brickwork above the lintel made good, the timber work is removed and the needle holes made good.

Metal props (figure 7.10) may be used instead of posts. Details of these are also given in chapter 20. It would be as well to get the concrete lintel in position on the floor before the work commences, since it may be difficult to do this once the posts or props are in position.

Figure 7.11 is an isometric view showing details of the underpinning problem mentioned in figure 7.9; it shows the folding wedges in between the brickwork and needle which are supported on posts extending down to floor level and resting on a plate.

Figures 7.12 and 7.13 show the elevation and a vertical section through another underpinning job that is much larger than those previously covered. This involves making a fairly large opening in an external wall of a building and inserting two British Standard beams across the top of the opening.

Basically, of course, the work is similar to that shown in figures 7.9a and b, although in this case the timbers will be larger and the work may involve the placing of raking shores on each side of the underpinning to ensure stability in the wall while the work is being carried out.

Two or more holes are cut in the wall — depending on the size of the opening and the positions of windows above the opening to be made — so that needles can be placed through the wall and supported at their ends with posts, see figure 7.13.

Care must be taken to see that there is a firm base inside the building as well as outside. If there is a hollow timber ground-floor inside, some floorboards must be removed to allow the posts to go down to the oversite concrete, not forgetting to include the plate.

Figure 7.14 shows isometric details of the underpinning shown in figures 7.12 and 7.13.

Now look at figures 7.15 and 7.16. They are not related to the underpinning problems already covered; they show a single raking shore. Try to interpret the two drawings and describe them and their purpose briefly.

....

....

....

....

....

(1) What is the difference between a raking shore and a dead shore?

....

....

(2) Place the missing details in the drawing below, which represents a raking shore supporting a wall. Name the various parts in the completed drawing.

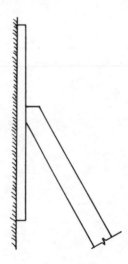

(3) Below is a list of the various stages in the preparation and fixing of a single raking shore that is to give support to a wall. Place a letter in each of the spaces provided to show the correct sequence that will lead to the safest completion of the job.

    (a) cut and prepare wall piece
    (b) cut and prepare needle and cleat
    (c) cut out brick from wall to receive needle
    (d) position and fix wall piece, needle and cleat
    (e) cut and prepare raker shore

(f) assemble wall piece, needle and cleat
(g) fix raker in position
(h) prepare base platform
(i) cut and fix stiffening boards
(j) tighten up raker and fix foot
(k) prepare ground for base

Correct sequence

(1) ....   (2) ....   (3) ....   (4) ....

(5) ....   (6) ....   (7) ....   (8) ....

(9) ....   (10) ....   (11) ....

(4) What is the purpose of a needle in a dead shore?

....

(5) Timbers in dead-shoring work are mostly butt jointed. How are they secured to prevent accidental movement?

....

....

(6) What items are used in dead shoring to assist in the tightening up and the dismantling of timbers?

....

....

(7) The angle between the lower end of a raker and the base it rests on should be approximately
(a) 95°   (b) 85°   (c) 110°   (d) 70°
Cross out those that are incorrect.

8. PITCHED ROOFS

There are two common types of roof used for domestic buildings: gable-end roofs and hipped roofs, although it must be said that the latter has gone out of favour in recent years, because of its higher cost in materials and labour. Figures 8.1 and 8.2 show the difference in the construction of these roofs; the names of the various components are also given.

The gable roof in figure 8.3 consists of a wall plate on each of the longest walls over which the common rafters are notched and extend downwards to form the overhanging eaves. The tops of the rafters are nailed securely to the ridge board which extends the full length of the building. If the rafters are 100 x 50 and more than 2.5 m long, centre supports — called purlins — must be provided to resist the tendency for the rafters to bend under the weight of the roof covering. The position of the purlins should be exactly half-way between the wall plate and the ridge board. If the verge of the roof extends beyond the face of the brickwork, common rafters have to be fixed outside the gable walls to support the roof covering at these points. The rafters are supported at their tops by the extended ridge-board and at their lower ends by the extended wall-plate. If additional supports are required between these two points, timbers nailed to the inside common rafters can be positioned as shown in figure 8.5. To finish the roof at the verge, barge boards are fixed, the top edge of these being slightly higher than the tile battens, to give a slight tilt at the verge, see figure 8.6.

The hipped roof in figure 8.4 consists of four sloping surfaces, as opposed to the gable roof's two. Common rafters extend downwards from the ridge board beyond the wall plate to the eaves overhang — the hip rafters are those forming the four corners of the roof, and the jack rafters extend downwards from the hips to the eaves.

JOINTS USED IN ROOF CONSTRUCTION

Figure 8.7 shows simple halving-joints used at the intersections of wall plates. Figure 8.7a shows the corner halving and figure 8.7b the tee halving used where external and internal walls meet.

Figure 8.8 shows the joint used to fit the top ends of the common rafters up against the ridge board.

Figure 8.9 shows how the common rafters are notched over the top outside edge of the wall plates. The depth of this notching should be approximately one-third of the depth of the rafters.

Figure 8.10 shows a hip rafter intersecting with a ridge board at its top end. Two bevels are required for this joint and these, with all the others required for the construction of a hipped roof, will be discussed later.

Figures 8.11a and b show how a hipped rafter is joined at the intersection of two wall plates at a corner of a roof. Notice that the hip is wide compared with a common rafter and its width has to be reduced from the wall plates down to its lowest end. Another important point to remember is that the hip must project above the wall plates exactly the same distance as the common rafters. Distance x in figure 8.11 should equal distance x in figure 8.9.

Figure 8.12 shows the two-bevel joint required for joining a jack rafter to a hip rafter; figure 8.13 shows another two-bevel joint so that the purlin can also be joined correctly to the hip rafter.

The most popular way of constructing roofs is the trussed-rafter method, where trusses are made to the dimensions of the section through the roof, their main components being a pair of common rafters and a ceiling joist. These trusses are frames bolted together with double-toothed connectors (figure 8.18) between each pair of timbers; they are capable of withstanding very heavy loads when made correctly. They can be used for both types of roof and the elevation of a truss suitable for a roof with a pitch of 40°, is shown in figure 8.14. The type of joint used in these frames is shown in figure 8.17. To make the truss easy to handle and lift up into position on the roof, it can be made in two halves, the halves being connected at the ridge and the gusset plates at G on the ceiling joist.

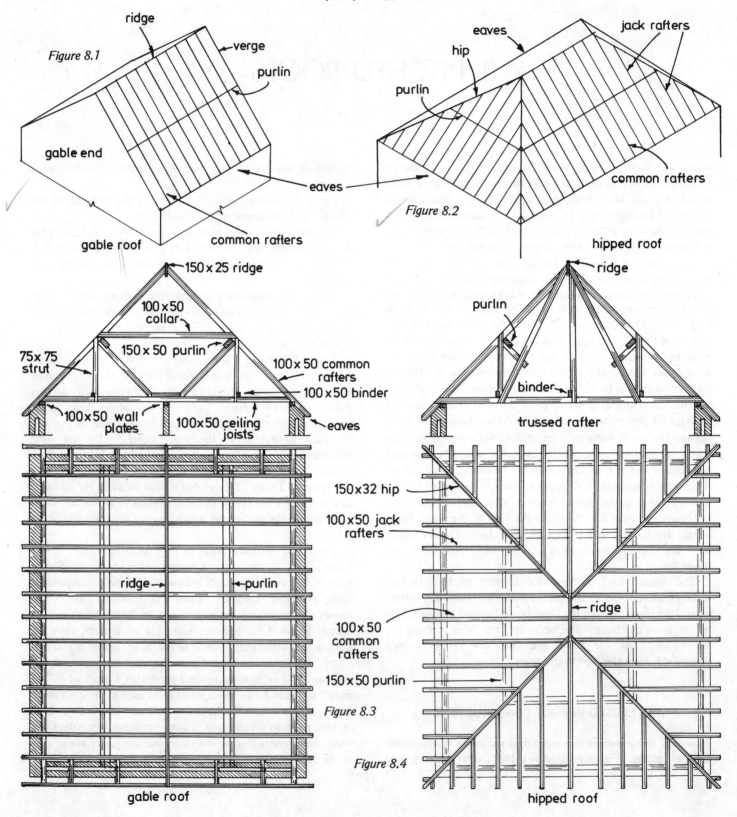

Figure 8.1

ridge

verge

purlin

gable end

common rafters

gable roof

eaves

Figure 8.2

eaves

jack rafters

hip

purlin

common rafters

hipped roof

150 x 25 ridge

100 x 50 collar

150 x 50 purlin

75 x 75 strut

100 x 50 common rafters

100 x 50 binder

100 x 50 wall plates

100 x 50 ceiling joists

eaves

ridge

purlin

gable roof

Figure 8.3

ridge

purlin

binder

trussed rafter

150 x 32 hip

100 x 50 jack rafters

ridge

100 x 50 common rafters

150 x 50 purlin

Figure 8.4

hipped roof

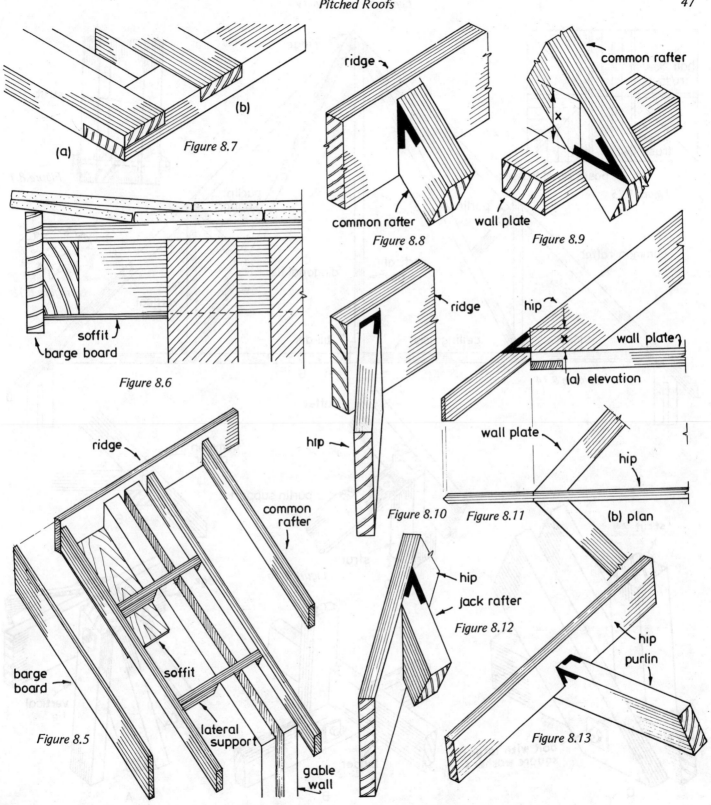

(a)

(b)

Figure 8.7

soffit

barge board

Figure 8.6

ridge

common rafter

barge board

soffit

lateral support

Figure 8.5

gable wall

ridge

common rafter

wall plate

Figure 8.8

common rafter

wall plate

Figure 8.9

ridge

hip

Figure 8.10

hip

x

wall plate

(a) elevation

wall plate

hip

(b) plan

Figure 8.11

hip

jack rafter

Figure 8.12

hip

hip

purlin

Figure 8.13

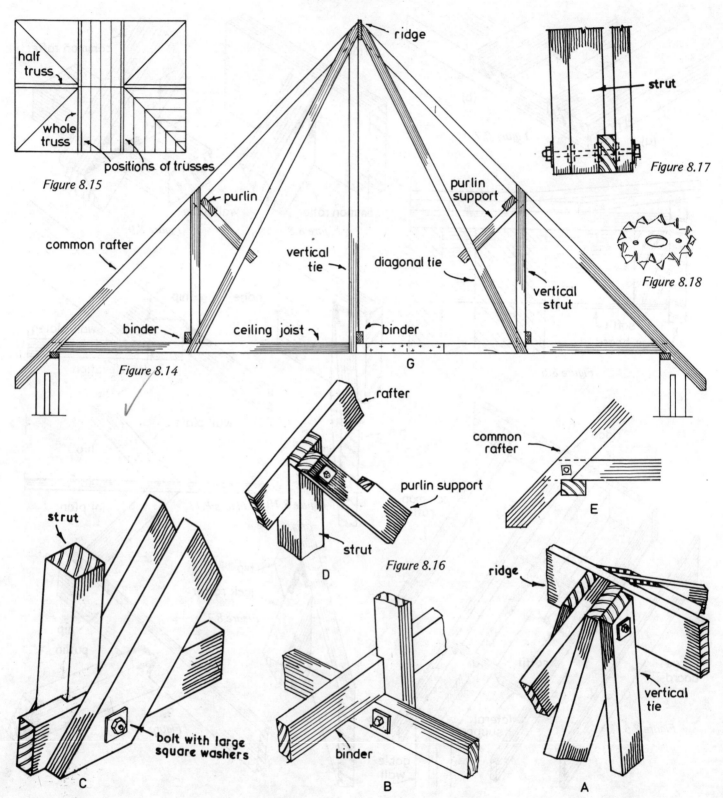

half truss

whole truss

positions of trusses

Figure 8.15

ridge

purlin

purlin support

common rafter

vertical tie

diagonal tie

vertical strut

binder

ceiling joist

binder

G

Figure 8.14

strut

Figure 8.17

Figure 8.18

rafter

common rafter

purlin support

strut

E

D

Figure 8.16

ridge

vertical tie

A

strut

bolt with large square washers

C

binder

B

The various joints in the truss are shown below the elevation (figure 8.16). At A is seen the joint between the common rafters and the diagonal and vertical ties. Note here, as well as in the other details, that the bolt passes through all the timbers on their centre lines. This is essential if strong joints are to be obtained. At B is seen the intersection between the vertical tie and the ceiling joist. A binder, one of three, passes across the ceiling rafter at this point and its job is to support the intermediate ceiling joists between the trusses, which should be placed every four to six rafters along the length of the roof (see figure 8.15). At C is the joint at the lower ends of the diagonal pieces and the vertical strut. D illustrates the top of the strut and shows the top end of the purlin support; note that the purlin is notched into the support very slightly. At E is seen the joint betwen the ceiling joists and the common rafters.

Figure 8.19 shows a view of a half truss that would be used at each end of a hipped roof. It is constructed similarly to a whole truss but in this case, the centre binder takes the place of the ceiling joists. (Figure 8.15 shows a line diagram with two half-trusses and two whole-trusses in position in the roof.)

Figure 8.20 shows an isometric view of one end of a hipped roof showing the position of a half truss and other components. Figure 8.21 shows the components necessary to join three pieces of timber with double-toothed connectors: two connectors (one is required for each pair of timbers), a 12 mm diameter bolt with nut and two 50 mm square 3 mm thick washers.

Figures 8.22a and b show why timber connectors are necessary for joints in roof trusses. Figure 8.22a shows what would happen if the connectors were left out: the piece of the tie behind the bolt would tend to split out. Figure 8.22b shows the same joint with the connectors included; in this case the forces within the joint are spread over a much larger area, making a much stronger joint.

Figure 8.23 is a view of a truss for a low-pitched gable roof, something we see much more of now than we do of the roof shown in figure 8.14. The pitches for this type of roof truss are betwen 22½° and 30°. A single ceiling-joist is used in its construction as well as two common-rafters. Diagonal pieces or ties are made to fit in between the common rafters at their top ends and the ceiling joists at their lowest ends, each joint being secured by two 12 mm plywood gusset plates, one on each side securely nailed to the timbers. This type of roof is usually assembled in a factory with the help of a jig; each component is cut on a crosscut saw and then placed in position in the jig. When all parts are in position, gang nail plates are tacked lightly in position over all the butt joints, the truss is moved into a press, which descends on to the plates, forcing the points completely into the timber surfaces. The result is a light, very strong roof truss. This truss is being used in roofs that have no common rafters as we know them but have a truss every 450 mm or so along the length of the roof, eliminating the necessity for purlins. Figures 8.24—8.26 show the various gusseted joints in the trusses and figure 8.27 shows the situations occupied by the trusses in a roof.

To be able to set out the various parts of a roof, be it a hipped roof or a gabled-ended roof, the carpenter must understand the geometry of a roof, even if he intends to use a steel square in the marking out, because the steel square is an instrument to which the basic geometry is applied. Figure 8.28a shows the plan and a section through a hipped roof. abcd is the outline of the plan, ef is the centre of the ridge board. a'd'g is the section through the roof showing the pitch. If the drawing has been drawn to scale, say 1 : 10 the section gives the length of the common rafter. All that is required is to multiply this length by 10 to get the correct length of a'g. Reference back to volume 1 will show that slight adjustments have to be made to this length: half the thickness of the ridge has to be deducted from the top end and the overhang for the eaves has to be added to the lower end. The bevels are shown in the section in figure 8.28b.

Let us revise the method of setting out a common rafter. Figure 8.29a shows the piece of timber to be set out. Near to its lower edge mark a parallel line one-third of the width away from the edge. Set a sliding bevel up to the plumb cut (at g in figure 8.28) and mark this bevel at the right-hand end to give point g. From g along the parallel line mark off ga' taken from the setting out (figure 8.28) to give a'. Set another sliding bevel up to the seat cut bevel and mark this through a'. Mark the plumb cut also through point a' to give the shape of the notching to be made in each of the common rafters. Next, the amount of overhang for each common rafter has to be calculated; this is shown in figure 8.30. Let us assume that the thickness of the wall is 275 mm, the width of the wall plate 100 mm and the overhang 125 mm. The horizontal distance from a' to a" is therefore 300 mm. Set up a right angle as in figure 8.31, making the lower arm 300; draw the hypotenuse at the pitch of the roof and the distance a"a' is the amount of overhang. This must be added from a' on the marking out to give a" on the parallel line. Figure 8.29b shows the completed rafter.

We now have to obtain the length and bevels for the hip rafters. Let us take hip ae; draw a right angle at e and make eh

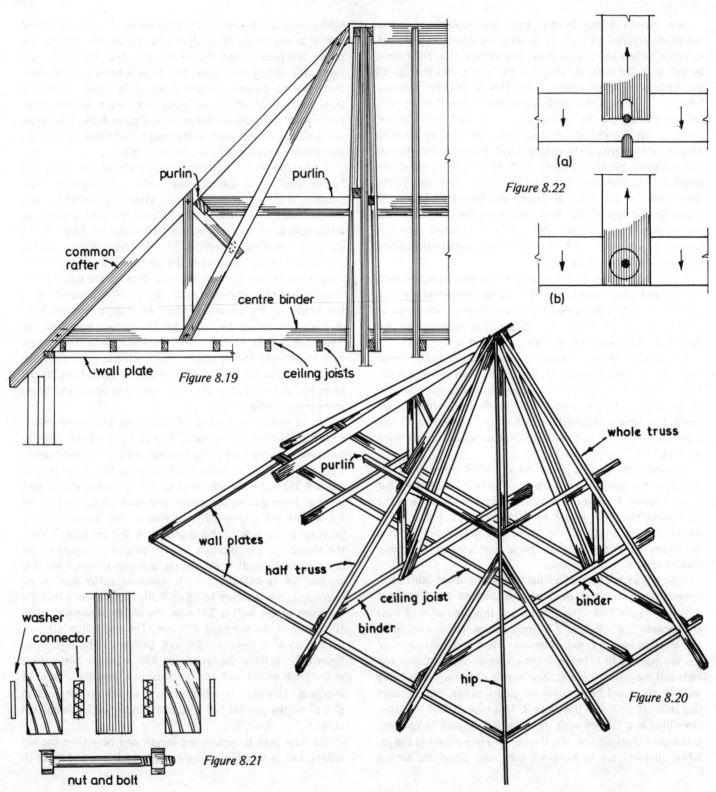

purlin

purlin

common rafter

centre binder

wall plate

ceiling joists

Figure 8.19

(a)

Figure 8.22

(b)

whole truss

purlin

wall plates

half truss

ceiling joist

binder

binder

hip

Figure 8.20

washer

connector

nut and bolt

Figure 8.21

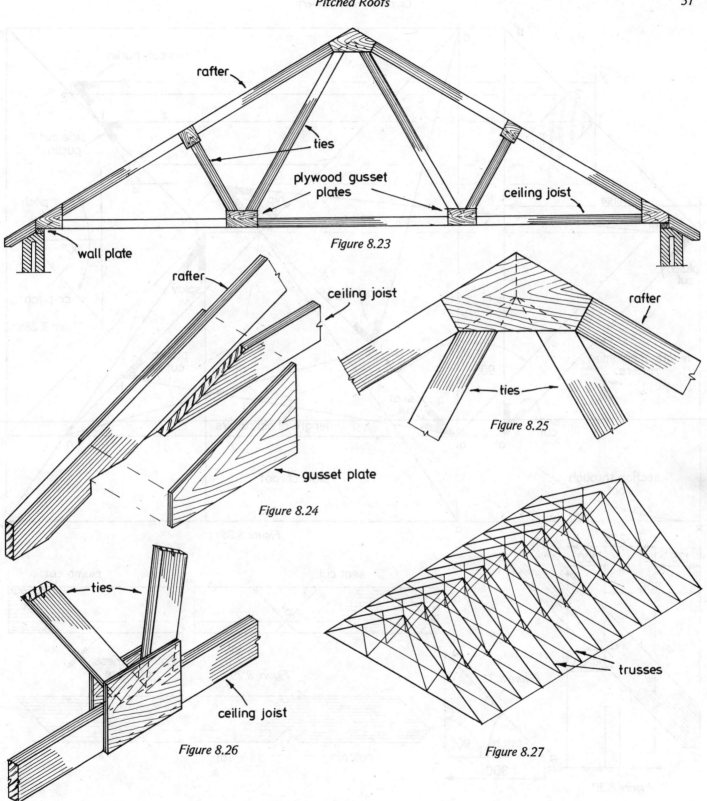

rafter

ties

plywood gusset plates

ceiling joist

wall plate

Figure 8.23

rafter

ceiling joist

gusset plate

Figure 8.24

rafter

ties

Figure 8.25

ties

ceiling joist

Figure 8.26

trusses

Figure 8.27

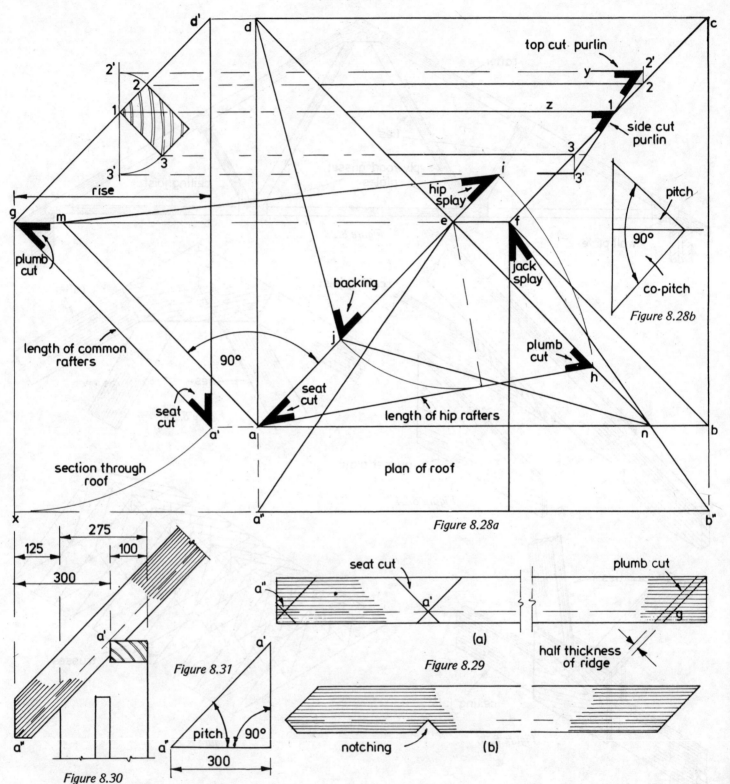

top cut purlin

side cut purlin

hip splay

pitch

90°

co-pitch

Figure 8.28b

rise

plumb cut

length of common rafters

90°

backing

jack splay

plumb cut

seat cut

seat cut

length of hip rafters

seat cut

section through roof

plan of roof

Figure 8.28a

275

125

100

300

Figure 8.31

pitch

90°

300

Figure 8.30

seat cut

plumb cut

(a)

half thickness of ridge

notching

(b)

Figure 8.29

equal to the rise of the common rafter (see section); join h to a — ha is the length of the hip rafter. Remember that we must deduct half the thickness of the ridge board from the top of the hip length and add on the overhang (which will be longer than that for the common rafters) at the lower end. The plumb and seat cuts are shown.

The hip-splay cut (to allow it to sit up against the ridge board) is found by placing the compass point in a, and with radius ah, describe an arc to give i on the extended ae line. Then draw a right angle at a to give point m on the extended centre-line of the roof. Join m to i. The angle a-i-m is the hip splay. The backing bevel (very seldom used these days but it sometimes crops up in examinations) is found by extending the hip de over to give n on the other edge of the roof. With compass point in e, and open just to touch ah, describe an arc to give j on ae. Join d to j and j to n. The backing bevel is dje, and the dihedral angle d-j-n.

The jack-rafters-splay cut (the plumb and seat cuts are the same as for the common rafters) is found by first developing a portion of a roof surface. Let us develop one end of surface efba. With compass point in g (in the section) and open to ga' describe an arc to give x on the vertical line from g. Draw a line from x parallel to the side of the roof and draw a line from b to give b″ on the line from x. Draw any vertical line from the hip bf to give the jack-splay cut.

The only remaining bevels are those for the purlins. Draw the section through one purlin as shown in the roof section. Make this as large as possible. Number the top three corners of the purlin 1, 2 and 3 to represent the two surfaces that have to be developed. Project these three points over to the hip cf to give points 1 2 3. To develop the top edge of the purlin, place the compass point in 1 in the section and with radius 1-2 describe an arc to give 2' on the vertical line passing through 1. Project this point over towards hip cf to give point 2' on the vertical line from 2. Angle y-2'-1 is the top edge cut for the purling to sit up against the adjacent hip rafter. The bevel for the sides of the purlin can be obtained in a similar manner and in this instance the bevel is z-1-3'.

THE STEEL SQUARE IN ROOFING

If the geometry just covered for the rectangular hipped roof is understood it should be quite simple to use a steel square for the same roof. A steel square with its fence is shown in figure 8.32.

Take the length of the common rafters, for example. If the span across the top outside corner of the wall plates and the required pitch are known, the length and bevels for the common rafters are found by marking off half the span on the blade and setting the fence from this point at the pitch; the length will be obtained by measuring along the fence from the outside edge of the blade to the outside edge of the tongue. Also obtained are the two bevels, the plumb cut at the tongue and the seat cut at the blade, see figure 8.33.

Figure 8.34 shows how to obtain the overhang for the common rafters. Dimension x is equal to the horizontal distance between the outside edge of the wall plate and the end of the rafters. To obtain dimension x the amount of required overhang must be known. Set the fence up at the pitch to obtain the amount of overhang to be left on the common rafters, starting from the notching that sits on the wall plate.

The length of the hip rafters is found as follows. First, the run of the hips is required: half the span on the blade and the same on the tongue will give the hip run (figure 8.35). Second, mark the hip run on the blade and the rise of the common rafters on the tongue to give the hip length. The plumb and seat bevels are obtained at the same time (figure 8.36). The overhang for the hip is found by first finding its run (figure 8.37) and then setting the fence at the hip pitch from the end of the run (figure 8.38). While the square is set up for the hip length, measure dimension y which is required for the backing bevel (figure 8.40). With the run of the hips on the blade and dimension y on the tongue, set the fence across these points to obtain the backing bevel.

The splay cut for the hips (figure 8.39) is found by marking off the length of the hips on the blade and the run of the hips on the tongue. The bevel is at the blade end of the fence.

The splay cut for the jack rafters is found by marking off the length of the common rafters on the blade and half the span on the tongue to obtain the bevel at the blade (figure 8.41).

To understand the purlin bevels on a steel square, refer back to figure 8.28b. The pitch line is drawn to the pitch of the roof, in this case 40°, and the co-pitch is drawn at right angles to the pitch. The procedure for developing the purlin bevels is as follows. Purlin top edge cut — mark the pitch length on the blade and half the span on the tongue to obtain the bevel (figure 8.42). Purlin side cut — mark the co-pitch on the blade and half the span on the tongue to obtain the bevel (figure 8.43). The co-pitch length can be obtained by marking half the span on the blade and setting the fence at the angle of the co-pitch. The angle of the co-pitch is 90° minus pitch. For example, if the pitch is 45°, the co-pitch is 45°. If the pitch is

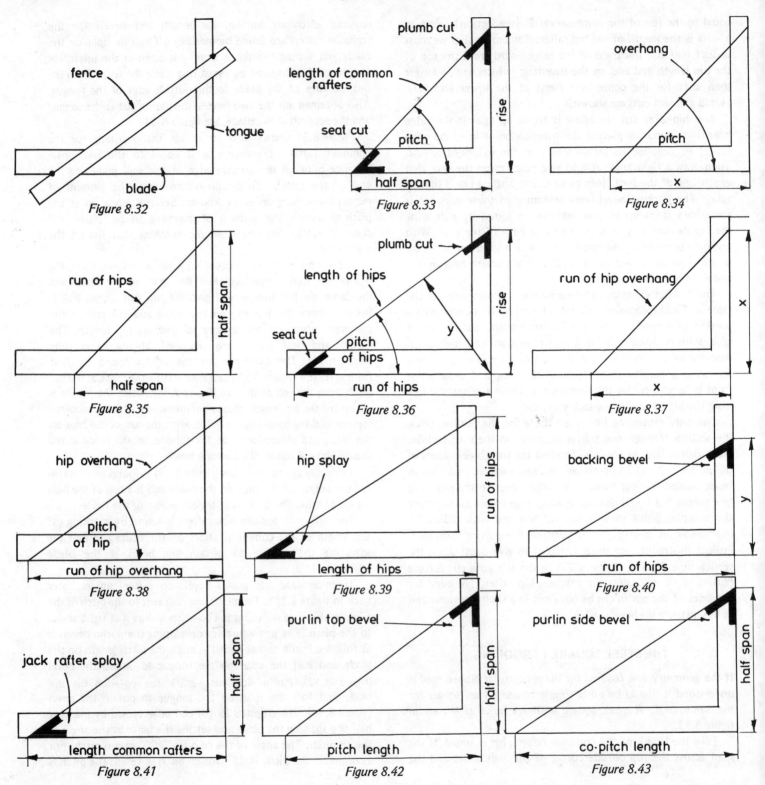

Figure 8.32

Figure 8.33

Figure 8.34

Figure 8.35

Figure 8.36

Figure 8.37

Figure 8.38

Figure 8.39

Figure 8.40

Figure 8.41

Figure 8.42

Figure 8.43

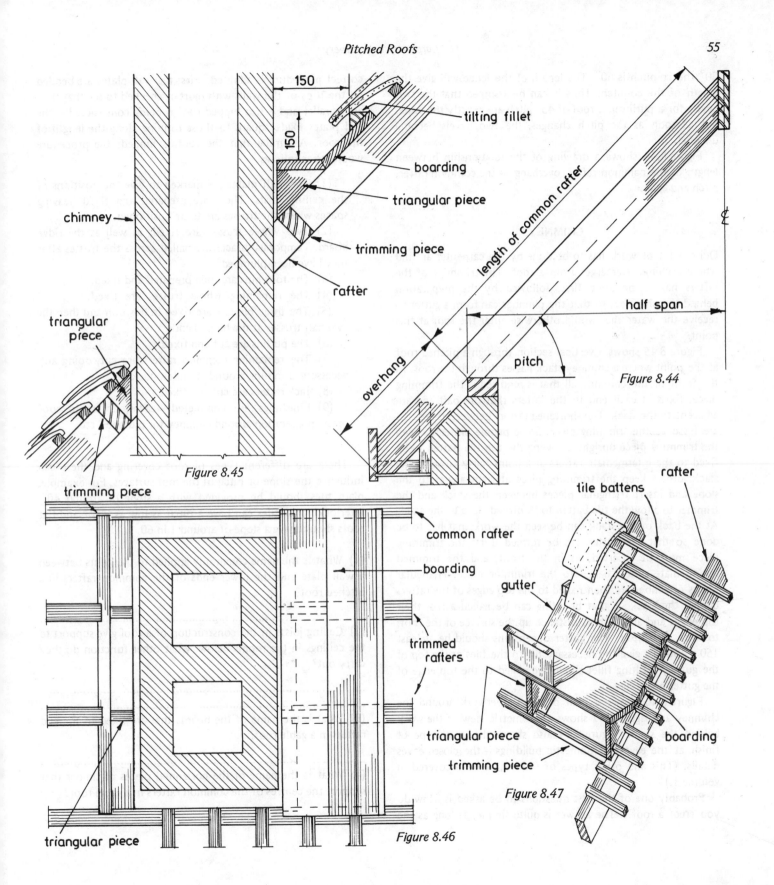

150

150

tilting fillet

boarding

triangular piece

trimming piece

chimney

rafter

length of common rafter

half span

overhang

pitch

Figure 8.44

triangular piece

trimming piece

Figure 8.45

common rafter

boarding

trimmed rafters

triangular piece

Figure 8.46

rafter

tile battens

gutter

triangular piece

trimming piece

boarding

Figure 8.47

30° the co-pitch is 60°. The length of the fence will give the length of the co-pitch. Thus it can be assumed that the two bevels for a purlin in a roof of 45° pitch are exactly the same, but as soon as the pitch changes, the two bevels become unequal.

Figure 8.44 shows a drawing of the relationship between length of the common rafter, overhang of the common rafter, pitch and span.

CHIMNEYS

Quite a lot of work has to be done by the carpenter around where a chimney emerges from a roof. The trimming of the rafters has to be done first, followed by the preparation behind the chimney, so that the plumber can form a gutter to receive the water that would otherwise enter the roof at this point.

Figure 8.45 shows a vertical section through a pitched roof at the point where a chimney stack passes through the roof. In the front of the chimney all that is required is the trimming piece, fixed at each end to the rafters that run past and are adjacent to the stack. The shortened rafters between these two are fixed to the trimming piece. Some people prefer to keep the trimming piece upright, allowing the top tile batten to be fixed to the intermediate rafters at a point fairly close to the stack; others keep the trimming piece at right angles to the slope and insert triangular pieces between the stack and the trimmer to allow the tile batten to be placed close to the stack. At the back of the stack can be seen the work that has to be done so that the gutter can be formed. First the trimming piece must be inserted, as in the front, and the trimmed intermediate rafters nailed to the trimming piece. Triangular pieces of timber are then nailed to the top edges of the rafters behind the stack so that boarding can be nailed across their top edges and also a short distance up the surface of the roof, to form the gutter. The gutter dimensions should be at least 150 x 150. To give the necessary tilt to the tiles at the top of the gutter, a tilting fillet should be nailed to the top edge of the gutter boarding.

Figure 8.46 shows a plan of the timberwork around the chimney and figure 8.47 shows an isometric view of the work behind the stack. Figure 8.44 also shows the usual type of finish at the eaves for domestic buildings — the closed-eaves details. (This and other types of finish have been covered in volume 1.)

Probably one of the first questions to be asked is 'How do you erect a roof?'. The answer is quite simple, as long as the correct procedure is adopted. First the wall plates are bedded on the tops of the walls with mortar, checked to see that they are parallel and — if a hipped roof is being constructed — the end plates made square to those running along the length of the roof. Assuming that the roof is hipped, the procedure would be as follows.

(1) The wall plates are marked to give the positions of the ceiling joists. These are prepared and fixed, leaving spaces where the trusses are to be positioned.

(2) Two whole trusses are fixed, as well as the ridge board. Temporary braces are nailed across the trusses after they have been plumbed.

(3) The four hips are then prepared and fixed.

(4) The remaining whole trusses are fixed.

(5) The three binders are fixed in position and then the two half-trusses at the hipped ends.

(6) The purlins are cut and fixed.

(7) The remaining common rafters are cut, doing any necessary trimming around chimney stacks.

(8) Jack rafters are cut and fixed.

(9) Finishings are completed — eaves, access to roof space, preparation around chimney for plumber, etc.

There are different types of roof covering and these can influence the slope or pitch of the roof surfaces. For example, plain tiles should be provided with a slope of around 40°, interlocking pantiles can have a pitch as low as 22½° and flat roofs should have a slope of around 1 in 60.

(1) What is the name commonly applied to the joints between a wall plate and the lower ends of the common rafters in a pitched roof?

....

(2) Ceiling joists in the construction of a roof give support to the ceilings in the rooms below. What other function do they carry out?

....
....

(3) What is the name of the boards that are fixed to the end rafters in a gable roof?

....

(4) What is the name of the horizontal pieces of timber that support the centres of the common rafters in a gable roof?

....

(5) What is the name given to factory-made frames?

....

(6) What is the name given to the piece of timber marked X in the drawing below?

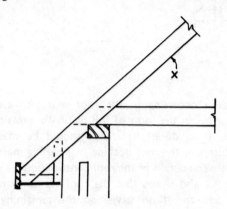

....

(7) What is the name of the eaves finish seen in the above drawing?

....

(8) What is the name of the galvanized plates that are used for fixing the butt joints in roof trusses?

....

(9) Make a sketch of a double-toothed timber connector.

(10) What is a gangnail plate?

....

9. FLAT ROOFS

Flat roofs are very prone to failure if the construction and finishings are carried out in a haphazard manner. Too often, neglect is shown in design and construction, leading to condensation, dampness, dry rot and subsequent damage to other parts of the main building.

Figure 9.1 shows the plan of a flat roof of a room adjacent to the main part of a building. The rafters run in the direction of the 'fall' (slope) of the roof. Although the surface of a flat roof is actually flat, it is by no means horizontal. Probably one of the most important considerations in the design of a flat roof is that adequate provision be made to get any water that may settle on the surface away as quickly as possible. This is done by sloping the roof surface slightly, say, to a 1 in 60 fall. The joists are laid level in position and tapering pieces of timber nailed to their tops to form the slope. The tapered strips are called firring pieces; their thinnest end should be no less than 25 mm in thickness. The covering material is laid and nailed to the firring pieces and can be in the form of tongued and grooved boarding, plywood, chipboard, etc. The joists, of course, must be positioned to suit the covering material: if boarding is used their centres can be up to 450 mm for ex 25 mm material but if 2400 x 1200 sheets of plywood are used, their centres should be 400 mm for 9 mm thick and 600 mm for 12 mm ply. For 19 mm chipboard the rafter centres should be 400 mm. Nogging pieces too must be used across the direction of the joists to strengthen the edges of the sheet material where they are butted together. In some cases the movement of the material must be allowed for when fixing to the joists.

Heavy-duty wood wool and compressed strawboard are two other sheet materials that may be used for flat-roof coverings, but care must be taken to follow the manufacturers' instructions: this is critical if an efficient roof is to be produced.

To stop the roof making the room below too hot in the summer and too cold in the winter, it is always a good idea to fix an insulating material to the top surfaces of the roof joists before the covering material is fixed. There is also a risk of condensation occurring in the roof space; to avoid this a vapour barrier, in the form of foil or plastic sheeting, may be necessary. If in doubt, reference should be made to the manufacturers of the roof decking or finishing materials, who will advise when details of the roof construction are given.

Figure 9.1 also shows that the roof has overhanging eaves on one side and flush eaves on the remaining side. To construct the overhanging eaves, short lateral joists are required to carry the joist adjacent to the fascia. Details of this and those for flush eaves are seen in figures 9.2 and 9.3. To avoid any tendency for lateral movement in the roof timbers, herringbone strutting should be included in the construction and this can be seen in figure 9.1. Folding wedges should be inserted between the first and last joists and the walls.

Figures 9.4 and 9.5 show two flat roofs, the first with its timbers spanning the width of the room without any other support, and the second using narrower joists with a beam running underneath their centres to give the required extra support. The beam should be boxed in as shown in the drawing.

Figures 9.6 and 9.7 show isometric views of the eaves details already mentioned.

(1) How is the fall to the tops of the joists in a timber flat-roof obtained?

....

....

(2) What should the fall be in mm per m?

....

(3) In what direction should the joists in a flat roof be placed? Give reasons for your answer.

....

....

....

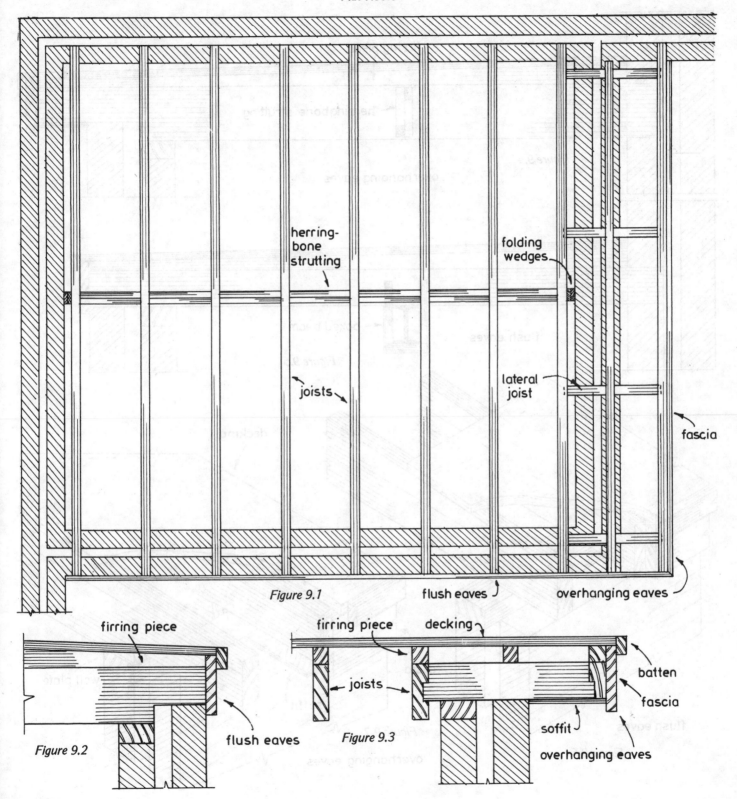

herring-
bone
strutting

folding
wedges

joists

lateral
joist

fascia

Figure 9.1

flush eaves

overhanging eaves

firring piece

firring piece

decking

joists

joists

batten

fascia

soffit

flush eaves

Figure 9.2

Figure 9.3

overhanging eaves

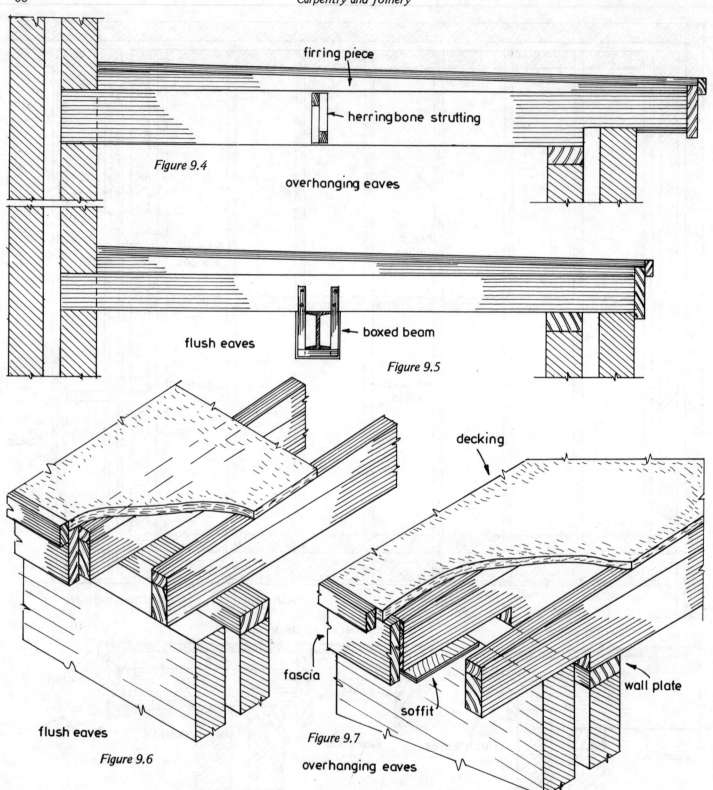

firring piece

herringbone strutting

Figure 9.4

overhanging eaves

flush eaves

boxed beam

Figure 9.5

decking

fascia

flush eaves

Figure 9.6

Figure 9.7

overhanging eaves

soffit

wall plate

(4) What should be done to prevent lateral movement in the joists?

....

....

(5) What would lead you to decide on the distance apart the joists would have to be placed?

....

....

(6) What should be included in the construction at the eaves of a flat-roof surface to prevent rainwater affecting the fascia?

....

(7) What would you do to insulate the spaces between the joists of a flat roof?

....

....

10. SINGLE TIMBER UPPER-FLOORS

Timber upper-floors can be divided into two types — single and double. Single floors are those that have their joists spanning from one wall to the other without any intermediate support; double floors are those that have their joists supported (by beams) between the supports at their ends. In this chapter we shall only deal with single upper-floors made from timber. Although fireplaces are fast disappearing in the upper floors of domestic buildings, a fireplace is included in these drawings to illustrate the trimming and hearth preparation required from the carpenter, should it be required.

Figure 10.1 shows the plan of a single upper-floor, with a fireplace opening that requires the adjacent timbers to be trimmed and allowing a concrete hearth to be formed in front of the opening.

Remember that timbers must not be built into a wall adjacent to a flue, any nearer than 200 mm to the flue. Thus the trimming joist nearest to the flue in the drawing should be positioned so that its nearest surface to the flue is 200 mm away. As an added precaution this joist may be supported on a metal shoe or a 9 mm metal plate acting as a corbel (figure 10.2) instead of building it into the wall.

The trimming and bridging joists are first placed in position, a 50 mm space being allowed for between each wall and the joist adjacent to it. The others are spaced evenly across the remaining spaces, keeping in mind that the trimmed joists should have approximately the same amount of space between them. The trimmer and trimming joists are usually a little thicker than the rest of the timbers, say 75 mm as opposed to the 50 mm of the rest of the joists. The trimmer joist is cut to fit exactly between the trimming joists and its ends supported on metal shoes (figure 10.6) the sizes of which are equal to that of the trimmer. The trimmed joists can then be cut to fit up against the trimmer, their ends being supported in the same way, with metal shoes equal in size to the timbers they support (see also figure 10.8).

To stop any lateral (sideways) movement of the joists when people are moving around on the floor, a row of herring-bone strutting is fixed by nailing between the joists near to their centres, if they are no longer than 3.5 m; otherwise an additional row of strutting should be fixed. Folding wedges are inserted and nailed in between the first and last joists and the walls to complete the row of strutting.

Figure 10.3 shows a vertical section through the floor and fireplace opening. It shows that a concrete hearth, 125 mm over-all thickness, has been formed by nailing battens to the timbers and wall; the battens support the rough boarding which in turn supports the concrete hearth. Figure 10.4 shows larger details of how the hearth is formed. The battens A and B are removed later to allow the shuttering to be taken away, leaving batten C to support the hearth. Support D is then fixed in position; it is used for fixing the sheet material forming the ceiling. Since the floorboards will be extending to half-way across the chimney breasts, a dovetailed batten (figure 10.7) is bedded into the concrete on each side of the opening, flush with its top surface, so that the boards can be nailed at their ends. These must be at least 150 mm from the fireplace opening. Figure 10.5 is an isometric view of the opening to the fireplace; one-half of the drawing shows the timbers and the other half shows the finished work.

Figure 10.9 shows the two types of flooring in common use. The first (figure 10.9a) is the normal tongued-and-grooved board and the second (figure 10.9b) is also tongued and grooved but shaped in such a way that the boards can be secretly nailed. Figure 10.10a is the type of nail to be used for the common tongued-and-grooved boards; figure 10.10b shows the lost-head nail which is most suitable for the secretly nailed boards.

Figure 10.11 shows how to make a simple trap in a floor so that services, such as electric-wiring junction-boxes, can be attended to. The tongues around the trap are removed and a shelf, supported on rough battens, made to fit in between the joists immediately below the trap. Only one screw is required to secure the trap in position if each end of the trap is cut on a bevel.

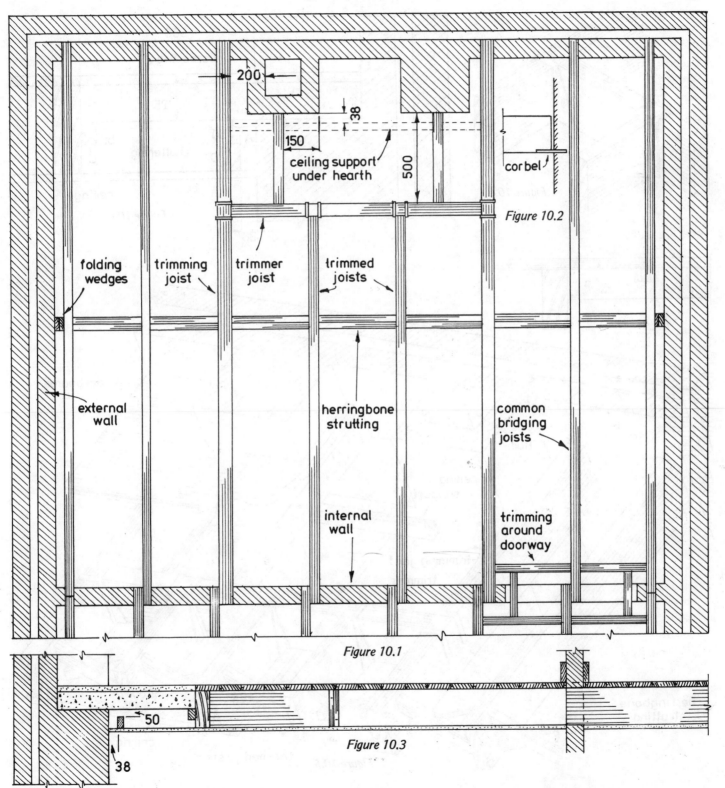

200

38

150

ceiling support
under hearth

500

corbel

Figure 10.2

folding
wedges

trimming
joist

trimmer
joist

trimmed
joists

external
wall

herringbone
strutting

common
bridging
joists

internal
wall

trimming
around
doorway

Figure 10.1

50

38

Figure 10.3

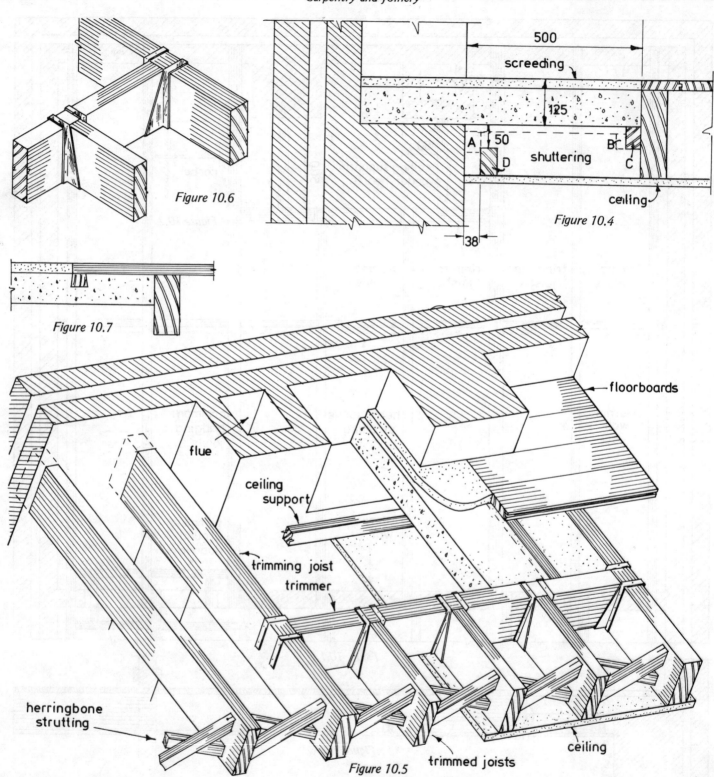

Figure 10.6

Figure 10.4

500

screeding

125

A   50

D   shuttering   B   C

ceiling

38

Figure 10.7

floorboards

flue

ceiling
support

trimming joist
trimmer

herringbone
strutting

Figure 10.5   trimmed joists   ceiling

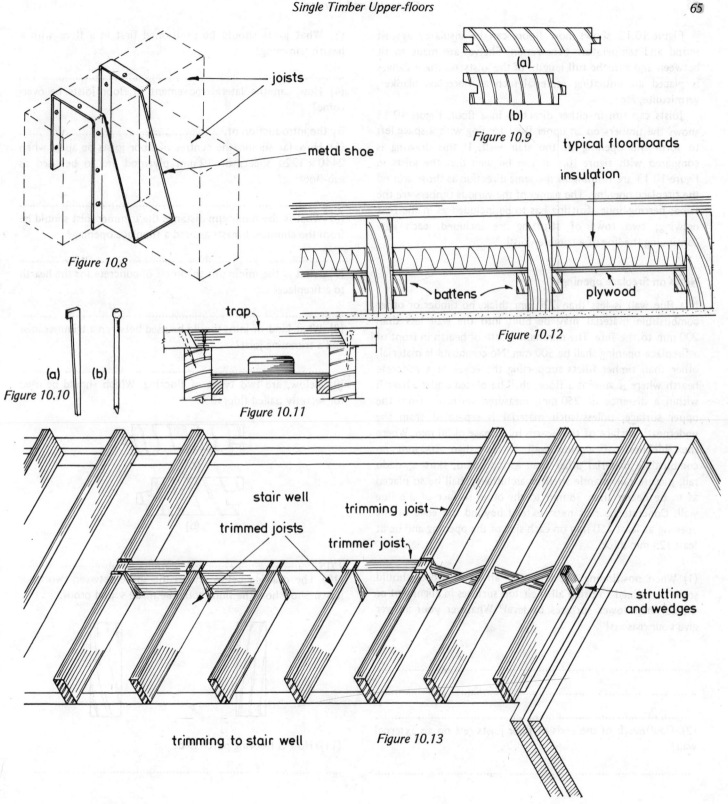

joists

metal shoe

Figure 10.8

(a)

(b)

Figure 10.10

trap

Figure 10.11

(a)

(b)

Figure 10.9

typical floorboards

insulation

battens

plywood

Figure 10.12

stair well

trimmed joists

trimming joist

trimmer joist

strutting
and wedges

trimming to stair well

Figure 10.13

Figure 10.12 shows how floors can be insulated against sound and temperature penetration. Shelves are made to fit between and run the full lengths of the joists; on these shelves is placed an insulating material such as fibreglass blanket, vermiculite, etc.

Joists can run in either direction in a floor. Figure 10.13 shows the timbers on an upper-floor landing with a space left to form the opening of the stair well. If this drawing is compared with figure 10.1 it can be seen that the joists in figure 10.13 are running in the same direction as those around the fireplace opening. The names of the various timbers are the same; herring-bone strutting has to be included as in the first drawing; two rows of strutting are included, each row continuing the line of a trimmer joist.

Notes on fireplace openings

If a flue wall is less than 200 mm thick, no timber or other combustible material may be built into the wall less than 200 mm to the flue. The minimum width of hearth in front of a fireplace opening shall be 500 mm. No combustible material, other than timber fillets supporting the edges of a concrete hearth where it adjoins a floor, shall be placed under a hearth within a distance of 250 mm, measured vertically from the upper surface, unless such material is separated from the underneath surface of the hearth by a space of 50 mm. Where the thickness of a flue wall is less than 200 mm no combustible material other than a floorboard, skirting, dado rail, picture rail, mantle shelf or architrave, shall be so placed as to be nearer than 38 mm to the outer surface of the flue wall. Concrete hearths must extend beyond the edge of the opening at least 150 mm on each side of the opening and be at least 125 mm thick.

(1) When positioning the joists for an upper floor, should some be packed to bring all their top surfaces in alignment or should their lower surfaces be level? Whatever your answer give your reasons!

....

....

(2) How much of the ends of floor joists rest on an external wall?

....

(3) What joists should be positioned first in a floor with a hearth trimming?

....

(4) How can the lateral movement in floor joists be overcome?

By the introduction of. ....

(5) How far should the centres of floor joists be apart when 2440 x 1220 sheets of 12 mm plywood are to be used as sub-flooring?

....

(6) What is the minimum distance the trimmer joist should be from the chimney breasts around a fireplace opening?

....

(7) What is the minimum thickness of concrete for the hearth to a fireplace?

....

(8) What kind of joint should be used between a trimmer joist and a trimming joist?

....

(9) Below, are two types of flooring. Which should be used for secretly nailed floors?

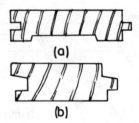

(a)

(b)

Type..

(10) The drawing below shows the space between two floor joists. Show how the floor could be made sound proof.

(11) How is flooring purchased?

....

(12) How are floor joists purchased?

....

(13) What types of nails are used for (a) tongued-and-grooved flooring, (b) secretly nailed flooring.

(a) ....

(b) ....

11. STUD PARTITIONS

Partitions are used mainly for dividing large areas up into smaller areas. For instance, a large room in a house may have to be divided up to make two or more smaller rooms. Sometimes partitions are required with no openings; at other times they may need to have doors or windows provided.

Before building a common timber partition — usually called a stud partition — it is necessary to find out what the surfaces of the partition are to be covered with. There are many forms of cladding material, for example matchboarding, sheet material such as plasterboarding, insulating board, plywood, etc. This information is necessary so that the studding (the vertical members of the partition) can be fixed at the correct distances apart.

Another important thing, of course, is to build the partition in a perfectly upright position. This can be done by first finding the position of the top plate, which is fixed to the ceiling joists with screws. If the joists are as shown in figure 11.1 parallel to the partition, it may be necessary to build in bridging pieces so that the top plate can be fixed adequately (see figure 11.2). Once the top plate has been fixed, a plumb bob can be dropped from the plate to give the exact position of the lower plate (figure 11.3) which can be fixed to the floor joists below. If the two floors are of a different material, such as concrete, naturally the plates will have to be fixed by other means — Rawlplugs or Rawlbolts (figure 11.5).

Figure 11.4 shows the preliminary steps completed in the construction of a simple stud partition, which is to be covered with 2440 x 1220 mm sheet material. The top and lower plates have been plumbed and fixed and the two wall-studs have also been fixed by screws and Rawlplugs (assuming the walls are of brickwork or concrete). The next step is to fix the studs to which the edges of the sheet material are fixed. If the dimension is to be 1220 mm, that length is measured from the wall surface to give the centre of the first stud to be fixed. The centre of the next stud to be fixed is found by measuring another 1220 mm from the centre of the first stud. This is repeated along the whole length of the partition; then the intermediate studs can be fixed. Most sheet materials require two intermediate studs for adequate support. Nogging pieces are the short horizontal timbers fixed in rows across the partition; they serve to stabilise the studs and give additional fixing surfaces. All the various members of a stud partition are butt jointed together and nailed unless otherwise requested. Figure 11.4 shows the elevation of a stud partition, prior to fixing the sheet material, and includes, in broken lines, the intermediate studs and nogging pieces.

Figure 11.6 shows the timbers round a doorway. Two studs and a head are required for the opening and the joints around the opening are seen in figures 11.7 and 11.8. The head is mortised and tenoned to the studs — the tenon shoulders are bevelled as seen in the drawing. The tenon is allowed to pass through the stud and beyond for a distance of, say, 100 mm and a hardwood wedge is driven through a small mortise at the back of the joint to keep the shoulders up tight. An alternative to this small wedge is a dowel through the centre of the tenon, similar to that shown for the joint at the foot of the opening. This is a dovetail joint, the pin being on the vertical stud. The joint, as seen in the drawing, is secured by a dowel. When marking out the position of the doorway, allowance must be made for the thickness of the door frame or lining, which will fit in between the studs and below the head; the size of the door must also be taken into account (see figure 11.9).

The linings must be made to a width equal to the thickness of the timber partition plus the thickness of the cladding material that is fixed on both sides. The joints between the cladding material and the linings are hidden by architraves, mitred around the opening on both sides.

The sound and thermal insulation of timber partitions can be done in several ways; the cheaper the job, the less efficient, usually, is the insulation. To make sound insulation to a partition more efficient, an insulating material should be placed between the top and lower plates, as shown in figure 11.10. Figure 11.11 shows what is probably the most

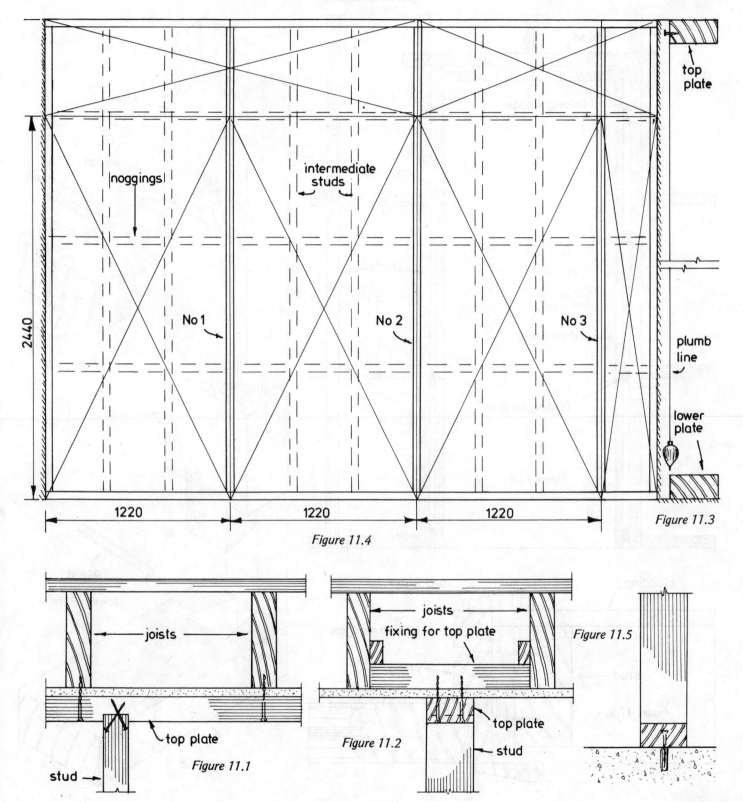

noggings

intermediate studs

No 1

No 2

No 3

2440

1220   1220   1220

top plate

plumb line

lower plate

Figure 11.3

Figure 11.4

joists

top plate

stud

Figure 11.1

joists

fixing for top plate

top plate

stud

Figure 11.2

Figure 11.5

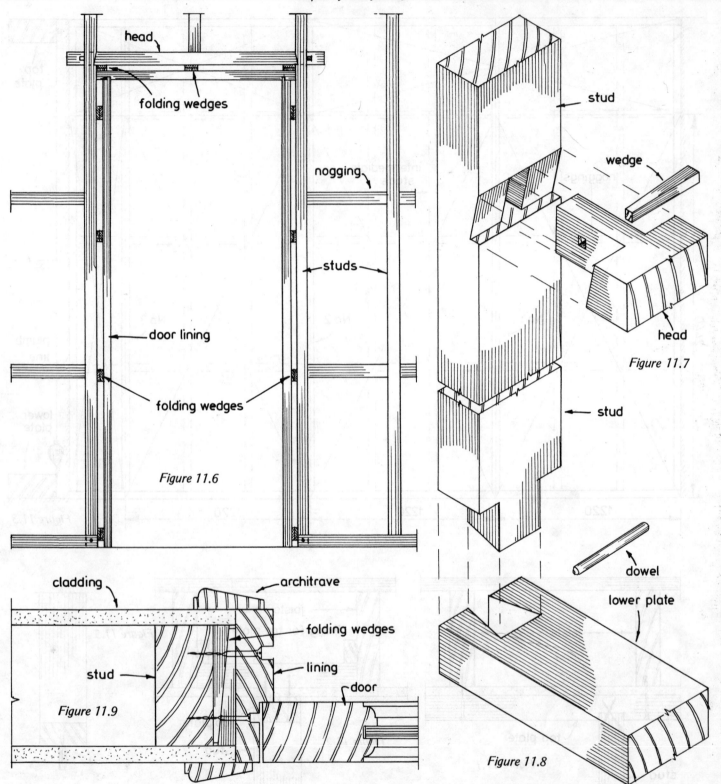

head

folding wedges

nogging

studs

door lining

folding wedges

Figure 11.6

stud

wedge

head

Figure 11.7

stud

dowel

lower plate

Figure 11.8

cladding

architrave

folding wedges

stud

lining

door

Figure 11.9

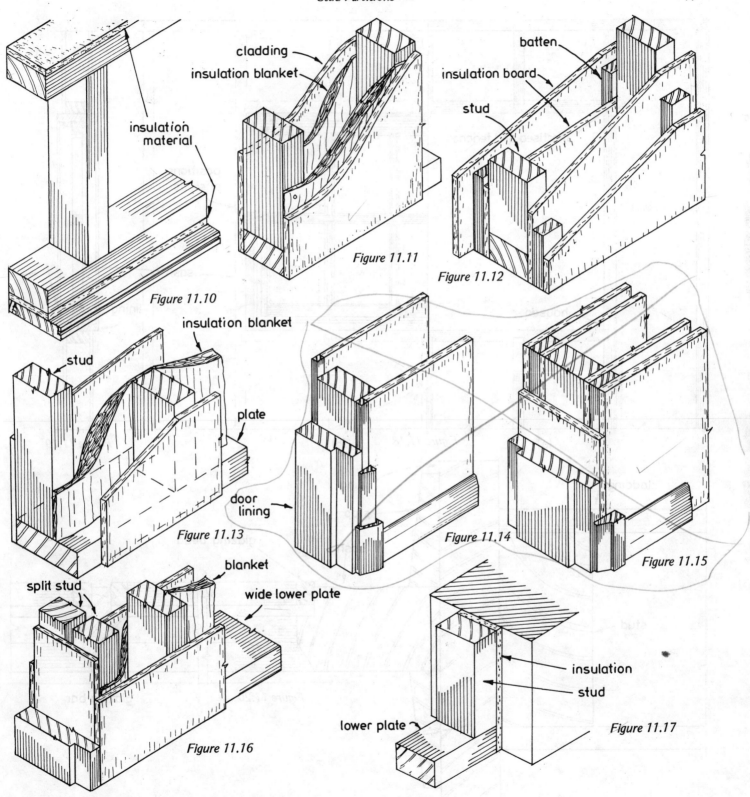

insulation
material

Figure 11.10

cladding
insulation blanket

Figure 11.11

batten
insulation board
stud

Figure 11.12

insulation blanket
stud
plate

Figure 11.13

door
lining

Figure 11.14

Figure 11.15

split stud
blanket
wide lower plate

Figure 11.16

insulation
stud
lower plate

Figure 11.17

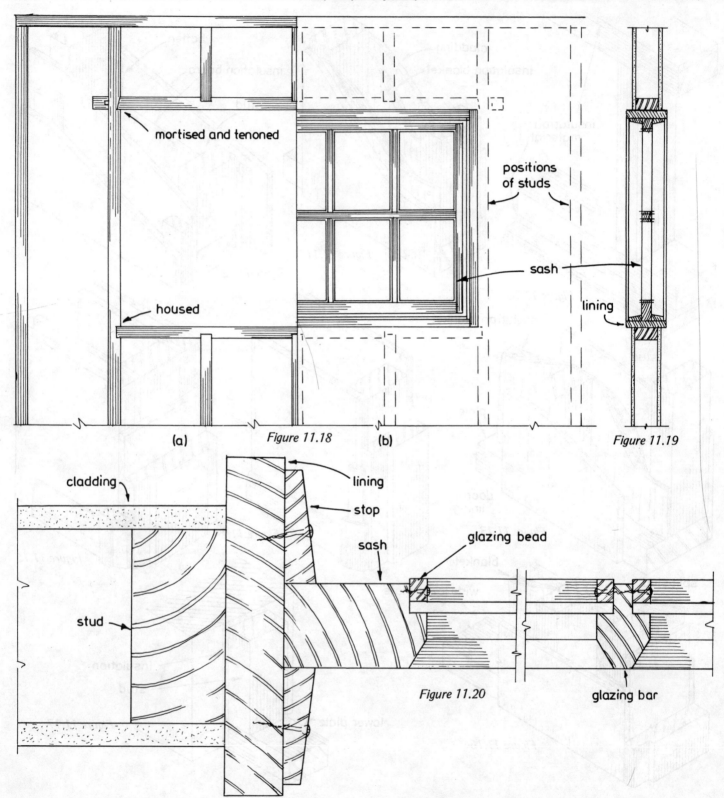

mortised and tenoned

housed

positions
of studs

sash

lining

(a)   *Figure 11.18*   (b)   *Figure 11.19*

cladding

lining

stop

sash

glazing bead

stud

Figure 11.20

glazing bar

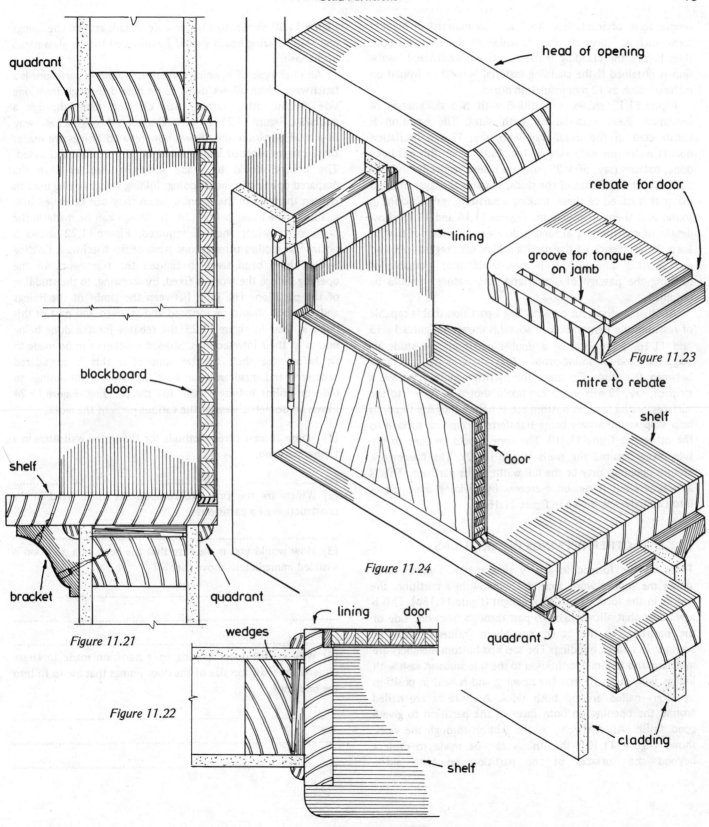

quadrant

shelf

blockboard door

bracket

quadrant

Figure 11.21

wedges

Figure 11.22

head of opening

rebate for door

lining

groove for tongue on jamb

Figure 11.23

mitre to rebate

door

shelf

Figure 11.24

lining

door

quadrant

cladding

shelf

simple form of insulation. An insulating material in blanket form, such as fibreglass, etc., is nailed to the studs on both sides before the cladding material is fixed. Additional insulation is obtained if the cladding material is itself an insulation material, such as 12 mm insulation board.

Figure 11.12 shows a partition with two thicknesses of insulation sheet material on both sides. The partition is constructed in the usual way with, say, 12 mm insulation boards nailed on each side of the studs. When this has been done, battens (say, 50 x 25 mm) are nailed vertically on both sides over the positions of the studs, and another layer of sheet material is nailed to these, making a partition very efficient in sound and thermal insulation. Figures 11.14 and 11.15 show details of partitioning around a doorway. Remember that to keep the efficiency of the partition high with regard to sound and thermal insulation, a purpose-made door — capable of resisting the passage of sound and temperature — should be obtained.

Another method for constructing a partition that is capable of resisting the penetration of sound is shown in figures 11.13 and 11.16. It consists of a double partition; the studs are staggered and a sound-proof sheet material is interlaced between the studs. To make the partition more effective, a strip of, say, 12 mm insulation board should be nailed to the surfaces of the top and bottom plates before they are fixed, to help stop sound waves being transferred from one surface to the other (see figure 11.10). The same should be done to the side pieces against the walls (figure 11.17). The framework around openings may be the full width of the partition. This is a weakness but it can be overcome by dividing these pieces into two halves as shown in figure 11.16.

OTHER OPENINGS IN PARTITIONS

These can be formed in a very simple way. Figure 11.18a shows the timber work around a window in a partition; the sash is in the form of a borrowed light (figure 11.18b). This is a window that allows light to pass through from one side of the partition to the other, possibly a formerly badly lit corridor in a large building. The top and bottom members are mortised and tenoned, or housed to the side studs. A sash with linings is made to fit into the opening and is held in position by stops nailed around both sides. Architraves are nailed around the opening on both faces of the partition to give a good finish. Alternatively, as the section through the work shows (figure 11.19), the linings can be made to project beyond the surfaces of the partition on both sides.

Figure 11.20 shows, to a larger scale, details around the linings and sash. Glazing beads should be provided for the glass panes in the sash.

Another type of opening sometimes found in partitions is a hatchway, which allows items to be passed through from one side to the other rather than carrying them through a doorway. Figure 11.21 is a vertical section through a hatchway in a stud partition and shows how rebated linings are made: these can be tongued and grooved at their corners and nailed. The linings should be made somewhat smaller than the prepared opening in the studding, folding wedges being used to tighten them up in the opening when they can be nailed into position. The lower portion of the linings can be made in the form of a wider shelf if required. Figure 11.22 shows a horizontal section through one jamb of the hatchway. Folding wedges have been used to tighten the framework in the opening before the work is fixed, by screwing, to the studding of the partition. The joint between the jambs of the linings and the shelf should be tongued and grooved and part of this joint is seen in figure 11.23 the rebates for the door being mitred at their intersections. Shaped brackets can be made to fit below the shelf to give support if this is considered necessary and quadrants can be fitted around the linings to hide the joints between them and the cladding. Figure 11.24 shows an isometric view of the various parts of the work.

(1) Name at least three methods for fixing the wall studs in a timber partiton.

(a) .... (b) .... (c) ....
(2) Which are the first two components to be fixed in the construction of a partition?

....

(3) How would you make sure that the head of a partition is situated immediately above the sill?

....

....

....

(4) Why is the door opening in a partition made to larger dimensions than the size of the door linings that are to fit into the opening?

....

....

....

(5) What are noggins and what is their purpose?

....

....

....

(6) Name at least three materials that can be used for sound
and thermal insulation in partitions.

(a) ....

(b) ....

(c) ....

(7) What is the common size of building board used in the
cladding of partitions, in millimetres?

....

(8) To what centres should the studs be fixed when using the
above size sheet material?

....

(9) Name the ironmongery item that could be used for fixing
a batten to the surface of the cladding to a partition.

....

....

(10) Make a sketch of an alternative piece of ironmongery
that could be used for the same purpose.

12. PREFABRICATED BUILDINGS

Site huts for workmen, site agents and foremen should be made in sections for easy assembly and transportation. Nothing elaborate is needed, but even so, a site hut must be well ventilated and draught proof and, in the colder weather, warm!

The smaller type of hut is made from a floor section, four frames for the walls and a roof section. Figure 12.1 shows a horizontal section through the four sides of a site hut. For rigidity and to avoid using braces in the frames they are clad on their external surfaces with 9 mm resin-bonded plywood. Figures 12.2 and 12.3 show pictorial views of two of the frames — top and bottom plates and vertical studding, with one or more rows of nogging pieces in between. The two frames also show openings for a window and a door. Most of the intersections between the timbers in the frames are butt jointed but some people prefer to house them together — the housing need only be 10 mm in depth. The joints are secured with two 125 mm wire nails.

If the hut is also to be lined inside, the lining need only be 6 mm plywood or even 3 mm tempered hardboard. This lining is nailed to the inside surfaces of the frames extending right through to the external edges. A thermal-insulation material, such as 50 mm fibreglass blanket, could be tacked between the studs before the internal lining is fixed (see figure 12.13). The four frames are bolted together at the four corners (figures 12.4 and 12.5) and openings left in the inside linings so that the nuts can be started on the ends of the bolts (figure 12.6). Failing this, bolts can be inserted in the framework and secured in position, as shown in figure 12.7, before the inside lining is fixed. This will involve sinking the head of the bolt into the surface of the stud and then screwing a cover plate of mild steel on to the surface of the stud. This will ensure the bolt being kept in position during assembly.

The floor is made of one or more sections made from 100 x 38 joists framed together and covered with 12 mm plywood (figure 12.8). If there is more than one section, they can be bolted together on site.

The roof section is made of tapered 150 x 38 timbers (figure 12.11) covered with 9 mm plywood on their top edges and secured together on their lower edges by two plates, positioned to coincide with the top plates of the side frames to which they are bolted. The roof is so constructed that the covering (two layers of bituminous felt) can be dressed over the sides to form drips and to receive a gutter at the lower end of the fall if necessary. A section through the eaves of the roof is seen in figure 12.12. Figure 12.9 is a vertical section through a door opening with a louvred ventilator above but, of course, this item plus the windows will be included only if required, or if other arrangements are not desired. Only a very cheap type of door is necessary (unless security is needed) — a ledged and braced door is most common. Windows, too, are quite simple in construction — no mouldings or other refinements are necessary (figure 12.10).

When assembling the hut on a site the position must be levelled as much as possible and sleepers or concrete blocks placed on the levelled ground (see figure 12.11). A little time spent on the preparation of the site will pay dividends later, and provision should be made for the disposal of water from the roof; duck-boards should be provided outside the hut to stop the entrance becoming muddy. Electricity must be provided to give light and possibly heat. Benches for the inspection and making of drawings will be required, as will seats, coat hooks, cupboards, etc.

DOMESTIC TIMBER BUILDINGS

A more sophisticated kind of timber building is the domestic type, which is more commonly one or two storeys high. Firms throughout the United Kingdom manufacture these buildings under factory conditions and several different designs can be obtained. These buildings may be clad on the outside with various types of timber boarding, or a brick outer skin may be built to make the building look more traditional. Whichever

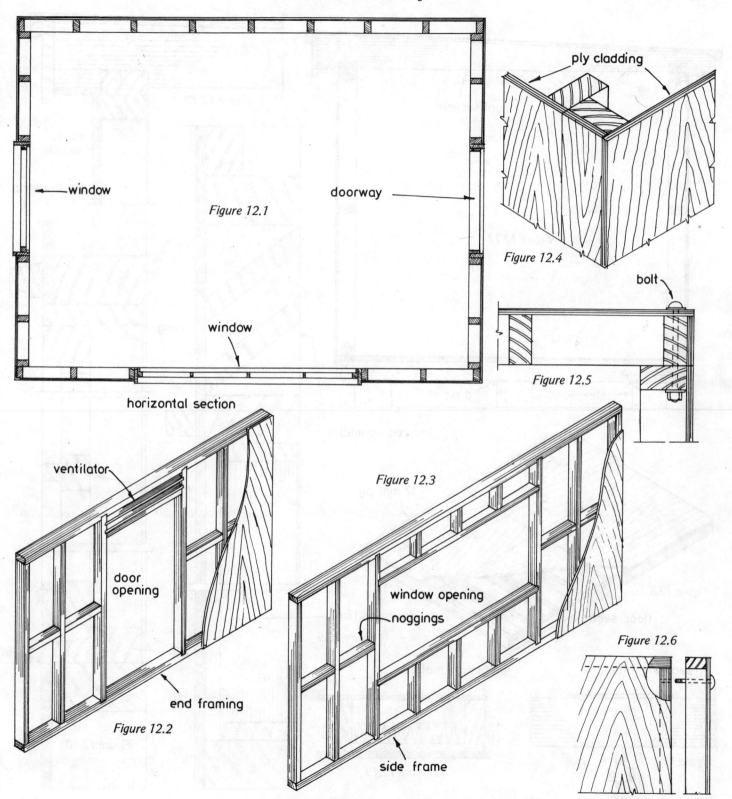

window

doorway

Figure 12.1

window

horizontal section

ply cladding

Figure 12.4

bolt

Figure 12.5

ventilator

door
opening

end framing

Figure 12.2

Figure 12.3

window opening

noggings

side frame

Figure 12.6

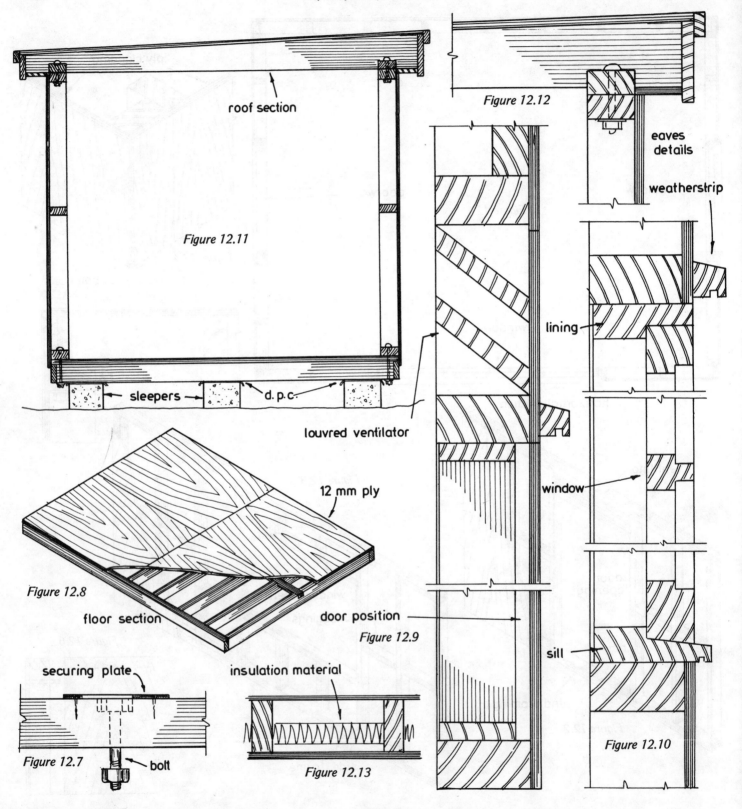

roof section

Figure 12.11

Figure 12.12

eaves details

weatherstrip

louvred ventilator

lining

window

sleepers   d. p. c.

12 mm ply

Figure 12.8

floor section

sill

door position

Figure 12.9

Figure 12.10

securing plate

insulation material

bolt

Figure 12.7

Figure 12.13

finish is chosen, the resulting building, which is basically timber, is extremely comfortable to live in.

There are two methods used for the construction of timber houses – the platform method and the balloon method. For single-storey buildings there is little advantage in either method, but in two- or more-storey timber buildings, the author prefers the platform method, because at each stage in the building a platform is constructed on which the workmen can be placed to start on the next stage.

Figure 12.14 shows a vertical section through a single-storey dwelling constructed by the platform method. The brickwork is brought up to a level and damp-proof courses are laid on all the walls at least 150 mm above ground level, when the plates are placed over them. The ground floor is then constructed and 12 mm plywood subfloor laid and nailed to the joists to form a working platform. Header boards should run along each end of the joists to support the plywood subfloor. The wall frames are then made and lifted into position. These have their studs spaced so that 12 mm thick sheets of external plywood can be nailed to their outside edges, making certain that a stud is spaced centrally below the edges of each sheet of plywood. (No braces are necessary in the framing because the plywood sheets will keep the frames square and rigid.) Double studs are required at points where external frames meet at a corner as shown in figures 12.15 and 12.16. Double head plates are also required to the frames; the reason for this is that the studs will be spaced at approximately 400 mm centres, whereas the roof trusses will be around 600 mm centres. Some trusses will not come directly over a stud, therefore the top plates to the frames will need strengthening. Figure 12.17 shows isometric details at floor level. At a later stage the plywood subfloor will be covered with the required finish.

Figure 12.18 shows a view of a roof truss suitable for a timber house. Each truss is made from fairly light material such as 75 x 25. All joints are butt joints, with 9 mm plywood gusset plates glued and nailed on each side. These are spaced around 600 mm centres, so that 2400 x 1200 x 12 mm plywood covering sheets can be fixed to them by nailing. Eaves details are shown in figure 12.19. The roof trusses are fairly low pitched, say 22½°, so, if required, a fairly wide overhang can be formed at the eaves without interfering with the windows and doorways.

The ceiling material will have to be supported on 50 x 32 mm battens (see figure 12.14) which are nailed and run in the opposite direction to the trusses. These battens, fixed at 400 mm centres, are provided because the roof trusses are fixed at 600 mm centres, which is too great to give adequate support to the ceiling material.

Figure 12.20 shows a part vertical section through the balloon type of construction. With this method the wall frames are placed directly on to the walls, with a damp-proof course in between and the joists placed on the tops of the lower plates. One disadvantage in this construction is that if a fire breaks out under the floor, the spaces between the studs in the frames tend to suck the flames up very quickly to the top of the building and possibly engulf it in a very serious fire in a short space of time. To prevent this, fire stops are nailed between the studs at floor level (figure 12.20) – these are not necessary in the platform method.

The lining to the walls of the building must be done efficiently if trouble is not to be met with at a later date. Probably the three most important things to think about when finishing the external walls to a timber building are insulation, condensation and the penetration of moisture. Condensation, if allowed to form in the cavities between the studs, could eventually lead to a fungus (such as dry rot) attacking the timbers. Condensation can be caused by water vapour passing through the inner linings of the walls and settling in the cavities in the form of water droplets. This water vapour must be avoided by covering the inside surfaces of the studs with, say, foil or a sheet of polythene before the inside lining is fixed (see figure 12.21); this sheeting is called a vapour barrier.

Moisture must also be prevented from entering the framework from the outside. This is done by tacking sheathing paper to the outside surface of the plywood sheets covering the studs; this is called a moisture barrier. The external cladding in the form of boarding is then nailed over the sheathing paper. A little of the water vapour may penetrate through into the cavities. The building paper will be able to breath, which means that although it is capable of preventing moisture entering the building, it will also allow any water vapour to pass through to the outside.

Window and door openings are constructed with double jambs, the inside half of each supporting the two pieces of 150 x 50 on edge, which form the lintels above each of the openings. Details of these two openings are shown in figures 12.22a and 12.23a, and horizontal sections through suggested finishings to these are shown in figure 12.22b and 12.23b.

Figures 12.24, 12.25 and 12.26 show details of internal wall frames intersecting with other wall frames. Figure 12.24 shows that two studs are required in the cross-wall frame where the intersection takes place to give adequate fixing and

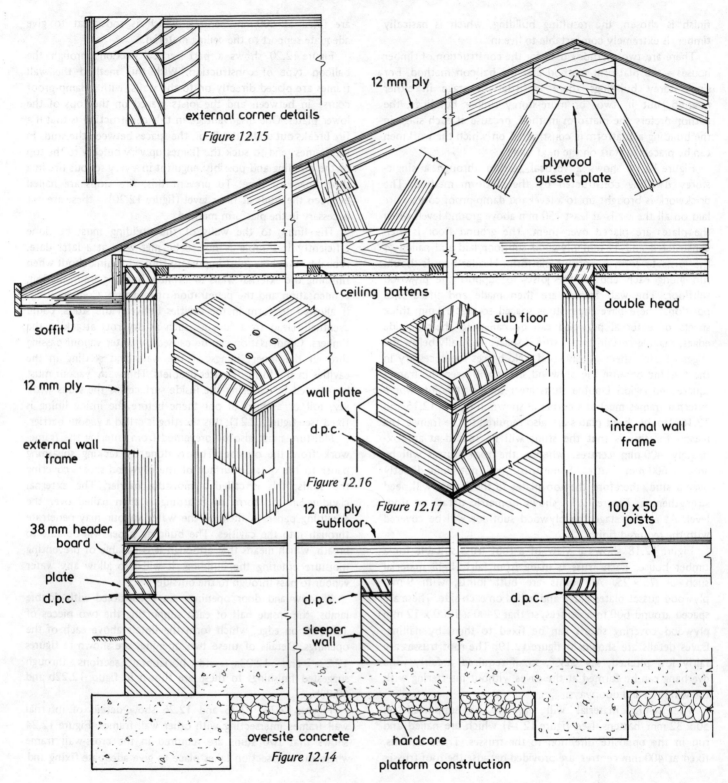

external corner details

Figure 12.15

12 mm ply

plywood gusset plate

ceiling battens

soffit

double head

sub floor

12 mm ply

wall plate

d.p.c.

internal wall frame

external wall frame

Figure 12.16

Figure 12.17

100 x 50 joists

12 mm ply subfloor

38 mm header board

plate

d.p.c.

d.p.c.

sleeper wall

d.p.c.

oversite concrete

hardcore

Figure 12.14

platform construction

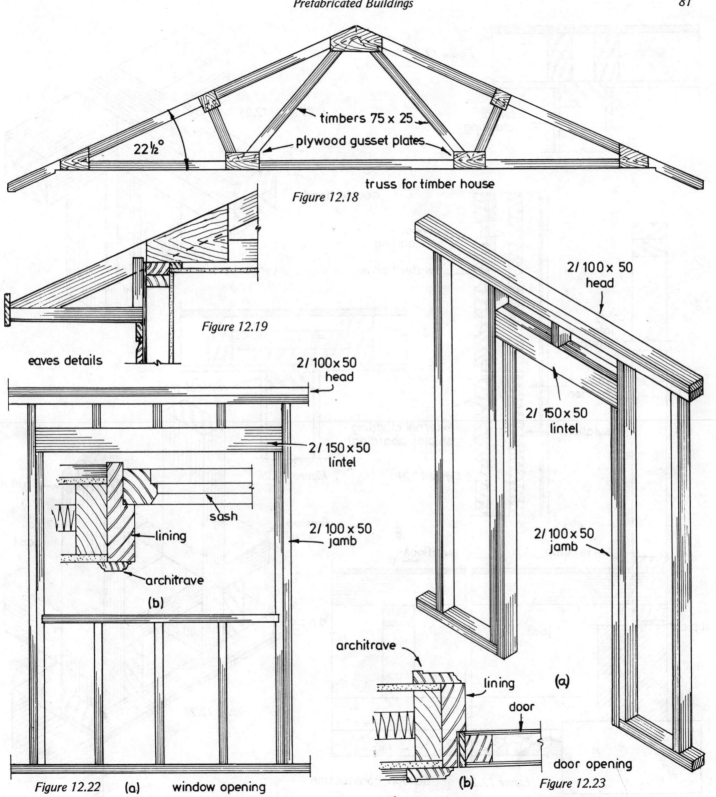

22½°

timbers 75 x 25

plywood gusset plates

truss for timber house

Figure 12.18

Figure 12.19

eaves details

2/ 100 x 50 head

2/ 150 x 50 lintel

2/ 100 x 50 jamb

2/ 100 x 50 head

2/ 150 x 50 lintel

2/ 100 x 50 jamb

sash

lining

architrave

(b)

architrave

lining

door

(a)

Figure 12.22   (a)   window opening

(b)   door opening   *Figure 12.23*

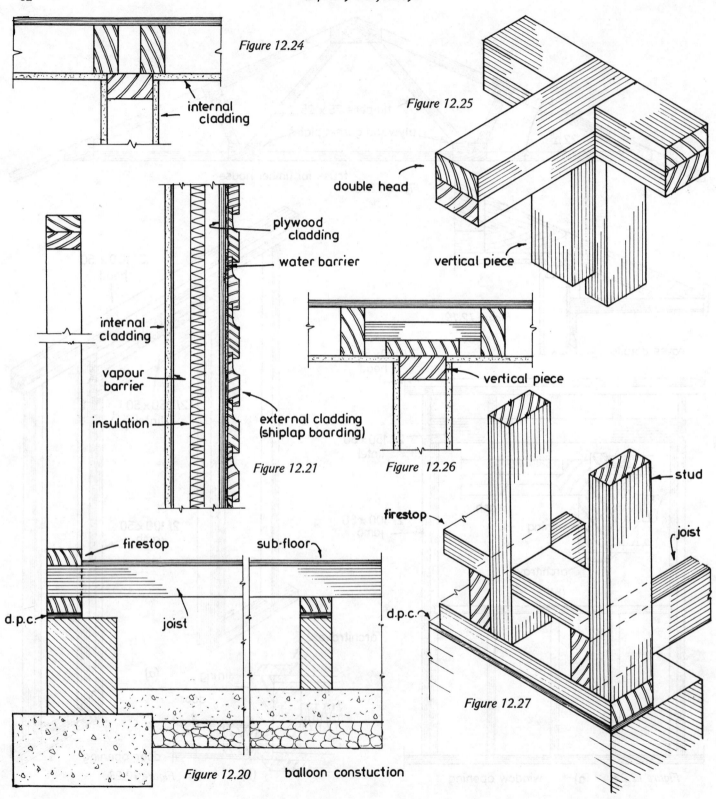

Figure 12.24

internal cladding

Figure 12.25

double head

vertical piece

plywood cladding

water barrier

internal cladding

vapour barrier

insulation

external cladding (shiplap boarding)

Figure 12.21

vertical piece

Figure 12.26

stud

firestop

joist

firestop

sub-floor

d.p.c.

joist

d.p.c.

Figure 12.27

Figure 12.20   balloon constuction

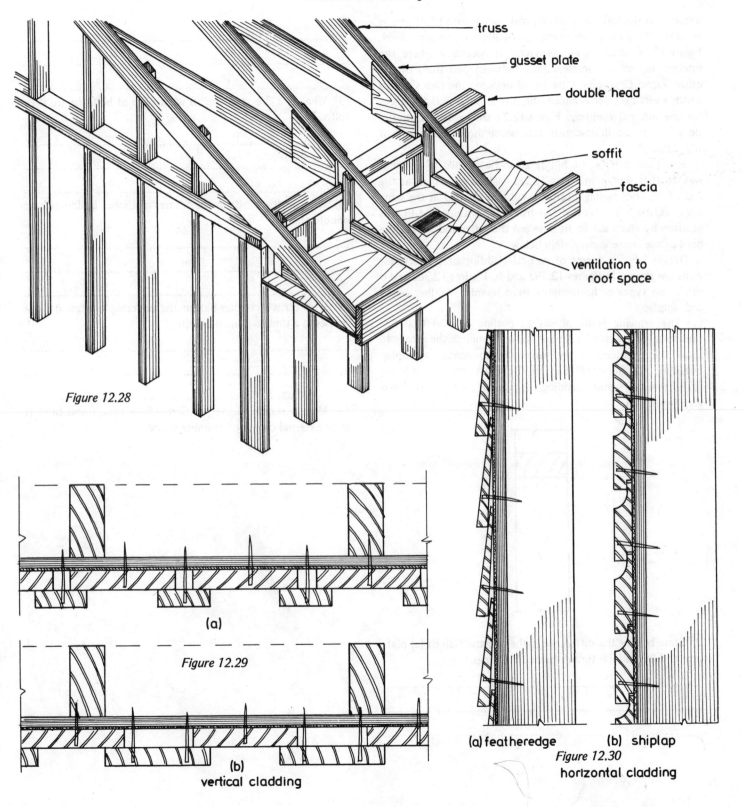

truss

gusset plate

double head

soffit

fascia

ventilation to
roof space

Figure 12.28

(a)

Figure 12.29

(b)
vertical cladding

(a) featheredge (b) shiplap
Figure 12.30
horizontal cladding

support to the internal cladding material. Figure 12.25 shows an isometric view of the same intersection at top-plate level. Figure 12.26 shows what provision is necessary where the intersection of one frame comes between two studs of the other frame. Cross-pieces are nailed between the two studs to which a vertical piece is nailed; this provides the fixing surfaces for the internal cladding. Figure 12.27 shows details around floor level to a balloon-constructed house showing positions of fire stops, etc.

The gable end to the building can be formed in a similar way to that shown in figure 12.28. Instead of a truss at the end of the roof, a single rafter is cut and pitched at the same angle as the top edges of the trusses and supported in this position by studs cut to fit between the rafter and the double head of the frame immediately below.

Details of two forms of vertical cladding of the exterior walls are shown in figures 12.29a and b. Figures 12.30a and b show two types of horizontally fixed boards — feather edged and shiplap.

(1) The drawing below shows an outline of a vertical section through a wall of a timber house. Complete the details to show the positions of the various components: (a) shiplap boarding, (b) moisture barriers, (c) plasterboard cladding, (d) 12 mm plywood cladding, (e) vapour barrier, (f) fibreglass insulation.

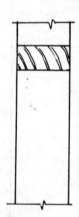

(2) State briefly the difference in the construction of (a) platform and (b) balloon timber-framed buildings.

....

....

....

....

....

....

(3) What is a fire stop and in what type of building are they found?

....

....

(4) Why do the heads in the frames of timber buildings have double plates?

....

....

(5) Why do we counter-batten the underneath edges of roof trusses in a timber-framed building?

....

....

(6) Make a sketch of the positions of the main frame timbers at an external corner of a timber house.

13. WINDOWS

Windows which give light and ventilation to areas can be divided up into several groups; the most common of these are (1) casements, which are usually hinged, (2) sash, which slide vertically or horizontally, and (3) pivot, which revolve round a central point.

CASEMENT WINDOWS

Figure 13.1 shows the elevation of a casement window; the frame consists of a sill, a head, two jambs, a mullion and a transom — which make it a four-light casement window. The two lower casements would each be hinged to one of their stiles and the top two — which are called fanlights — would be hinged to their top rails if they opened outwards and to their bottom rails if they were required to open into the room.

Figure 13.2 shows a vertical section through the frame and casements, showing the shapes and sizes of the head, transom and sill of the frame, and the shapes and sizes of the rails of the casements. Notice that capillary grooves are included in the frame and sash members, drips are made in the bottom surfaces near to the front edges of the sill and transom and grooves are also included in the sill to receive a water bar (on the lower surface and the tongue to the window board on the inside surface).

Figure 13.3 shows a part horizontal section through the frame and a casement and shows the shapes and sizes of the jambs, mullion and stiles of the casements.

Figures 13.4 to 13.9 show the various joints involved in the manufacture of a casement window.

Figure 13.4 shows one of the mortises in the head to receive the tenon on the top end of one of the jambs (figure 13.6). Note in both drawings that the mouldings have been prepared to be scribed at their intersections.

Figure 13.5 shows one end of the sill and also shows the preparation necessary for scribing the mouldings. Remember that the sill is weathered — this is the slope provided on its top surface so that water will run off fairly quickly; thus the outside shoulder to the tenon on the lower end of each jamb must be bevelled to allow for the slope on the sill. The amount of slope necessary will, of course, be obtained from the workshop roll but a glance at figure 13.2, which is similar to the details that would be seen on the rod, will show the amount of slope required.

Figures 13.7 and 13.8 shows the mortise and tenon joint for the casements and again show that the mouldings are scribed. Incidentally, if the depth of the mouldings is kept exactly the same as the depth of the rebates, the result will be level shoulders on the tenons.

Figure 13.9 shows an exploded isometric view of the frame and special note should be made of the joint between the jamb and the transom. It shows the mortise and tenon with the mouldings scribed as before but the front edge of the transom is recessed into the front edge of the jamb. This makes for a more weather-resistant joint.

Another type of casement window is the French casement; the elevation, horizontal and vertical sections are shown in figure 13.10. (Many people regard this type of construction as a door.) A French casement can be arranged in several ways. The one shown in figure 13.10 shows a single door and two fixed side lights. If necessary, of course, double doors can be included with no lights or single or double lights — it depends what is required. The joints for the frame would be very similar to those already mentioned and those for the opening light or door would be similar for those shown for framed doors (see p. 102). The joints at the intersections of the glazing bars can be treated in one of two ways. Figures 13.11a and b shows one of these joints and the drawings show how the bars are prepared for halving. Figure 14.17 shows the second method, that of mortising and tenoning.

SLIDING SASH WINDOWS

There are two fairly common methods for the construction of frames to receive sliding sashes — those with and those without

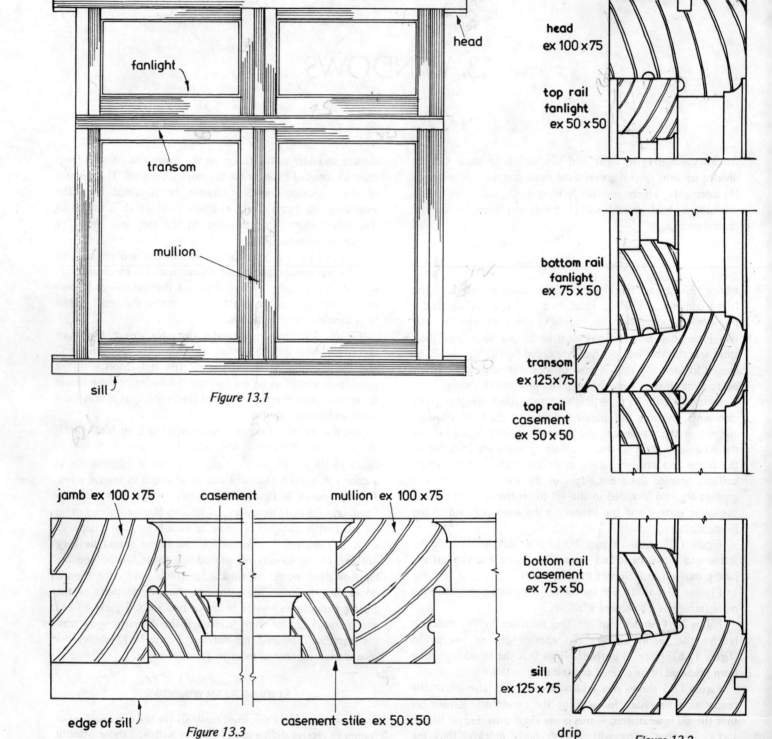

fanlight

head

transom

mullion

sill

Figure 13.1

head
ex 100 x 75

top rail
fanlight
ex 50 x 50

bottom rail
fanlight
ex 75 x 50

transom
ex 125 x 75

top rail
casement
ex 50 x 50

bottom rail
casement
ex 75 x 50

sill
ex 125 x 75

Figure 13.2

jamb ex 100 x 75   casement   mullion ex 100 x 75

edge of sill

Figure 13.3

casement stile ex 50 x 50

drip

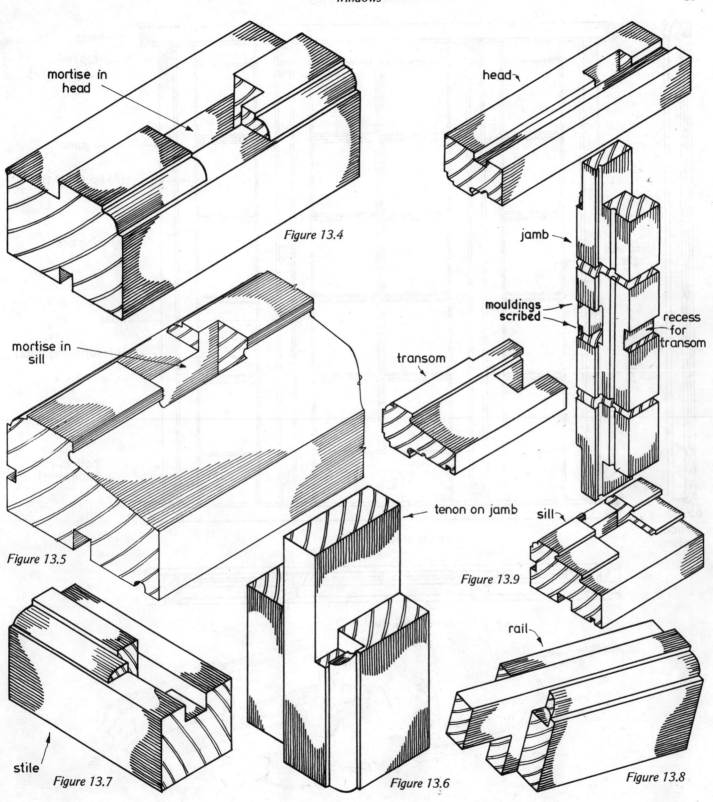

mortise in head

Figure 13.4

head

jamb

mouldings scribed

recess for transom

mortise in sill

transom

Figure 13.5

tenon on jamb

sill

Figure 13.9

stile

Figure 13.7

Figure 13.6

rail

Figure 13.8

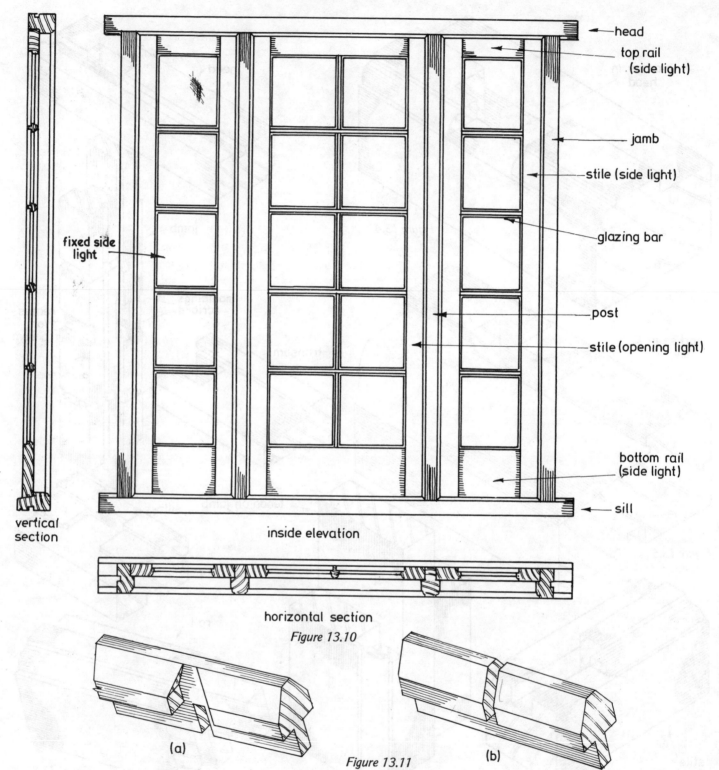

head

top rail
(side light)

jamb

stile (side light)

glazing bar

post

stile (opening light)

bottom rail
(side light)

sill

fixed side
light

vertical
section

inside elevation

horizontal section

Figure 13.10

(a)

Figure 13.11

(b)

side boxes. When the frames are made with boxes, these boxes house the weights to counterbalance the sashes. Let us first consider the frame without the boxes.

Figures 13.12a, b and c show part elevation, vertical section and part horizontal section of a window with sliding sashes. Little information can be obtained from the elevation other than what a window of this type looks like. A glance at the vertical section shows that there are two sashes — the top sash and the bottom sash. These are separated by a parting bead (see horizontal section) and the gap between them is closed by the two meeting rails when both sashes are in the closed positon. The head and jambs of the frame are from material about 38 mm thickness and the joints where they intersect can be tongued and grooved, with the tongue stopped near to the inside surface. The sill is from 75 mm material, preferably a timber that is resistant to dampness. The joint between the jambs and sill can be open mortise and tenons, using twin tenons in each joint (these joints are indicated in the diagram).

The sashes are retained in their respective positions by a lining which is fixed to the outside surface of the frame and a loose bead around the inside edge of the frame. The outside edge of the sill and that of the lining are in the same plane so the edge of the sill has to be recessed to receive the lining; this recess is similar to that shown in figure 13.17.

Since there are no weights to counterbalance the sashes, something has to be provided to keep the sashes in any required position. For instance, if the lower sash were opened or raised without some means of keeping it in that position, the sash would just fall to the bottom of the frame because of its weight. A fairly modern device in current use is the Unique balance, details of which are seen in figures 13.13a and b. Two of these are used for each sash and can be obtained in various sizes to suit the lengths of the sashes. Recesses must be made in the edges of the sash stiles (some prefer to recess the jambs) to receive the tube of the balance (see figure 13.14) and the device is fixed at the top of each jamb by a small hole provided. The plate at the lower end of the spiral rod is secured to the lower edge of the frame it is supporting (figure 13.13c) — the friction set up by the rod and the tube is sufficient to hold the sash in any required position.

The type of joint between the stiles and rails of the sashes adjacent to the recesses for the balances is shown in figure 13.14. This is an open mortise and tenon joint and if designed as in the drawing it will provide ample glueing surfaces.

Figures 13.15 and 13.16 show details of a sliding sash window where provision is made for the sashes to be counterbalanced with weights. Figure 13.16 shows a part horizontal section through the frame showing details of one of the jambs. The jamb consists of a pulley stile, an inside and an outside lining and a back lining, forming the box in which the weights are housed. Figure 13.15 shows that a parting bead separates the sashes and the gap taken up by the parting bead is closed by the meeting rails of the sashes when they are in the closed position. The head of the frame is constructed in a similar manner to the jambs but no back lining is necessary in this case and the head is strengthened by glueing blocks in the angles between the head and the two linings.

Figure 13.17 shows how each end of the sill has to be prepared to receive the lower end of the pulley stile, inside and outside linings. The outside linings run past the front edge of the pulley stiles so that the outside or top sash can be kept in position. The inside lining finishes flush with the pulley stile, the bottom sash being held in position by a bead fixed around the inside edge of the frame. This is needed because it may be necessary to remove the sashes for some reason — to renew the cords holding the weights, for instance — so all that is needed is to remove the beads, when the sashes can be taken out of the frame. Note that the tongues on the pulley stiles (and head) are on opposite corners. The parting beads also fit into grooves in the pulley stiles and across the head of the frame. *Do not glue these in position.*

Figure 13.18 shows the first stages in the assembly of the frame. (Before this is done, of course, holes or pockets must be prepared in each of the pulley stiles to allow the weights to be removed from the boxes; this is necessary, for instance, if the chords have to be renewed.) Cutting of pockets will be covered later. The recesses of the pulleys must also be made near the tops of the pulley stiles — both of these are shown in figure 13.18. The figure shows the sill, head and the two stiles assembled as a frame, all joints being glued and nailed. When this has been done, the inside and outside linings can be placed in position and nailed; they are not usually glued. The fitting of the feathers (narrow strips of plywood or hardboard) hanging from the head down through the centres of the two boxes is to stop the weights from jamming against one another. Glue blocks, back linings and parting beads can then be fitted to complete the work of the frame.

Figure 13.19 should give the student an idea of the positions of the components of a boxed frame. The sashes are counterbalanced by weights, a chord (or chain) being attached to the sash at one end, passing over a pulley to the weight at the other end. The pulley is housed in the pulley stile near to its top; one of these pulleys can be seen in figure 13.20.

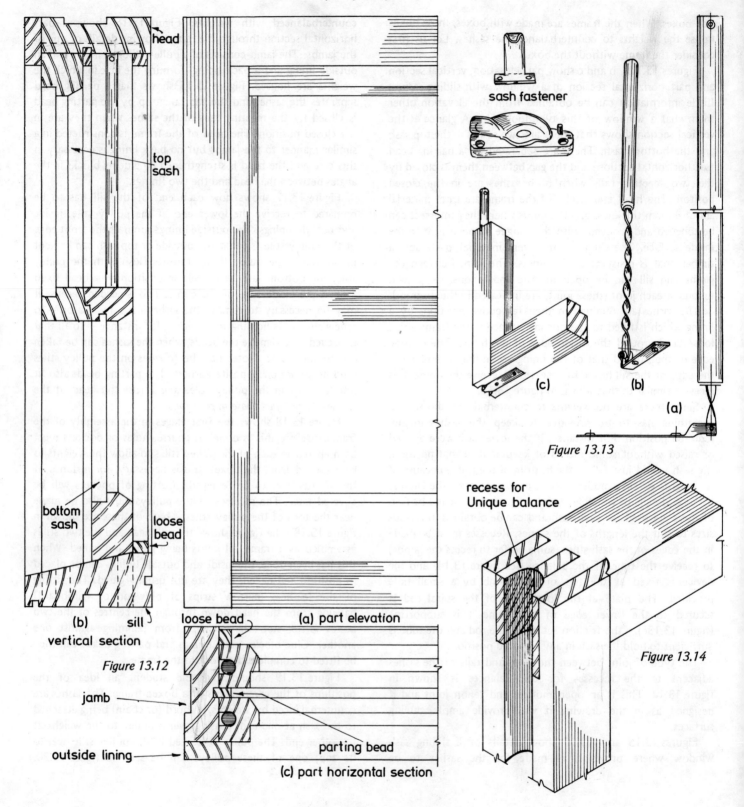

head

top sash

bottom sash

loose bead

(b)   sill
vertical section

Figure 13.12

loose bead

(a) part elevation

jamb

parting bead

outside lining

(c) part horizontal section

sash fastener

(c)   **(b)**

(a)

Figure 13.13

recess for
Unique balance

Figure 13.14

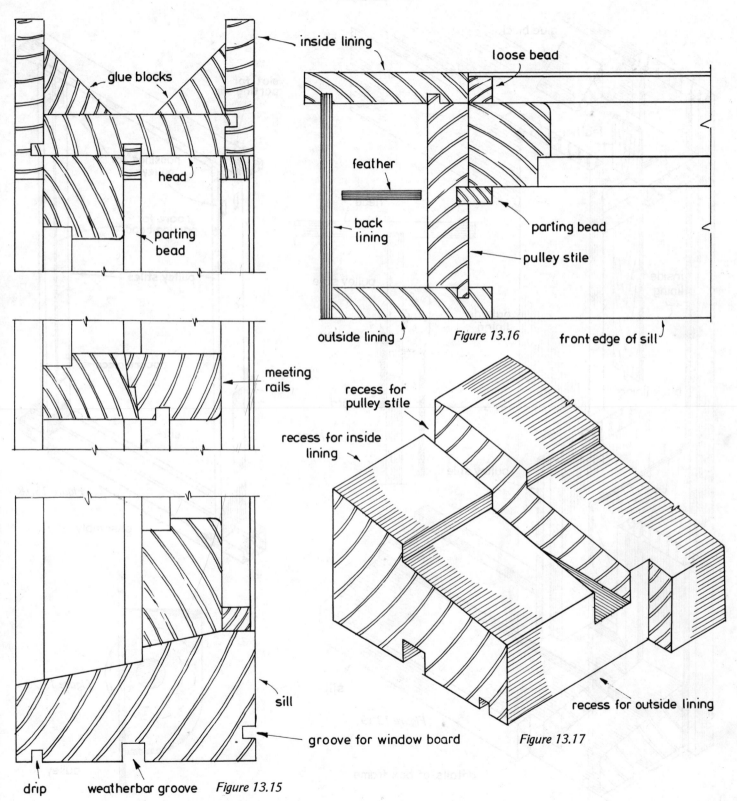

inside lining

glue blocks

head

parting bead

loose bead

feather

back lining

parting bead

pulley stile

outside lining

Figure 13.16

front edge of sill

meeting rails

recess for pulley stile

recess for inside lining

recess for outside lining

Figure 13.17

sill

groove for window board

drip

weatherbar groove

Figure 13.15

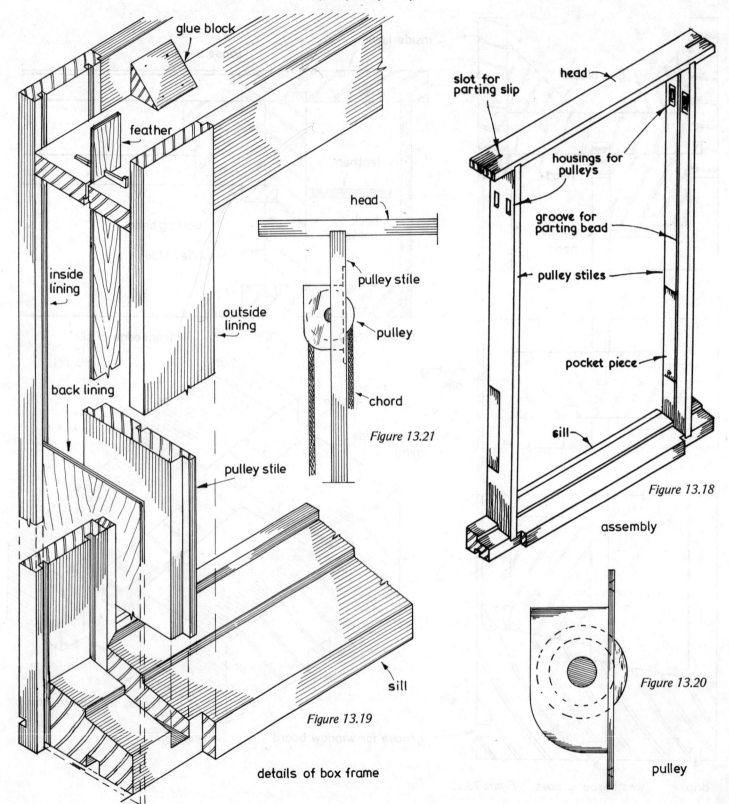

glue block

feather

inside
lining

back lining

outside
lining

pulley stile

sill

details of box frame

Figure 13.19

head

pulley stile

pulley

chord

Figure 13.21

slot for
parting slip

head

housings for
pulleys

groove for
parting bead

pulley stiles

pocket piece

sill

Figure 13.18

assembly

Figure 13.20

pulley

Figure 13.21 shows the pulley's general position in the frame, with the chord passing over it to enter the box in which the weight is situated. As explained previously, pockets must be made in the pulley stiles to enable the weights to be removed. Figure 13.22 shows an elevation and a side view of a pocket in a pulley stile. The method of preparation is as follows.

(1) First remove the tongue on the edge of the pulley stile adjacent to the pocket.

(2) Bore two small holes in the parting bead groove and with a keyhole saw cut down the centre of the groove between the holes.

(3) With a tenon saw, make the four cuts shown in the side view of the pocket.

(4) With a hammer give a sharp rap to the back surface of the lining near to each pair of saw cuts. This should split the wood between the pairs of saw cuts and release the pocket piece.

Figure 13.23 shows what the pocket piece will look like when removed from the stile. Only one screw is needed to fix it back in its original position.

Figures 13.24a and b show the joint for the top rail of the top sash. This is slightly different to the conventional haunched mortise and tenon joint because the haunching (franking) is left on the piece with the mortise. The reason for this is that if the conventional haunched mortise and tenon joint were used, the joint would be weakened because the groove for the chord has to be cut into the outside edge of the stile (figure 13.25).

Figures 13.26 and 13.27 show the sash joints around the meeting stiles. If mortise and tenon joints are to be used (figure 13.26) it is usual to allow the stiles to run well beyond the joint because of the narrow depth of the meeting rail. The horn may be shaped as shown in the drawing. If the shaped horns are not required (some consider them unsightly) the type of joint seen in figure 13.27 should be used. This is a dovetailed joint providing plenty of glueing surface, and gives a much stronger joint than if a mortise and tenon joint were used without the shaped horn.

BAY WINDOWS

Casement bay windows, which project outwards beyond the main face of a building, can be constructed in various shapes — angular (figure 13.28), square (figure 13.29), or segmental (figure 13.30), etc. The main difference in the construction of these frames, compared with an ordinary casement window, is, of course, the manufacture of the sills, heads, mullions and the jambs. The mullions (figure 13.31) which are angular even in the segmental bay, can be obtained from solid timber (figure 13.31a) where there will be a large percentage of waste, or they can be made by mitring two smaller pieces together (figure 13.31b), when the amount of labour will be greater than for the former type. The sills (figure 13.32) and heads (figure 13.33) must also be mitred at their intersections; also involved at these points are the mortise and tenon joints connecting the jambs and mullions to the sills and heads. The various parts of the head and sill at the mitres are connected together by using a handrail bolt (figure 13.34) and two hardwood dowels. Positioning the handrail bolts is important because mortises must be cut in the head and sill sections to receive the tenons at the top and bottom ends of the mullions.

Square bays are constructed in a similar way to angular bays, the plan shape being the only difference. Segmental bays are also constructed in a similar manner, the difference being that the sills are curved on their front edges. Their window boards, too, are curved on the edges facing the room.

The bricklayer who builds the brickwork below the bay windows usually needs some help from the carpenter. He will require a templet, made from plywood, hardboard, or solid timber, suitably strengthened with battens, so that he can keep the profile of his brickwork to the correct shape. Two templets are shown in figure 13.35 and would be suitable for the brickwork to an angular bay (a) and a segmental bay (b).

PIVOT-HUNG SASH WINDOWS

This type of window has several advantages, among which are: (1) they can be opened and closed easily when out of normal reach by having chords attached and (2) both surfaces of their panes of glass are easily cleaned from inside the building.

Figure 13.36 shows a vertical section through a frame with a single pivoted sash. Since the sash is situated centrally in the frame, it is necessary to bevel the rebate in the head of the frame to ensure that the sash opens without touching the frame. Because the rebate of the sill of the frame also has to be bevelled (for weathering purposes as well as for the reason given for the head) these two components can be shaped exactly the same as each other. The two jambs of the frame have no rebate worked on their inside surfaces because stops are fixed to them with screws. To obtain the positions and lengths of these stops, and those fixed to the sash, the vertical section should be constructed as shown in figure 13.36 and the

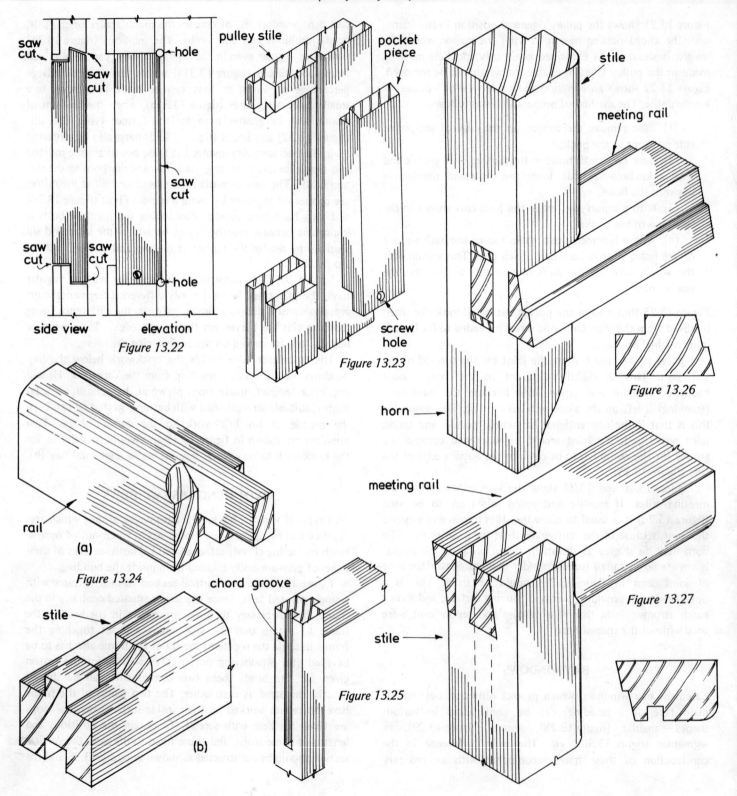

saw cut
saw cut
saw cut
saw cut
saw cut

hole

hole

side view   elevation

Figure 13.22

pulley stile

pocket piece

screw hole

Figure 13.23

rail

(a)

Figure 13.24

stile

(b)

chord groove

stile

Figure 13.25

stile

meeting rail

Figure 13.26

horn

meeting rail

stile

Figure 13.27

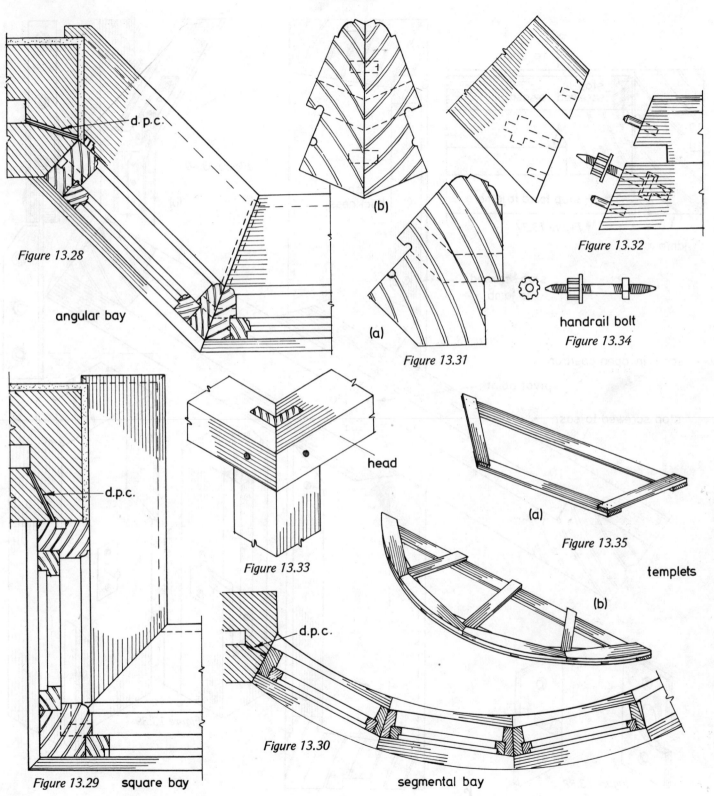

Figure 13.28

angular bay

d.p.c.

(b)

(a)

Figure 13.31

Figure 13.32

handrail bolt
Figure 13.34

head

Figure 13.33

Figure 13.29 **square bay**

d.p.c.

(a)

Figure 13.35

templets

(b)

d.p.c.

Figure 13.30

segmental bay

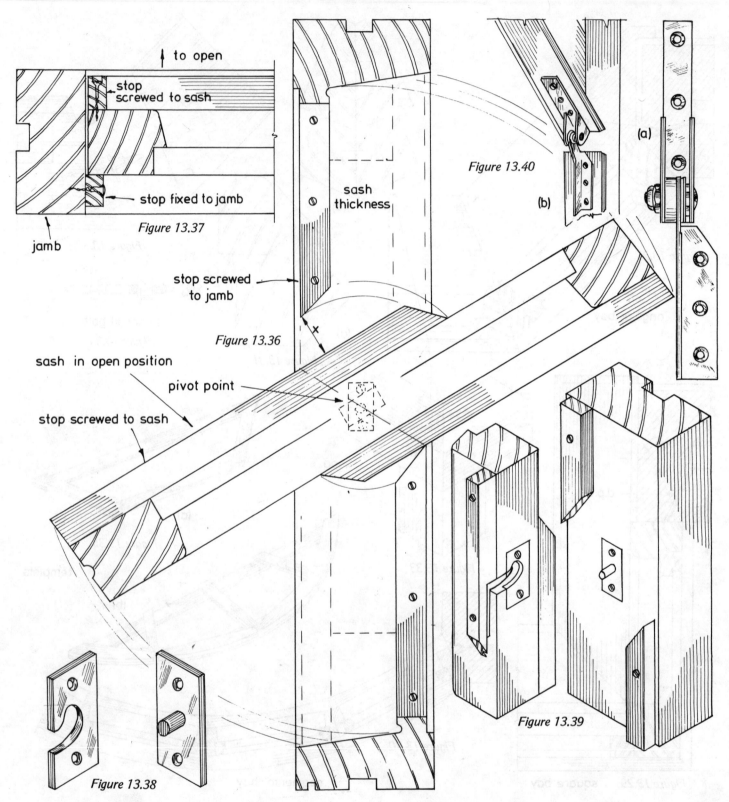

↑ to open

stop
screwed to sash

stop fixed to jamb

jamb

Figure 13.37

sash
thickness

stop screwed
to jamb

Figure 13.36

x

Figure 13.40

(a)

(b)

sash in open position

pivot point

stop screwed to sash

Figure 13.38

Figure 13.39

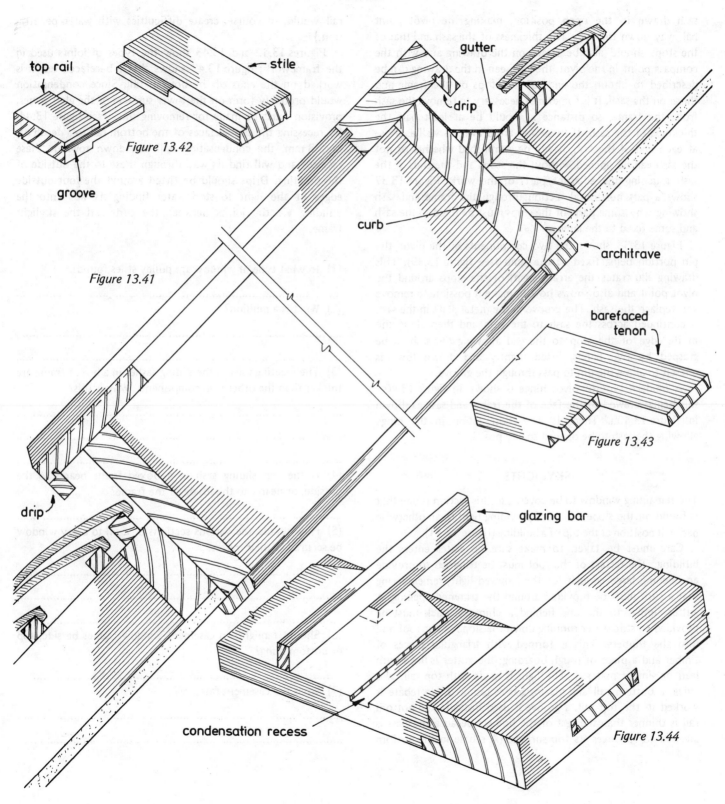

top rail

stile

Figure 13.42

groove

Figure 13.41

drip

gutter

drip

curb

architrave

barefaced tenon

Figure 13.43

glazing bar

condensation recess

Figure 13.44

sash drawn in the open position, making the pivot point half-way down the sash. The thickness of the sash and that of the stops should also be placed on the drawing and with the compass point in the pivot, the arcs seen in the drawing can be described to obtain the ends of the stops on the frame and those on the sash. It is sometimes necessary to remove the sash from the frame, so distance x should be at least half the thickness of the sash. If these arcs are drawn, as well as those at each end of the sash, it will be established whether or not the sash can be opened without the stops and the ends of the sash touching the adjacent parts of the work. Figure 13.37 shows a part horizontal section through the frame and sash showing why some parts of the stops must be fixed to the sash and some fixed to the jambs.

Figure 13.38 shows the two components of the pivot, the pin portion being fixed to the jamb (see figure 13.39). This drawing illustrates the arrangement of the stops around the pivot point and also shows how to make it possible to remove and replace the sash. The groove in the metal plate in the sash is continued across the sash to the stop and then along the inside edge of the stop to the end allowing the sash to be grasped by two hands, lifted slightly and drawn towards oneself to allow the pin to pass through the groove.

A modern type of pivot hinge is shown in figure 13.40a, this being screwed to the face of the frame and sash as shown in figure 13.40b. There is a friction action in the hinge allowing the sash to be opened to any position.

SKYLIGHTS

The remaining window to be covered in this section is one that is found on the slope of a roof providing light to an otherwise badly lit position at the top of a building (figure 13.41).

Care must be taken to make sure no water enters the building. The rafters of the roof must be trimmed to provide an opening large enough for the required light, remembering that a curb must be provided around the trimmed opening. A gutter similar to the one behind a chimney stack must be provided to stop water running down the slope of the roof and into the timbers. This is formed with triangular pieces of timber and a piece of rough boarding; the gutter is lined with lead or similar material. The light is made with top rail, two stiles, a bottom rail and glazing bar as required. No rebate is worked in the top rail, a groove is used instead. The bottom rail is thinner than the rest of the timbers because the glass is allowed to run over its top surface. (A rebate in the bottom

rail would, of course, create difficulties with water penetration.)

Figures 13.42 and 13.43 show the types of joints used in the framework; figure 13.43 shows that a barefaced tenon is worked on the ends of the bottom rail. Since condensation would probably form on the lower surfaces of the glass panes, provision must be made for removing this — see figure 13.44. By recessing the top surfaces of the bottom rail to a depth of, say, 3 mm, the condensation will run down towards these recesses and will find its way through these to the outside of the building. Drips should be fitted around the four outside edges of the light to stop water finding its way into the building via the joints between the curb and the skylight frame.

(1) In what type of window are pulley stiles found?

....

(2) What is a mullion?

....

....

(3) The meeting rails to the sliding sashes in a boxed frame are thicker than the other sash components. Why is this?

....

....

....

(4) Is the top sliding sash in a boxed frame nearer to the outside, or nearer to the inside of the frame?

....

(5) How should the various sections of a sill to a bay window be secured at their mitres?

....

....

....

(6) Should fanlights in casement window frames be side, top or bottom hung?

....

(7) What is a casement fastener?

....

....

(8) Make a sketch of a sash fastener.

(9) Make a sketch of a casement stay.

(10) Moisture movement in wooden sashes must be overcome as much as possible to avoid trouble with 'sticking' sashes. How?

....

....

....

(11) What is the name of the horizontal window-frame member situated between the sill and head?

....

(12) Make a list of the ironmongery required for a single-light casement window frame.

(a)..(b)...............................

(c). ....

14. DOORS

Doors can be divided up into two groups — external and internal. These groups can be subdivided into matchboarded doors, panelled doors, partly or fully glazed, flush, etc. Except for a few minor details, internal and external doors of each type are constructed similarly. External doors are usually made to a greater thickness than internal doors, the common thickness for external doors being ex 50 mm and that for internal doors ex 38 mm. Of course, there are exceptions to these thicknesses, circumstances often demanding lesser or greater dimensions.

Matchboarding doors consist of ledged and braced doors and framed, ledged and braced doors. The former have been covered in volume 1 of this series; the front and rear elevation of the latter, primarily an external door, are shown in figures 14.1 and 14.2. The door consists of two stiles, top, middle and bottom rails and a panel of matchboarding. Also included are two braces, the lower end of each being nearest to the edge of the door to which the hinges are fixed. It is traditional to include the braces because, in the past, when only animal glues were obtainable, the mortise and tenon joints were secured with dowels. Today, with synthetic adhesives, the joints can be glued without the fear of disintegration because of dampness. Such adhesives are very strong making the braces superfluous, but the traditional braces are shown in the drawings.

The stiles and top rail are equal in thickness to that of the finished door but the thickness of the middle and bottom rails is the thickness of the door less the thickness of the matching. This enables the matchboarding to pass over the front surfaces of the middle and bottom rails.

Figure 14.3 shows a part vertical section through the door indicating that the matchboarding is tongued and grooved to the top rail and passes over the surface of the middle rail. Figure 14.4 shows a part horizontal section through the door and shows that the matchboarding is tongued and grooved to the stiles. Also indicated on the rear elevation are the mortise and tenon joints and in each case, the total width of the haunchings is equal to the total width of the tenons.

Figure 14.5 shows how the tops of the stiles are prepared to receive the top rail and figure 14.6 is an elevation of one of the joints.

Figure 14.7 shows the elevation of one of a pair of framed ledged and braced doors suitable for a garage; that part of each door above the middle rail is glazed. The construction of these doors is similar to the previous one apart from the fact that here the middle rail is equal to the over-all thickness of the door and only one brace is required for each. The top rail, middle rail and a portion of each stile must be rebated to receive the glass panes and glazing bars can be included as required. Figure 14.8 shows a vertical section through the glazed portion of one of the doors and figure 14.9 shows how the intersections between the stiles and middle rails can be treated, avoiding bevelled shoulders that are found in better-class doors.

PANELLED DOORS

Panelled doors of the type illustrated in figure 14.10 are usually internal doors. This is a three-panelled door but, of course, the number of panels can be increased or decreased as desired. This door consists of two stiles, top, bottom and middle rails, a muntin and three plywood panels. Indicated on the right of the drawing are the types of mortise and tenon joints used.

Figure 14.11 shows a setting-out rod for the door. Since the door is constructed below the middle rail in a different way to that above, it is necessary to draw two horizontal sections on the rod to indicate the difference in the construction.

There are several ways of finishing the door round the inside edges of the framing and one of these is shown in figure 14.12. This shows that the two ovolo mouldings are worked on the inside edges of the framework; they are called stuck mouldings.

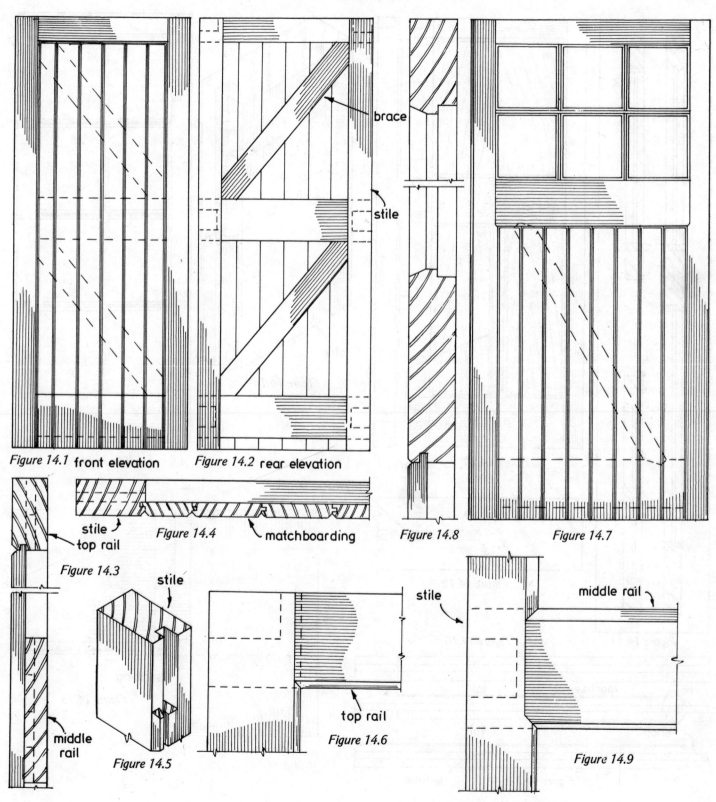

Figure 14.1 front elevation

Figure 14.2 rear elevation

brace

stile

stile
top rail

Figure 14.3

Figure 14.4

matchboarding

Figure 14.8

Figure 14.7

stile

middle
rail

Figure 14.5

stile

top rail

Figure 14.6

middle rail

stile

Figure 14.9

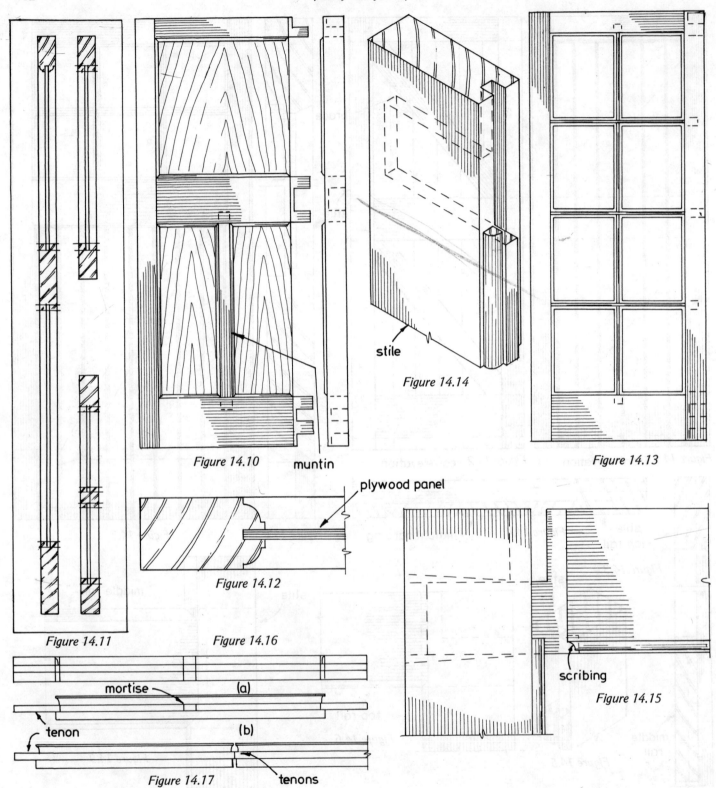

Figure 14.10

muntin

Figure 14.11

Figure 14.12

plywood panel

Figure 14.16

stile

Figure 14.14

Figure 14.13

scribing

Figure 14.15

mortise   (a)

tenon

(b)

Figure 14.17   tenons

The next door to be considered is an internal fully glazed door. Figure 14.13 shows the elevation of such a door consisting of two stiles, top and bottom rails and glazing bars. Each component is rebated at the rear to receive glass and moulded in the front. This particular door has eight panes of glass, all equal in size, but the number is not important – this can be decided to suit the circumstances. On the right of the elevation the mortise and tenon joints are indicated; it is often thought that it is unnecessary to have all the tenons on the ends of the horizontal glazing bars passing right through to the outside edge of the stile – the centre one must do so, but the others can all be stub mortise and tenons.

Figure 14.14 is an isometric view at the top of a stile, indicating the work that must be done to allow the top rail to intersect with the stile.

Figure 14.15 is an elevation of the top joint and the joints at the bottom rail should be treated likewise. As seen in the drawing, the mouldings are scribed at their intersections. When this can be done it is preferable to mitring but it must be borne in mind that some mouldings do not lend themselves to successful scribing.

Figures 14.16a and b show how a horizontal glazing bar should be set out and prepared. First, one of the bars should be placed on the rod and the shoulder positions marked. The scribings should also be marked as well as the tenons, rebates and mouldings. The scribes should be cut as in figure 14.16b before the tenons, rebates and mouldings. Figure 14.17 shows one end of the vertical bar showing the tenon that fits into one of the stiles. During assembly the vertical bars are cut into sections at the centres of the intersecting points, leaving short tenons that fit into the mortises of the horizontal bars.

Figure 14.18 shows the elevation of a half-glazed external door with a raised and fielded panel below the middle rail. A glance at the elevation will show that the stiles have been reduced in width above the middle rail, the purpose being to let as much light into the building as possible. The mortise and tenon joints are all indicated on the drawing and sections through the various parts are seen in figures 14.19 and 14.20. Figure 14.19a is a section through the stiles above the middle rail; figure 14.19b is a section through the stiles below the middle rail. Figure 14.20a is a section through the middle rail; figure 14.20b is a section through the bottom rail. When setting out the mortise and tenon joints for the middle and bottom rails, allowances must be made for the panel grooves in these two members.

Figure 14.21 shows how the diminished joints for the middle rail are marked out on the stiles. First, the over-all width of the rail is marked on the timber, its correct position being obtained by placing the stiles on the setting-out rod. The depth of the groove in the middle rail is then subtracted from the lower edge and the remainder divided into four equal parts, the two outer quarters being the positions of the two mortises. The positions of the diminished shoulders to the joints $(x - y)$ are found by first marking dimension 'a' from the inside or face edge of the material to give the inside edge of the stile above the middle rail. Then by marking the width of the moulding (c) from this point and also marking downwards from the top edge of the rail, point x will be obtained. This is the top end of the diminished shoulder. The lower end of the shoulder is at point y at the bottom edge of the middle rail position. The end of the middle rail is shown in figure 14.22 and the method for marking the diminished shoulder on this member is also shown. It is really very similar to that for marking the shoulders on the stiles. Incidentally, if the depth of the moulding (c) is exactly the same as the depth of the rebate, the two shoulders for each joint will be the same.

Figure 14.23 shows the joint assembled; figure 14.24 shows an isometric view of one end of the middle rail prepared. Figure 14.25 shows a section through a stile with the raised and fielded panel. The fielding is usually made to finish flush with the face of the framing. Bolection mouldings, are often used to finish around this type of panel. A bolection moulding is that which extends outwards beyond the face of the framing; it is usually rebated to fit over the inside corners. They are fixed with screws through the panel, the holes being slotted so that any movement in the panel will not result in splitting. The screws are hidden on the other side of the door with simple planted mouldings.

FLUSH DOORS

Figure 14.26 shows one method used in the construction of flush doors. These have very simple framing, the main components often being butt jointed and secured with corrugated fasteners. In addition to the stiles and rails, slats are incorporated in the framework to provide surfaces to which the plywood or hardboard panels, which form the outer surfaces of the door, are glued. Also included, between the two intermediate rails in this case, are two strips of wood, one on each side of the door, which provide extra width in the framing into which a mortise lock can be recessed. The door is completed by glueing a sheet of hardboard or plywood to each

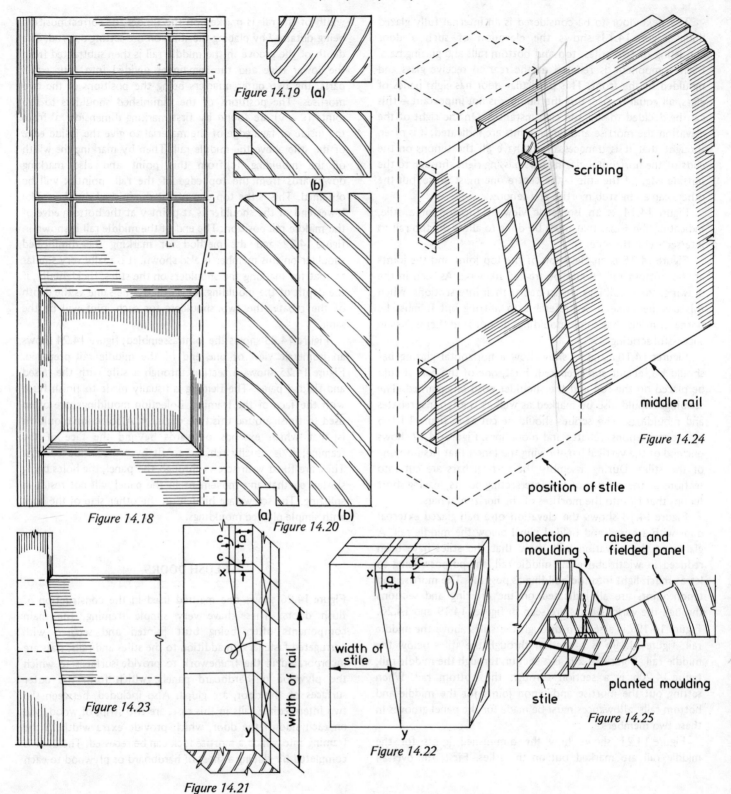

Figure 14.19 (a)

(b)

Figure 14.20

(a)   (b)

Figure 14.18

Figure 14.23

Figure 14.21

Figure 14.22

Figure 14.24

scribing

middle rail

position of stile

Figure 14.25

bolection moulding

raised and fielded panel

stile

planted moulding

width of rail

width of stile

c a

c

x

x a

c

y

y

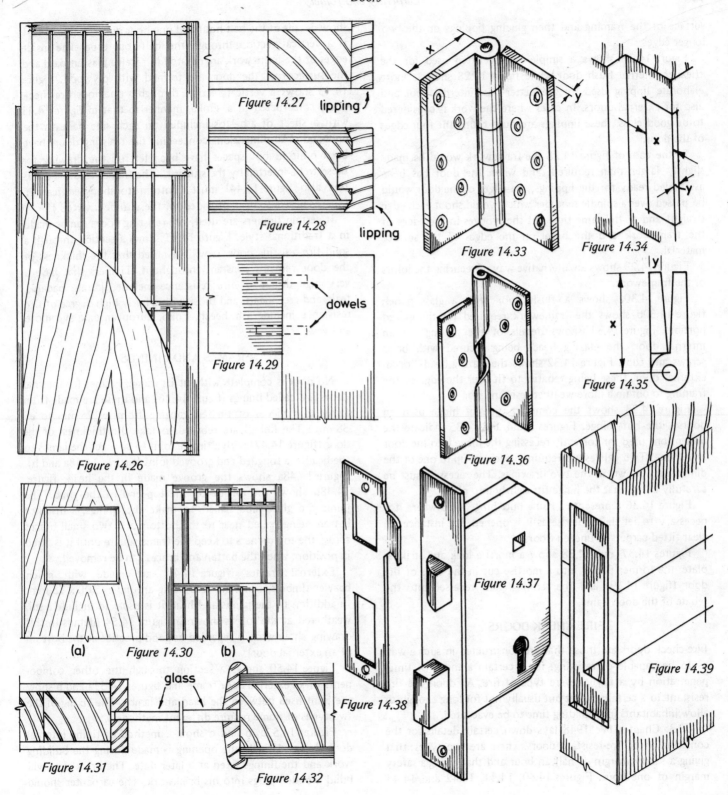

Figure 14.26

Figure 14.27 lipping

Figure 14.28 lipping

Figure 14.29 dowels

(a) *Figure 14.30* (b)

Figure 14.31

glass

Figure 14.32

Figure 14.33

Figure 14.34

Figure 14.35

Figure 14.36

Figure 14.37

Figure 14.38

Figure 14.39

surface of the framing and then glueing lippings on the two longer edges.

Figure 14.27 shows a simple lipping often used for the cheaper internal flush door while figure 14.28 shows a more elaborate lipping used for the better-class internal door and also for external doors. In cases where the work is considered to be good class, these lippings are glued round the four edges of the door.

In the case of figure 14.28 the framework would be made slightly larger than required, and when the door has been assembled ready for the lippings, the edges of the door would be passed over a spindle moulder which would shoot each edge straight and at the same time cut the grooves in the edges of the framework and the bevel on the edges of the surface material.

Figure 14.29 shows an alternative way of securing the joints of the framework.

Figure 14.30a shows a flush door with a glass panel; figure 14.30b shows the framework required for the glazed portion. Figure 14.31 shows details of the glazing for an internal door, the glazing beads being secured with brass screws and cups. Figure 14.32 shows the glazing beads for an external door, these being rebated to fit over the edge of the framing to obtain a more weather-resistant job.

Figure 14.33 shows the common type of hinge used on doors — the butt hinge. Figures 14.34 and 14.35 indicate the dimensions used for correctly recessing the hinge into the door and frame. Two gauges are required, each set up to one of the dimensions shown in the two drawings. The recesses must be carefully cut so that the hinge fits tightly into place.

Figure 14.36 represents a rising butt hinge, used where it is necessary to let the door rise as it is opened, for instance, to clear fitted carpets or uneven floors.

Figures 14.37 and 14.38 show a mortise lock and striking plate, the former fitting into a mortise cut in the edge of the door (figure 14.39) and the striking plate recessed into the rebate of the door frame.

FIRE-CHECK DOORS

Fire-check doors are those that are constructed in such a way as to be capable of resisting, for a certain amount of time, penetration by a fairly severe type of fire. All doors are fire resistant to a certain extent but usually not for long enough to allow inhabitants in a building time to be evacuated.

CP 3: Chapter IV: 1948 lays down certain details for the construction of fire-resistant doors. There are two types: that giving a safety margin of half an hour and that giving a safety margin of one hour. Figures 14.40, 14.41, 14.42 and 14.43

show details of the half-hour and one-hour doors. Figure 14.41 is a vertical section through the half-hour type. The inside edges of the framework are rebated to receive plasterboard and the surfaces of the door are formed with plywood. Figure 14.43 shows a vertical section through a one-hour fire-check door, constructed in a similar manner to that in figure 14.41 with a sheet of asbestos included on each side beneath the plywood. (All dimensions concerning fire-resisting doors have been omitted but spaces have been left on the drawing for these to be inserted by the student.) The frames to these doors (see also figure 14.44) must conform to the specification. (Spaces have also been provided for these to be inserted.)

If certain timbers are used, fire-resisting doors can be made in a traditional style. Figure 14.45 shows a section through a solid fire-resisting door. It will be noted that the thickness of the door remains constant throughout. Timbers that have a very high degree of fire resistance include, jarrah, padauk, teak, and greenheart; and those with a fairly high degree of fire resistance include ash, beech, iroko, European oak, sycamore and yew.

FRAMES AND LININGS

No door is complete without its frame. Frames for internal doors are called linings (figure 14.46) and these are made from fairly thin pieces of timber, ranging from ex 25 mm to ex 38 mm. The linings are rebated to take the thickness of the door (figure 14.47) with a simple joint to connect the jambs to the head — a tongued and grooved joint (figures 14.48a and b). Figure 14.48a shows the groove made in the head; figure 14.48b shows the tongue on the top end of the jamb. The joints are glued and nailed to make the linings, a distance batten being nailed near to the bottom and two small braces across the top corners to keep the frame square until it is fixed in position, when the batten and braces can be removed.

External frames (figure 14.49) are made with much heavier timbers, common sizes being around ex 100 x 75 mm. In addition to the jambs and head it is usual to include a sill, weathered at the top as shown in figure 14.54 (details in this drawing show what is regarded as good practice at the bottom of an external door).

Figure 14.50 shows a section through the other components of an external door frame and figures 14.51a and b show the joint used between the head and jambs. The fixing of the two types of frame require different methods.

Figures 14.52a, b and c show a method of fixing internal door linings. Usually the opening is made during the building work and the linings fixed at a later date. The bricklayer will build wooden plugs into his brickwork. The carpenter should

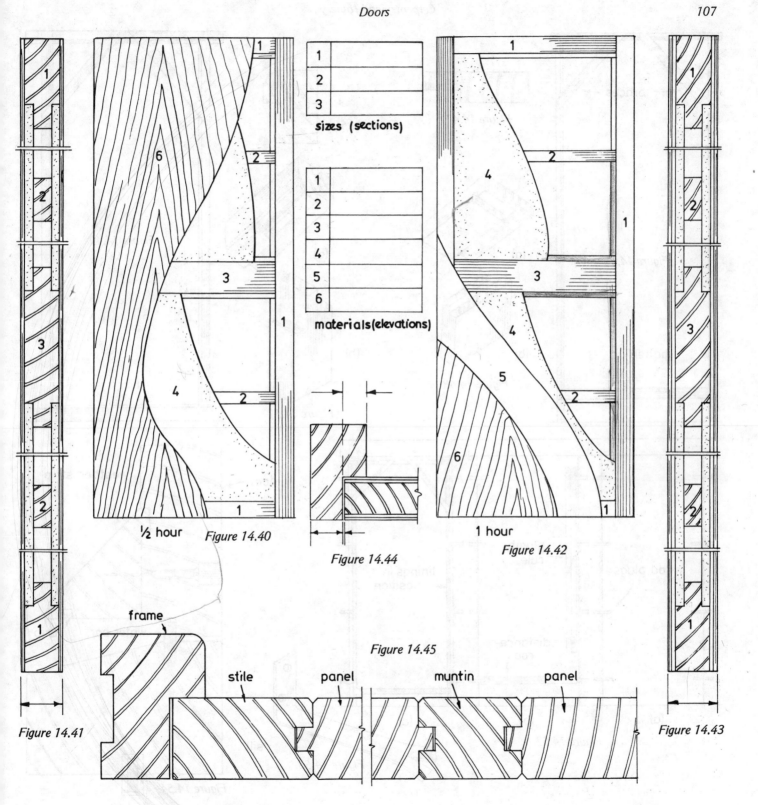

sizes (sections)

materials (elevations)

½ hour   *Figure 14.40*

Figure 14.44

1 hour
Figure 14.42

frame

Figure 14.45

stile   panel   muntin   panel

Figure 14.41

Figure 14.43

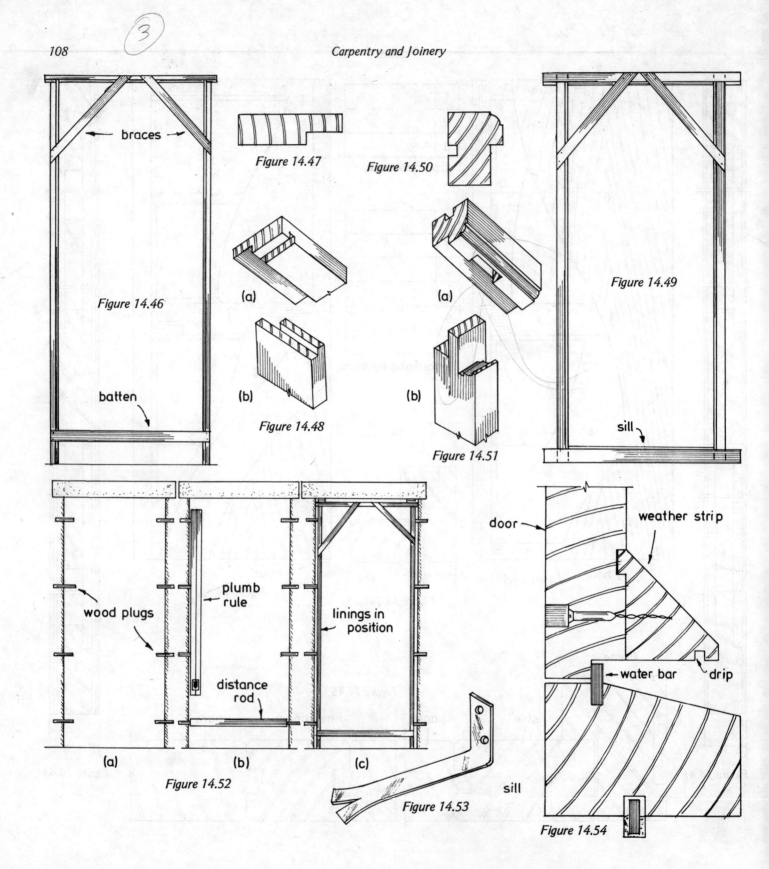

braces

batten

Figure 14.46

Figure 14.47

(a)

(b)

Figure 14.48

Figure 14.50

(a)

(b)

Figure 14.51

Figure 14.49

sill

wood plugs

plumb rule

distance rod

linings in position

(a)

(b)

(c)

Figure 14.52

Figure 14.53

sill

door

weather strip

water bar

drip

Figure 14.54

then offer the linings up to the opening to get an idea of how much is to be trimmed from the plugs to allow the frame to fit between their ends. He then trims off the ends of the plugs on one side of the opening, making sure that their ends are in vertical alignment (figure 14.52b). Then with a batten cut to the width of the frame, the ends of the plugs on the opposite side of the opening are marked and trimmed off to allow the frame to fit exactly between their ends (figure 14.52c). The linings are then nailed to the plugs and a pair of folding wedges driven in between the top of the opening and the frame immediately above the jambs.

The external frames are usually placed in position while the brickwork is being built; the galvanised metal ties shown in figure 14.53 are used for this purpose. As the brickwork proceeds the bricklayer or carpenter will screw one of the ties to the outside surfaces of the jambs, so that these are built into the brickwork, making a secure fixing.

A water bar is usually included in the sill of the frame (figure 14.54) so that the door, when closed, fits up tightly to the bar to exclude draughts and moisture.

(1) A framed door is found to be in winding before it is glued up. What could be the cause of this?

....

(2) How could the defect be overcome?

....

....

(3) What type of hinge would be most suitable for a door leading into a room with fitted carpets?

....

(4) When setting out a haunched tenon, the width of the haunching should equal the width of the tenon. Is this statement true or false?

....

(5) What type of adhesive should be used for an external door? ....

(6) A door is found to be slightly in winding at the time of hanging. How could this defect be overcome?

....

....

(7) The figure below shows the end of a middle rail of a panelled door. Show on the drawing how the tenons should be marked out prior to cutting.

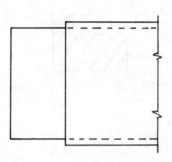

(8) How should door frames be stacked and protected on a site prior to being fixed in position?

....

....

....

(9) What type of sealer should be used on new doors and frames that are to be painted before they leave the joiner's shop?

....

....

(10) What should be done to the tongues and grooves of the matchboarding panel in a framed, ledged and braced door before they are fixed in position and why?

....

....

....

(11) What type of lock would you use on

(a) an internal door?...

(b) an external door?...

(c) a shed door?...

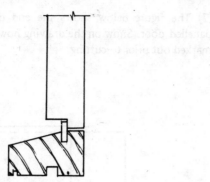

(12) The figure (left) shows the bottom of an external door. Show any additional details which should be included in the drawing to make the joint between the door and frame more weather-proof.

(13) What type of plywood should be used for the panels in an external door?

....

(14) What should be the minimum depth of rebate in the frame for a fire-resisting door?

....

(15) What kind of glue is suitable for an internal door?

....

15. STAIRS

Before a staircase can be manufactured, a knowledge of the Building Regulations applied to staircase work must be obtained (Building Regulations, Part H). There are two types of stairs as far as the Regulations are concerned — common stairways and private stairways. The first are those in buildings of a public nature; private stairways are those found in buildings that are usually occupied by one family.

DEFINITIONS

Parallel steps are steps that have their nosings parallel to those above and below them or are parallel to the landings above or below. *Tapered steps* are those which do not have their nosings parallel to those above or below them or to the landing above or below. (These steps were called winders before the Regulations were published.)

The *pitch line* is an imaginary line that runs parallel to the pitch of the staircase and is drawn to pass through the extreme outside edge of all the nosings of the steps.

The *going* is the horizontal distance measured from the extreme outside edge of one nosing to the extreme outside edge of the nosing above or below it.

The *rise* of a step is the vertical height measured from the top surface of one tread to the top surface of the tread immediately above or below it (all the steps in a single flight must have the same rise).

The *pitch* is the slope or angle of the flight and is measured in degrees (for private stairs the maximum pitch is 42° and for common stairs it is 38°).

Headroom is the amount of space between the flight and the landing or floor above, measured from the pitch line and in a vertical direction.

Figure 15.1 illustrates the above mentioned parts of the Regulations and also includes maximum or minimum dimensions for each, where appropriate. Remember, too, that the rise of each step in a straight flight must be equal to the rise of all the other steps in the flight and the going of each parallel step must be equal to that of all the other parallel steps in the flight.

When constructing steps with no risers (open stairs) the nosing of the step or landing must overlap the back edge of the tread immediately below by at least 15 mm — see figure 15.2. Also, the space between the treads adjacent to one another must be reduced to below 100 mm (see also figure 15.2).

Before a staircase can be constructed, a visit to the site should be made so that sketches can be drawn to give the site dimensions. In addition to noting wall-to-wall dimensions and the positions of doorways, windows, etc., a storey rod must be prepared to give all the vertical dimensions needed in the construction. A storey rod is a piece of timber, say approximately 32 mm square, used to measure the distance between the lower floor level and the upper-floor timbers (see figure 15.1). It is possible that, if the lower floor is of concrete, the screeding and floor finish will not be completed, so the amount of finish to finished floor-level (FFL) must be obtained from the person responsible for carrying out this work. If the floor is a suspended timber floor, like most upper floors, then the distance between the top surfaces of the lower-floor joists and the upper-floor joists will give the amount of over-all rise for the stair flight.

When designing a flight of stairs, remember that the total number of risers in the flight will be greater by one than the total number of treads (the landing at the top of the flight, of course, taking the place of the tread for the top riser).

For an example of staircase work, let us take the short flight shown in figure 15.3. The elevation shows that the flight has six steps. Let us also assume that the stair is for a private dwelling and that the over-all height from floor to floor is 1224 mm. If this figure is divided by the maximum rise for a private dwelling (220 mm) we obtain

$$1224 \div 220 = 5.564 \text{ steps}$$

The answer to this problem should lead us to the conclusion

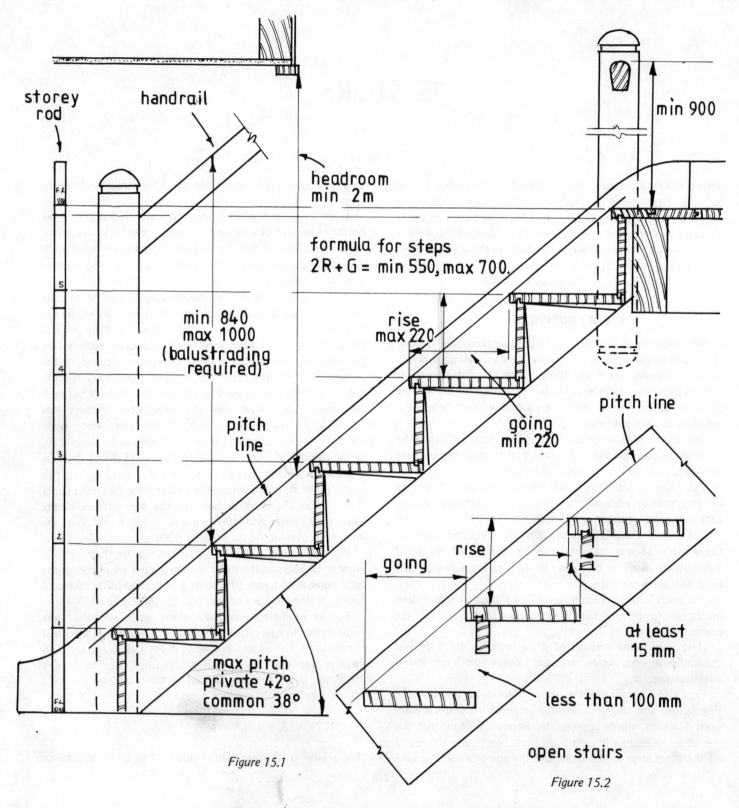

storey rod

handrail

headroom
min 2m

formula for steps
2R + G = min 550, max 700.

min 840
max 1000
(balustrading
required)

rise
max 220

pitch line

pitch
line

going
min 220

pitch line

rise

going

max pitch
private 42°
common 38°

at least
15 mm

less than 100 mm

open stairs

Figure 15.1

Figure 15.2

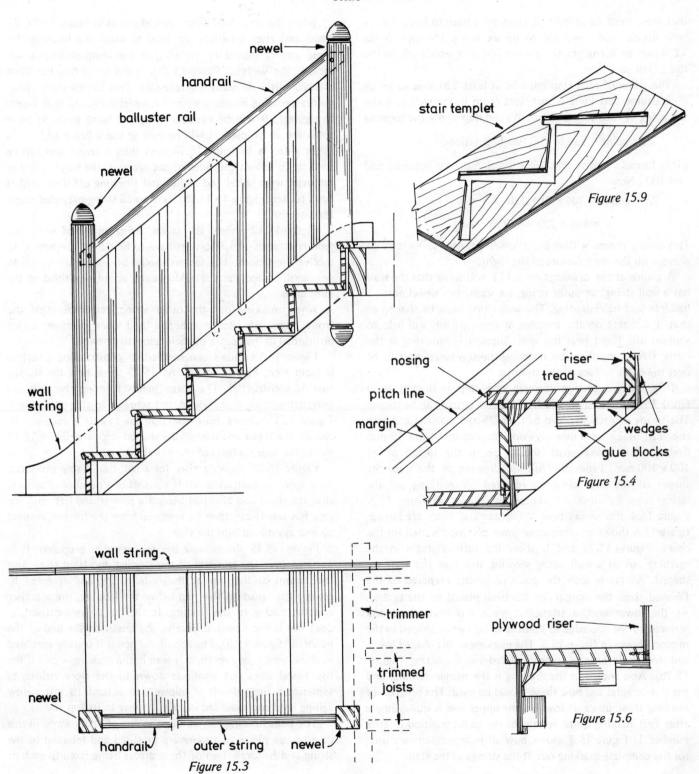

newel

handrail

balluster rail

newel

wall string

stair templet

Figure 15.9

nosing

pitch line

margin

riser

tread

wedges

glue blocks

Figure 15.4

wall string

trimmer

trimmed joists

plywood riser

Figure 15.6

newel

handrail

outer string

newel

Figure 15.3

that there must be at least six steps from floor to floor. Let us now decide that there are to be six steps. We then divide 1224 mm by 6 and get the answer 204 mm, which will be the rise (R) of each step.

The going of each step must be at least 220 mm, so let us now assume that there is sufficient room in the well to make the going of each step 220 mm. We can now apply the formula

$$2R + going = 550 \text{ to } 700 \text{ (see Regulations)}$$

(This formula means that $2R$ + going must be between 550 and 700.) Now

$$2R + going = (204 \times 2) + 220$$

$$= 408 + 220 = 628$$

This figure comes within the allowable range, so we can go ahead with the manufacture of the flight.

A glance at the drawings on p.113 will show that the stair has a wall string, an outer string, six steps, two newel posts, a handrail and ballustrading. The wall string must be shaped so that it will rest on the trimmer at the top; this will help to support the flight near the wall. Support is obtained at the outer side of the flight by notching the top newel post to fit over the outer surface of the trimmer.

If a full-size section through one step is drawn, as in figure 15.4, the over-all width of the two strings can be found. The treads of each step can be from 25 mm material and each riser can be either 9 mm plywood or prepared from 19 mm timber. The newel posts should be in the region of ex 100 x 100 mm. From the full-size drawing of the step, the shapes of the four templets required for marking out the strings can be obtained. These are shown in figure 15.5. Figure 15.4 also shows how the treads and risers are joined; figure 15.6 shows an alternative when plywood is used for the risers. Figures 15.7a and b show the various stages in the marking out of a wall string showing also how the ends are shaped. At (a) is seen the piece of timber prepared to the finished sizes; the margin line has been placed on the timber. At the lower end, a triangular piece has been glued and screwed to the top edge so that the string can be shaped in the manner shown in figure 15.3. The marking of the shaped lower and top ends have also been placed on the string (figure 15.7b). Also shown in the drawing is the margin templet and the step templet and how these should be used. The progress of marking these upwards towards the upper end is quite simple after first making quite certain of the exact position of riser number 1. Figure 15.8 shows how all four templets are used for the complete marking out of the strings to the stair.

When the steps have been marked out as in figure 15.7a, the tread and riser templets are used to mark the housings for these and it should be noted that the templet shapes will include the wedges (figure 15.7b). When the string has been marked out it is ready for recessing. This can be done either with a portable router — when a templet similar to that shown in figure 15.9 will be needed — or using hand tools. If hand tools are to be used, it will be best to use a brace and bit to begin with, as in figure 15.10, and then a tenon saw can be used to cut down the sides of the recesses, the surplus timber removed with chisel and mallet and finishing off done with a hand router. Figure 15.11 shows the wall string prepared ready for assembly.

Figure 15.12 shows the outer string prepared with the tenons at each end. Mortises have to be cut in the newels to receive the tenons. The tenons should be kept equal in size to one another and each should occupy about one-third of the joint area.

When marking out the outer string, remember that the front edges of riser number 1 and riser number 6 are positioned in the centre of their respective newels.

Figure 15.13 shows one method of constructing a shaped bottom step. Figures 15.14 and 15.15 show how the shaped riser is constructed. The three pieces forming the riser are mitred together, being glued and screwed to shaped formers. Figure 15.16 shows how the bottom newel is recessed to receive the tread and riser of the shaped step, and figure 15.17 shows the four surfaces of the newel marked out.

Figure 15.18 shows a riser for a half-round step produced by a more modern method. It consists of a number of veneers that are glued and clamped behind a former and left until the glue has set. It can then be removed from the former, cleaned up and assembled into the stair.

Figure 15.19 shows how the top newel is prepared. It is notched over the trimmer of the landing, mortised to receive the tenons at the top of the outer string and recessed to receive the tread to the step below the landing, the top riser and the nosing to the landing. It also has to be mortised, as does the lower newel to receive the tenon on the end of the handrail (figure 15.3). The top of the newel is usually moulded in some way — one method is seen in the drawing — and if the top newel does not continue down to the floor below, as sometimes they do, it is allowed to extend to just below ceiling level and moulded in a similar way to its top end.

The ballustrading can be done in one of many ways, in this case square pieces of timber are mortised and tenoned to the string and handrail, two of these pieces being fixed to each of

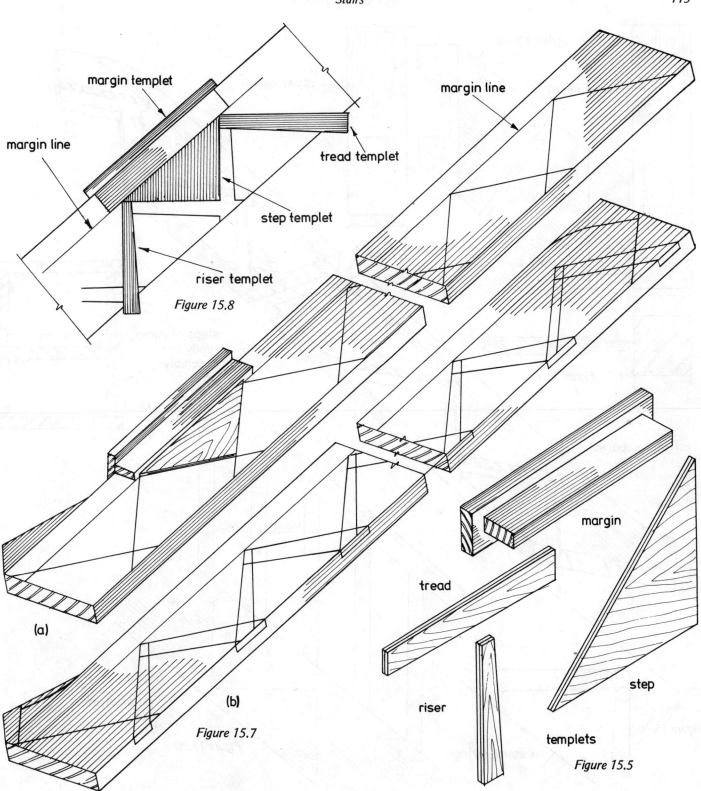

margin templet

margin line

tread templet

step templet

riser templet

Figure 15.8

margin line

(a)

(b)

Figure 15.7

margin

tread

riser

step

templets

Figure 15.5

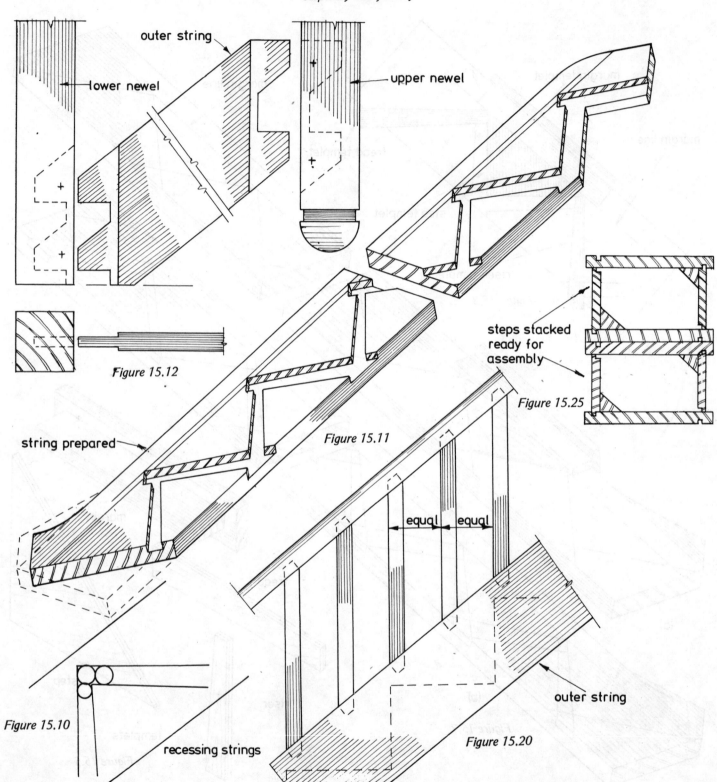

outer string

lower newel

upper newel

Figure 15.12

string prepared

steps stacked
ready for
assembly

Figure 15.25

Figure 15.11

equal   equal

outer string

Figure 15.10

recessing strings

Figure 15.20

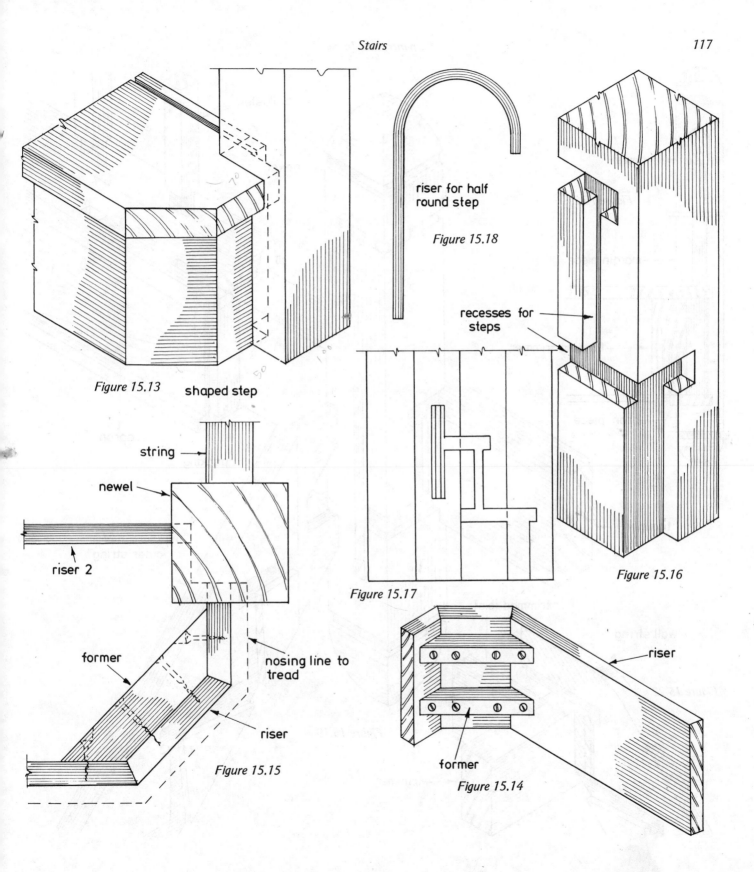

Figure 15.13 shaped step

riser for half round step

Figure 15.18

recesses for steps

Figure 15.16

string

newel

riser 2

former

nosing line to tread

riser

Figure 15.15

Figure 15.17

riser

former

Figure 15.14

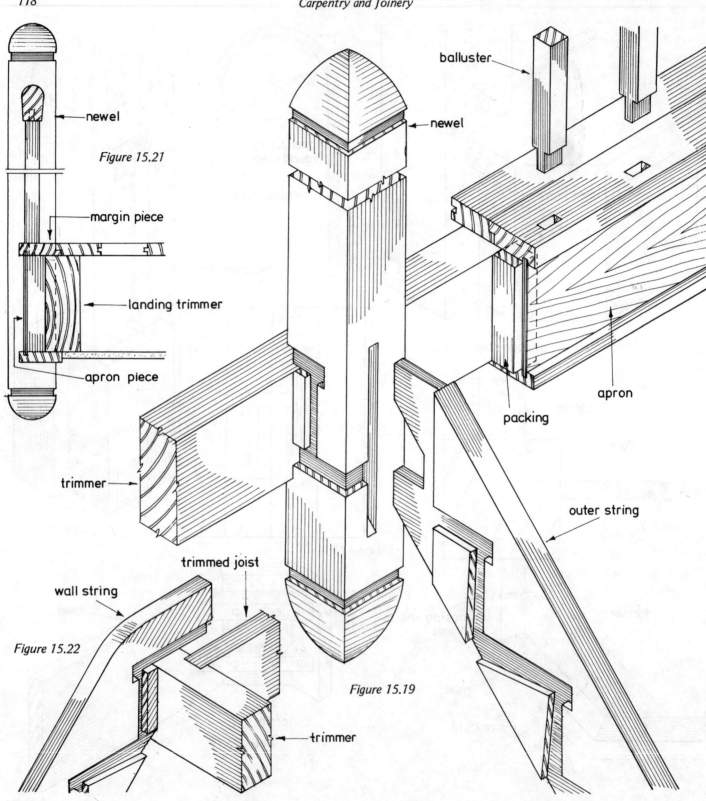

newel

Figure 15.21

margin piece

landing trimmer

apron piece

trimmer

trimmed joist

wall string

Figure 15.22

balluster

newel

apron

packing

outer string

Figure 15.19

trimmer

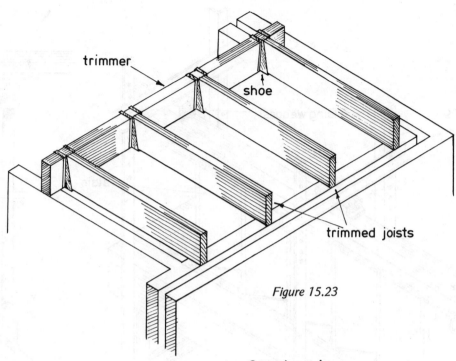

trimmer

shoe

trimmed joists

Figure 15.23

Open-riser stairs

the treads and spaced evenly throughout the flight — figure 15.20.

Figure 15.21 is a vertical section through the landing at the top of the flight. The newel is shown notched over the trimmer and the handrail along the edge of the landing placed central to the newel. So that the ballustrading along the landing can be fixed at the lower ends, the apron piece will have to be packed out so that mortises can be cut in the margin piece to receive the tenons on the ends of the ballustrading.

Figure 15.19 also shows an isometric view of details around a landing that would be suitable for a staircase such as the one described. It consists of a trimmer, 200 x 75, and trimmed joists, spaced at approximately 450 mm centres are jointed to the trimmer by means of notched joints or metal shoes. All joists are built into the walls as the brickwork proceeds.

Figure 15.22 shows an isometric view of the top end of the wall string where it is cut to fit over the landing trimmer.

Figure 15.23 shows an isometric view of one arrangement for the landing timbers, which are built into the walls as the brickwork proceeds. They consist of a trimmer and a number of trimmed joists connected to the trimmer with metal shoes. An alternative to these joints is, of course, a simple housed joint.

Figure 15.2 shows how an open-riser stair string would be set out. As the name implies, there are no risers to this staircase and since there is no additional support for the treads (supplied by the risers in a traditional-type stair) the treads of an open-riser staircase should be increased to 32—38 mm in thickness. Remember too that the front edge of each tread must project at least 15 mm in front of that immediately below. Also, the space between each pair of treads must be reduced to less than 100 mm.

Figure 15.24 shows two methods for jointing the treads, which are all recessings, into the strings: the first (a) showing that two square tenons have been left on the ends of each tread, these being fitted to mortises in the string. They are glued and wedged in position. An alternative to tenoning each tread is to tenon every other one, or even fewer, but whatever method is used, the resulting stair must be strong enough for its use. Figure 15.24b shows that the treads can be recessed into the strings and in addition, metal brackets may be screwed to the bottom surface of the tread and to the inside face of the string to give the additional strength required.

During the assembly of the staircase it is customary to assemble the steps individually; figure 15.25 shows them stacked to one side to await the general assembly work, which,

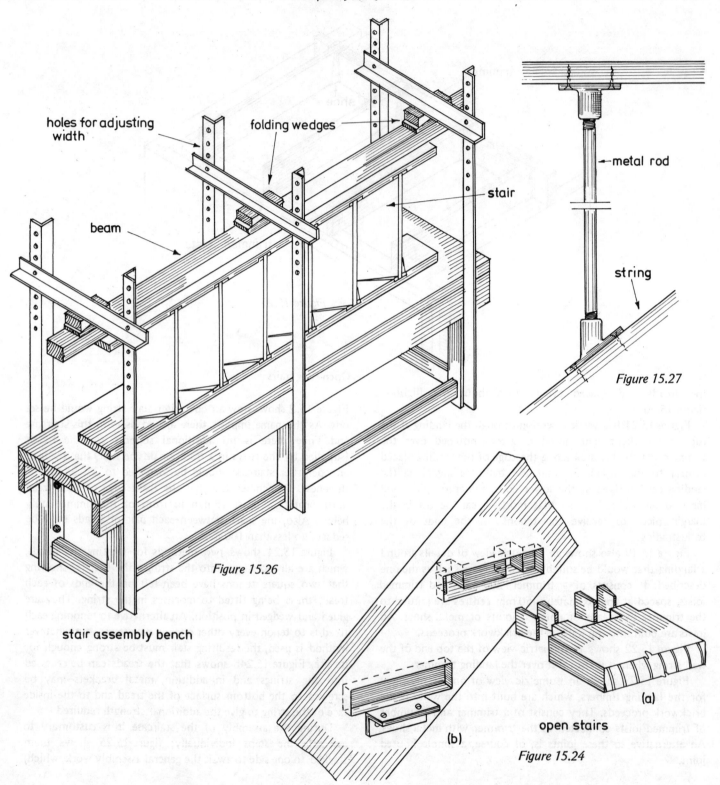

holes for adjusting width

folding wedges

stair

beam

Figure 15.26

stair assembly bench

metal rod

string

Figure 15.27

open stairs

(a)

(b)

Figure 15.24

in larger firms, is carried out with the use of a special stair-assembly bench. This type of bench is shown in figure 15.26 and consists of a strong firm bench on which the stair flight can be placed with a beam passing over and in contact with the top string with a means of clamping the work tightly between the bench top and beam, so that the wedges and glue blocks can be glued into position.

Figure 15.27 shows an alternative to the traditional type of ballustrading and consists of metal rods suitably fixed between string and ceiling.

(1) What is a storey rod?

....

....

(2) What is the difference between a 'private' stair and a 'common' stair as layed down in the Building Regulations?

Private stairs. ....

....

Common stairs. ....

....

(3) What is the maximum rise for the steps in a private stair?

....

(4) What is the minimum going for the steps in a private stair?

....

(5) What is the maximum pitch, in degrees, for a private stair?

....

(6) What does the term 'headroom' mean?

....

....

(7) What is the height of a handrail above a flight of stairs?

....

(8) What is the height of a handrail on a landing?

....

(9) What is the recommended maximum number of steps in a flight?

....

(10) How is a wall string supported at landing level?

....

....

(11) How is an outer string supported at landing level?

....

....

(12) What type of adhesive would you recommend for the glueing up of a stair?

....

(13) What items can be introduced during the assembly of a staircase so as to provide additional strength to the flight?

....

....

....

(14) What does the term 'shaped step' mean and where are they found?

....

....

....

(15) How is a shaped step secured in position in a flight?

....

(16) Make a sketch of the tenons at the bottom of an outer string where it is joined to a newel post.

(17) Name the templets required to mark out the housings for the steps in the strings of a staircase.

(a) ....   (b) ....

(c) ....   (d) ....

(18) Draw a section through a step in a stair showing (a) string, (b) riser, (c) tread, (d) glue blocks, (e) screws, (f) wedges, (g) joints between riser and tread.

(19) What is the purpose of spandrel framing?

....

....

(20) What is the minimum headroom for a staircase in a private dwelling?

....

(21) What is the rise of each step in a flight of fourteen, when the floor-to-floor dimension is 2.640 m?

....

16. JOINERY FITMENTS

Manufactured boards play a large part in the construction of internal fitments, both built-in and free-standing.

Figures 16.1 and 16.2 show two different vertical sections through built-in wardrobes. The vertical section in figure 16.1 shows the front of the cupboard, formed by a frame, mortised and tenoned together, rebated on its inside edges into which the doors fit. Battens are first fixed to the ceiling and the side walls against which the frame can be placed and fixed, with screws. Before the front frame is fixed, any shelves that are required must be fitted with their supporting battens to the side and back walls. When the front frame is fixed, small moulded cover fillets should be mitred around the outside edges of the frame to cover any gaps between it and the walls, ceiling and floor.

Figure 16.2 shows vertical details through a built-in wardrobe that does not have a front frame. The bottom of the cupboard is formed by a shelf or pot board that rests on battens screwed to the walls and also on top of a recessed toe board. Prepared timbers are screwed to walls and ceiling; the doors are hung on the wall timbers, so they must be strong enough to take the weight. Any shelf battens should be fixed at this stage, and these should be long enough to allow the shelves to extend outwards just to clear the back surfaces of the doors.

The doors to the wardrobes are made from two sheets of 3 mm plywood glued to battens to form hollow flush doors. If necessary, their edges can be lipped to give a clean finish.

AIRING CUPBOARD

Figures 16.3 and 16.4 show plan and elevation details of an airing cupboard enclosing the hot-water cylinder and space for shelves made from, say, 50 x 25 battens, spaced apart from one another to promote the circulation of warm air.

The side of the cupboard (figure 16.4) is formed with studding clad both sides with plasterboard and insulated with fibreglass blanket between the studs. The door opening is formed by fitting two upright studs, one plugged to the wall and the second securely screwed to the side studding. Two horizontal pieces, the first fixed to the ceiling joists and the second notched to the two door jambs, will complete the framing. The spaces across the top of the opening will be insulated as before and plasterboard fitted on both sides. A plain door lining can be fitted in the opening with stops planted to suit the thickness of the door. Figure 16.5 shows a large-scale drawing of details around the top of the door opening.

TABLE CONSTRUCTION

Figure 16.6 shows the elevation of a traditionally constructed table with two drawers. The four legs are connected to the rails with mortised and tenoned joints; provision is made on one of the larger sides for the two drawers. Figure 16.7 shows a plan view of the construction and Figure 16.8a shows, to a larger scale, construction details around one corner, with the provisions made for the drawers. Figure 16.8b shows how the openings for the drawers in the framing can be divided into two or more sections. To ensure good fixings at these points the vertical piece should be dovetailed to the horizontal timbers as shown in the drawing.

Traditionally the table top would be solid timber, but a more convenient material would be laminated board or blockboard. If solid timber is used for the top, provision must be made for the timber to move by using shrinkage plates (figure 16.9). These are not necessary with manufactured board but they are still desirable because they allow the top to be fixed without damage to the surface; also the top can be removed easily if necessary.

Figure 16.10 is an elevation of a table constructed in a slightly different way. A drawer has been provided and the front to this is the same depth as the rails connected to the

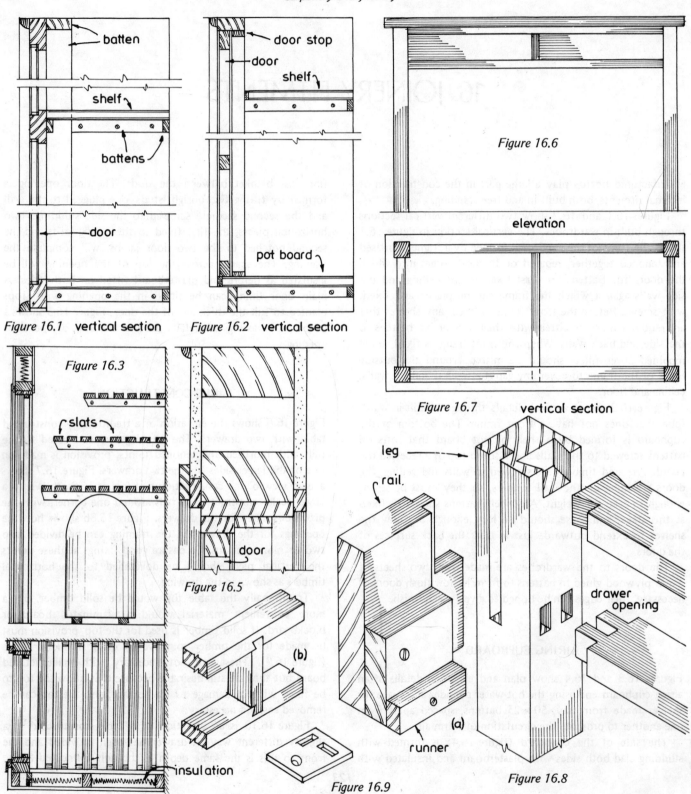

Figure 16.1   vertical section

Figure 16.2   vertical section

Figure 16.3

slats

Figure 16.5

insulation

Figure 16.4

Figure 16.6

elevation

Figure 16.7   vertical section

leg

rail.

drawer opening

runner

(a)

(b)

Figure 16.9

Figure 16.8

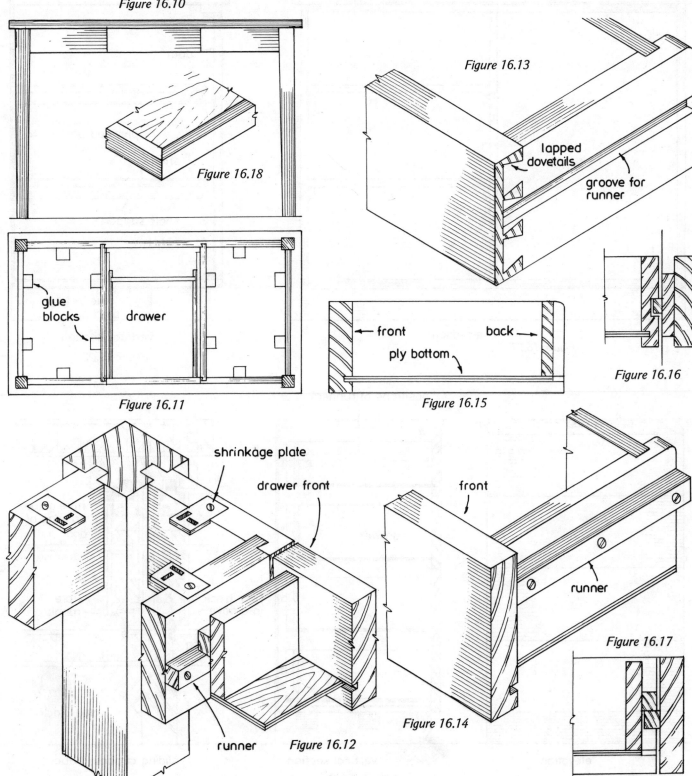

Figure 16.10

Figure 16.18

Figure 16.13

lapped
dovetails

groove for
runner

glue
blocks

drawer

front   back

ply bottom

Figure 16.16

Figure 16.11

Figure 16.15

shrinkage plate

drawer front

front

runner

runner

Figure 16.14

Figure 16.17

Figure 16.12

elevation

Figure 16.21

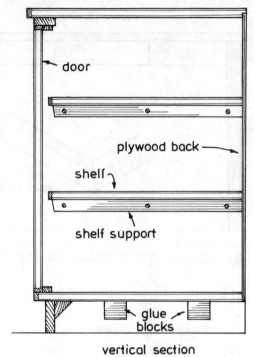

door

plywood back

shelf

shelf support

glue blocks

vertical section

Figure 16.22

positions of runners

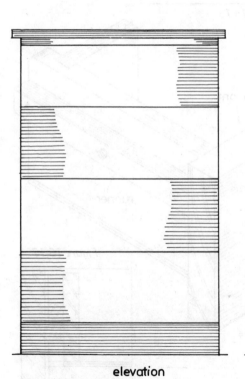

elevation

Figure 16.19

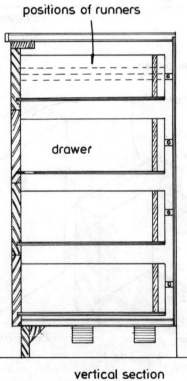

drawer

vertical section

Figure 16.20

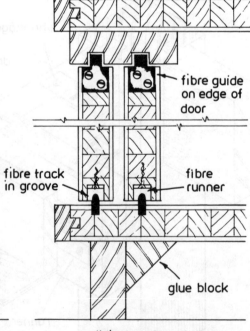

fibre guide on edge of door

fibre track in groove

fibre runner

glue block

sliding cupboard doors

Figure 16.23

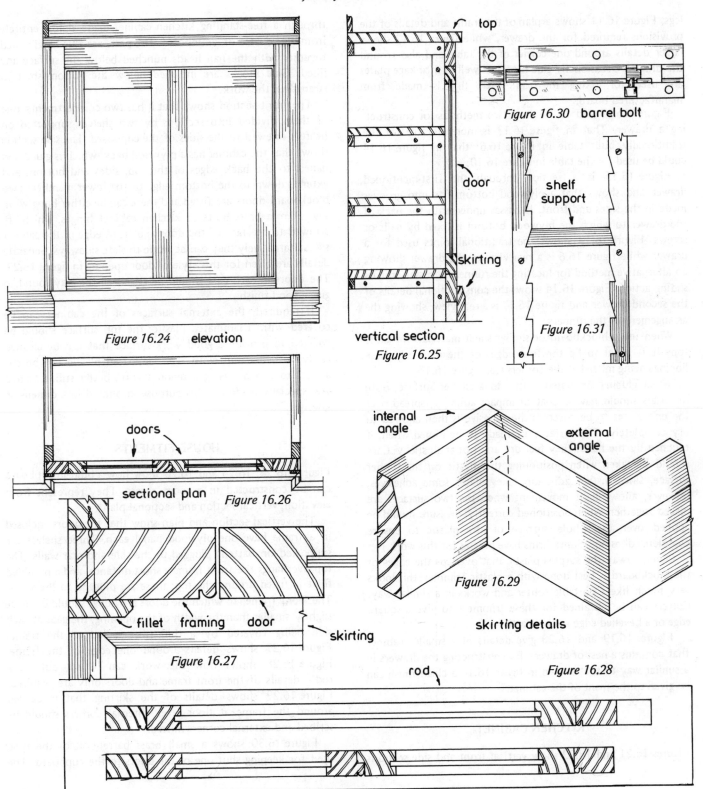

Figure 16.24 elevation

vertical section
Figure 16.25

top

Figure 16.30 barrel bolt

door

skirting

shelf
support

Figure 16.31

doors

sectional plan *Figure 16.26*

fillet framing door

skirting

Figure 16.27

internal
angle

external
angle

Figure 16.29

skirting details

rod

Figure 16.28

legs. Figure 16.11 shows a plan of the frame and details of the provisions required for the drawer, while figure 16.12 shows larger details around one corner of the table and also around the drawer. Occasionally glue blocks as well as shrinkage plates are used for fixing the top when this is made from manufactured board.

Figures 16.13 and 16.14 show two methods for constructing a drawer. That in figure 16.13 is more suitable for the traditionally built table in figure 16.6; that in figure 16.14 could be used for the table in figure 16.10.

Figure 16.15 is a section through the first-mentioned drawer and shows that a plywood bottom fits into grooves made in the sides and front. It passes underneath the back of the drawer to which the plywood bottom is fixed by nails or screws. Figure 16.13 shows the traditional joints used for a drawer while figure 16.6 is a rear view of the drawer showing an alternative method for locating the runners necessary for its sliding action. Figure 16.14 shows the constructional details of the second drawer and figure 16.17 is a rear view, showing the arrangement of the runners.

When using blockboard or similar sheet materials for table tops it is usual to lip the four edges of the material, these lippings being mitred at the corners (see figure 16.18).

When glueing laminated plastic to a timber surface, both materials should have a coat of impact adhesive, spread over the entire area to be covered; the adhesive is then allowed to dry completely. The surfaces are ready to be joined when, if touched by the hand, they feel dry and not at all sticky. Care should be taken when positioning the plastic on the timber surface, since instant adhesion takes place; some adhesives, however, allow slight movement when the two surfaces are placed together. When positioned correctly, pressure should be applied over the whole surface of the plastic to ensure complete adhesion. (Some firms have presses for this work.)

Planing away the surplus plastic that overlaps the edges of the blockboard is best done with a plastic trimmer; this looks very much like a portable router and works in a similar way. Cutters can be obtained for these trimmers to give a square edge or a bevelled edge to the plastic.

Figures 16.19 and 16.20 give details of a smaller cabinet that contains a nest of drawers. By constructing the drawers in a similar way to that shown in figure 16.14 a clean finish can be given to the front of the cabinet.

KITCHEN CABINET

Figures 16.21 and 16.22 show vertical front and side sections through a free-standing kitchen cabinet made almost entirely from blockboard or laminboard. The parts are glued and nailed together with the nail heads punched below the surface and filled. Glue blocks are included below the bottom shelf to strengthen the work.

The front section shows that it has two compartments, one of them divided into sections by two shelves supported on bearers screwed to the sides of the cupboard. The side section shows that the cabinet has a plywood back, which is glued and nailed to the back edges of the top, sides and bottom and extends down to the bottom edge of the lower member. Two blockboard doors are fitted and these can be either hung with, say, 50 mm brass butts or kitchen cabinet hinges, which are screwed to the face of the door and front edge of the cabinet side; alternatively they can be made to slide sideways. Separate details are given for this style of door opening in figure 16.23. The doors in each case should be edged all the way round to give a good finish.

If required, the external surfaces of the cabinet can be covered with a laminated plastic; the top surface should be covered to provide a good work-surface that can be cleaned easily with a damp cloth. The laminated plastic can be cut almost to size by using a tenon saw or, better still, a tipped saw specially made for this purpose, mounted in a dimension saw.

HOUSE FITMENTS

Figures 16.24, 16.25 and 16.26 show how a built-in cupboard can be constructed in a room recess. They represent front elevation, vertical section and sectional plan.

The vertical section and plan show that the doors enclosed in a frame have one plywood panel each. Three shelves are supported on battens plugged to the side and rear walls. The top overhangs the front frame a short distance, and a moulded fillet is fitted around the top; these are plugged to the walls. The front frame, to which the doors are hung, should be made slightly smaller than the width of the opening, the gaps at each side being covered by a thin fillet nailed to the frame. Figure 16.27 shows details around one edge of the frame. Figure 16.28 shows how the work can be set out on a rod — details of the front frame and doors only are required. Figure 16.29 shows details of the skirting that is carried around the frame at floor level. Internal corners should be scribed and external corners mitred.

Figure 16.30 shows a small brass barrel-bolt of the type used for keeping shut one of the doors to the cupboard. The other can be secured with a cupboard lock and key, a bales catch or magnetic catch.

Figure 16.31 shows how adjustments to the shelf positions can be carried out. Two vertical battens, notched as shown, are fixed at each end of the cupboard; into these shaped battens can be fitted at any desired position. The ends of the shelves should be cut to fit round the vertical battens to rest on the shaped supports.

In the space below, and to any convenient scale, draw the elevation and sectional plan of a built-in bookcase with a cupboard at each end, constructed entirely of blockboard, to the following dimensions: 2.5 m long, 0.75 m high and 0.5 m in depth.

17. SIMPLE WALL-PANELLING

Simple wall-panelling — a name usually applied to decorative timber framework fixed to the face of a wall up to a height of approximately 1 m — is quite a simple job to carry out if one or two points are remembered when setting out and carrying out the work.

One of the most important things to provide for a piece of panelling is a flat surface to fix it to. Nothing looks worse than a panelled frame fixed to a surface that is in winding. Nothing can be done to hide the twist that will be seen when looking along the length of the panelling. So what must be done? Grounds are usually fixed to the wall on which the panelling is to be situated so it is the grounds that must provide the flat surface to which the panelling is fixed. There will, no doubt, be irregularities in the brickwork or blockwork of the wall. So that the grounds, when fixed, will be perfectly straight and all in line with one another, the joints of the brickwork or blockwork must be cut out at regular intervals and wooden plugs like the one shown in figure 17.1 must be driven into the joints to provide a secure fixing. When all plugs are fixed, they are trimmed off with a saw so that their ends are all in line. If the vertical row of plugs at each end of the run of panelling is first trimmed in vertical alignment (figures 17.2 and 17.3; this will mean using a plumb rule) and then a line stretched between each horizontal row as in figure 17.4, the required end positions of all the intermediate plugs will be obtained. When these have been trimmed, all the plug ends should be in one vertical plane. The grounds are then nailed to the plugs to which the panelling is fixed. Figure 17.5 shows the elevation and vertical section through some simple panelling that can be fixed in the way described.

There are several methods that can be used for fixing the panelling to the grounds; the simplest of these is to screw through the face of the panelling, being sure to position the screws so that they will be hidden from view. Those at the top are driven through the top edge of the top rail so that the screws are hidden by the capping which is nailed to the top rail. The screws at the bottom of the panelling are hidden by the skirting as seen in the drawing of the larger details (figure 17.6).

Details of the skirting are also shown in figure 17.6. This shows the bottom edge of the skirting tongued, the tongue fitting into a groove in the moulded strip which is screwed to the floor. This method will prevent a shrinkage gap appearing along the bottom edge of the skirting.

Two other methods for fixing the framework to the grounds are shown in figures 17.7 and 17.8. Figure 17.7 shows that the grounds are rebated and lipped buttons screwed to the back surface of the panelling. This arrangement will allow the panelling to be 'hooked' on to the grounds, the work being secured in this position by the fixing of the capping. Figure 17.8 shows the method whereby slotted plates are recessed into the back surface of the panelled frame and screws fixed to the grounds with their heads protruding. The heads of the screws are allowed to enter the openings in the lower ends of the plates and the panelling tapped downwards to secure it in position. The capping, again, will secure the work in its final position.

Figures 17.9 and 17.10 show how internal and external angles can be treated.

(1) Write down in the correct sequence how a flat surface can be produced over a wall with irregularities so that some wall panelling can be fixed correctly.

(a) ....

(b) ....

(c) ....

(d) ....

(e) ....

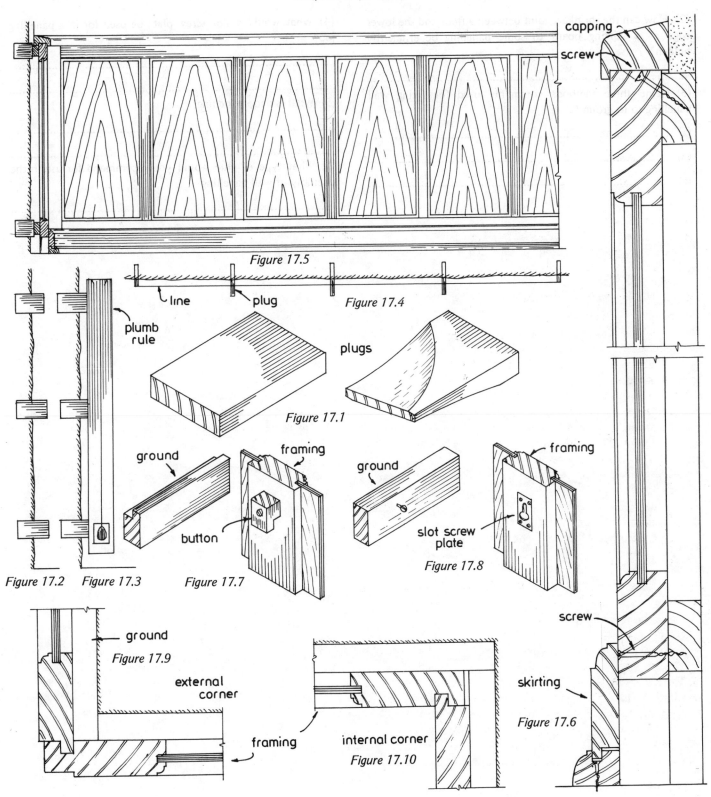

Figure 17.5

Figure 17.4

line

plug

plumb rule

plugs

Figure 17.1

Figure 17.2   Figure 17.3

ground

framing

button

Figure 17.7

ground

framing

slot screw plate

Figure 17.8

capping

screw

screw

skirting

Figure 17.6

ground

Figure 17.9

external corner

framing

internal corner

Figure 17.10

(2) How can the shrinkage joint between a floor and the lower edge of a skirting board to some panelling be efficiently hidden?

....

(3) Name three methods commonly used for fixing wall panelling to its grounds.

(a) ....

(b) ....

(c) ....

(4) What would a slot screw plate be used for in a panelling job?

....

....

(5) What is dado panelling?

....

....

(6) What type of glue would you recommend for use in the assembly of wall panelling?

....

18. PORTABLE TOOLS

The subject of safety in the use of portable electric tools used in the woodworking industries was well covered in volume 1 of this series, but since safety is so important it is considered necessary to go over these points briefly once again.

(1) The operator must understand the correct way of using an electric tool.

(2) He must know the type of work it is capable of doing and not expect it to go beyond its limits.

(3) The tool must be in good working order, it must be maintained regularly and if a fault develops it must be returned to stores, with a note stating why it has been returned.

(4) Repairs should only be carried out by a skilled person.

(5) The cables from the power supply to the tool should be inspected regularly and renewed if damaged. They should be protected from traffic passing over them and should never be bundled up (which allows kinking).

(6) Portable tools should be carried from one place to another correctly, *not by their cables* since this will cause the connections to separate.

(7) Never adjust a portable tool while its plug is in the socket. This could lead to someone switching the tool on and a serious accident resulting. Always disconnect the tool from the power supply when an adjustment is to be made.

(8) Be sure that the starting switch is in the 'off' position before reconnecting the tool to the power supply.

(9) Never disconnect the tool from the socket by pulling on the cable.

(10) If the material being worked on produces dust or abrasive particles, use a mask and/or a pair of goggles (goggles are absolutely essential when cutting materials with an abrasive disc).

(11) Never fix the trigger switch of a machine in the 'on' position unless provision has been made for this by the manufacturers. If an accident occurs the machine will continue running, possibly causing further damage. Some machines have a built-in device in the trigger switch which allows the machine to run when pressure is released from the switch. An additional squeeze of the trigger will switch off the tool. This is, of course, different to fixing the 'on' switch by some other means.

(12) Safety guards supplied with a machine should always be used.

(13) Always clamp the work down on a solid surface unless this is impossible or impracticable.

(14) Never let another person distract your attention from the work being done.

(15) Never put a machine down while it is still running — let it stop first.

(16) Never allow the cable of a tool to get near to the cutting edges. This could cause a severe shock to the operator if the cable is damaged.

(17) Protective clothing should always be worn when using portable tools (and woodcutting machinery, of course). Hair should be short or tied up so that there is no danger of it being caught up in the tools.

Many tools these days are what is known as 'double insulated'. In these tools there is a second protective insulation barrier over and above the normal insulation found in standard tools. These two barriers of insulation provide a positive form of protection against shock. No earthing wire is required for these tools. When connecting a two-core cable to a three-pin plug in a double-insulated tool, the earth terminal (marked E) should be ignored. The brown (live) wire must be connected to the terminal marked L and the blue (neutral) wire must be connected to the terminal marked N. Where the cable passes out of the plug there is a cable grip that is loosened or tightened with two screws. When the connections have been completed these screws are turned so that the cable is securely fixed in the grip. The cover is then replaced.

It is also advisable to mention that tools that are not

double insulated *must* be earthed. Failure to do this may lead to serious injuries. In addition to securing the brown- and blue-covered wires to the terminals mentioned above, the earth wire — coloured green and yellow — must be secured to the largest of the three terminals, which is marked E. (Older machines, if these have not been brought up to date with new cables, will have the outdated coloured wires: live wire — red; neutral wire — black; earth wire — green.)

A fair amount of safety is obtained by using portable tools that require 110 V supply. Whereas a few years ago most were driven with a current of 240 V, 110 V tools are especially advisable where double insulation is unobtainable, because if the operator receives an electric shock, it will be mild compared with one from a 240 V supply.

When the supply is received at 240 V and a 110 V tool is available, the voltage must be stepped down with a transformer. A transformer can be obtained with several outlets so that it will not be dominated by one tool. Be sure to check the required voltage of the tools available before connecting to the power. In fact it should be a rule that supplies of different voltage have their own particular plugs and sockets so that, for example, it should be impossible to connect a tool of 240 V to a supply of 110 V and vice versa. This will prevent mistakes and damage to the machines, especially since in some establishments there are two supply ratings — 110 V in sockets above the joiners benches and 240 V on the walls around the work area.

Never insert bare wires in a socket — get the electrician to fit the correct plug.

MANUFACTURERS' INSTRUCTIONS

When a portable tool is purchased, the manufacturer will always issue notes on the correct use and maintenance of the machine. These should be read carefully and the instruction sheet placed in a position where it can be found easily.

The maintenance of the tool should be carried out as directed by the manufacturers' instructions. These usually include such items as

(1) the wiring of the plug
(2) the recommended extension cables that should be used with the machine
(3) at what stage the carbon brushes should be changed
(4) lubrication of the machine and general instructions such as blowing out the machine after use to ensure adequate ventilation and never allowing the machine to work under too much load, etc.

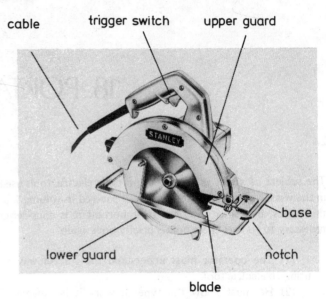

STANLEY CIRCULAR SAW

Figure 18.1

Figure 18.1 shows the Stanley 1½ h.p. heavy-duty circular saw. It has a blade speed of 500 rev. per minute and the blade diameter is 178 mm. It has a maximum depth of cut of 54 mm when cutting vertically and 51 mm when cutting at an angle of 45°. It is useful for straight ripping and cross-cutting. Its base plate can be adjusted for cutting up to an angle of 45°, making it useful for bevelled and splayed cuts.

Saw blades can be obtained for ripping and cross-cutting, and carbide-tipped blades for such materials as asbestos. Silicon carbide discs are also available for cutting asbestos sheets, etc. Fences — or ripping guides, as the manufacturers call them — are supplied for straight cutting. All portable rip saws have a spring-loaded lower guard that covers almost the whole of the lower portion of the blade. As the saw is fed on to the timber, the leading edge of the timber pushes back the guard, which comes to rest on the top surface of the wood during the cut. As the cutting is completed and the saw removed from the work, the guard will spring back over the exposed blade. Never fix the guard back in the open position because this will expose the operator to serious injuries if the saw is allowed to fall against him when the cut is completed. If the lower guard is fixed back in the open position, the operator could be seriously injured if he tripped up.

Figure 18.2 shows a Stanley saw being used for simple cross-cutting. Note that the lower guard has been pushed backwards as the saw is fed towards the timber.

Figure 18.2

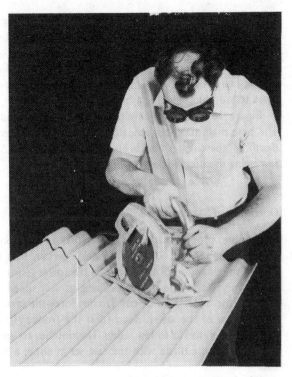

Figure 18.3

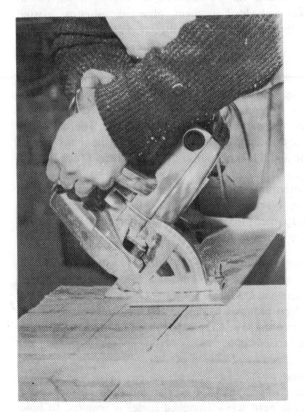

Figure 18.4

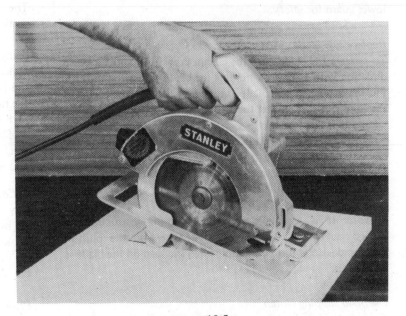

Figure 18.5

Figure 18.3 shows a tool being used for cutting asbestos cement sheets. In this case a silicon carbide disc is being used for the cutting. Note that the operator is wearing goggles; this is necessary when cutting this type of material and also when a disc is being used in the machine. The operator is wearing a mask to stop him inhaling asbestos dust.

Figure 18.4 shows a saw being used for bevelled cutting. The base plate has been adjusted to the angle required and the depth of the cut has also been adjusted. Figure 18.5 shows a saw being used for pocket sawing.

Operation of Stanley saw 272

Install the proper blade for the work to be done — rip, cross-cut, combination or mitre. Make certain that the teeth face in the direction of the arrow on the lower guard. Hold the saw firmly. Have the blade revolving at full speed before it contacts the material to be cut. Do not force the saw.

The base of the saw is notched at the front right corner to help the operator to follow a line. The notches are in line with the inside of the blade with the saw set at either a 90° or 45° cut.

If you wish to operate the lower guard by hand, as in the case of entry into the work from above, use the knob on the lower guard for *safety*.

Replace saw blade
To remove the blade, turn the clamp screw in an anticlockwise direction with a spanner, holding the blade with a rod through the small hole in the blade stopped against the underside of the sole plate. Remove the outer flange to leave the blade exposed.

When refixing the blade, ensure that the engraving on the blade is always to the front, replace the outer flange, then screw in the clamp screw finger-tight and lightly turn with a spanner to obtain sufficient torque loading of the slipping device.

Note: It is essential that the foregoing instruction be carried out when replacing blades, otherwise the built-in slipping device will not function when the load on the blade is excessive.

Overload slipping clutch
The saw is fitted with a built-in overload slipping device so that in the event of excessive pressure being applied to the saw blade causing it to stall, the motor will continue to rotate. If the pressure cannot be relieved immediately, release the switch trigger.

Bevel adjustment
To adjust for bevel 0°–45° loosen the bracket lever, swing the saw housing, read off the required angle on the pivot bracket, tighten the bracket lever firmly.

Depth of cut adjustment
To adjust the depth of cut, loosen the depth clamp knob, swing the saw housing up or down until the correct amount of blade is exposed below the sole plate, tighten the clamping knob firmly.

Note: Use minimum depth adjustment when cutting thin materials to give a longer contact arc for smooth cutting.

Stanley all-purpose saw

Figure 18.6 shows the Stanley 458 all-purpose saw which is particularly simple to use and is useful for many sawing purposes. Blades can be obtained for cutting wood, boards with nails embedded in them, plywood, asbestos, plaster, plastics, fibreglass and even metals.

Blades
The Stanley all-purpose saw has been designed for both vertical and horizontal flush cutting. Satisfactory performance of the saw depends on careful selection of the correct Stanley blade for the particular material to be cut. The blades are locked in the clamp by means of a hole in the shank area of the blade and a locking pin in the blade clamp which fits into the hold.

For smoothness of cut use 82 mm long blades for wood up to 50 mm thick, 150 mm long blades for wood up to 100 mm thick. Edge-hardened blades are recommended for plywood and where nails may be encountered.

Caution: Use sharp blades. A dull blade will slow work and may damage the saw by overloading the motor. Most blades are positioned at a 3° angle for tooth clearance on the forward stroke which prolongs blade life and increases cutting speed. Do not force the saw. Keep extra blades on hand to use when the blade becomes dull.

Blade clamp
The same clamp is used for regular and flush cutting, but a countersunk head screw (supplied loose) is required to hold the clamp in the flush-cutting position.

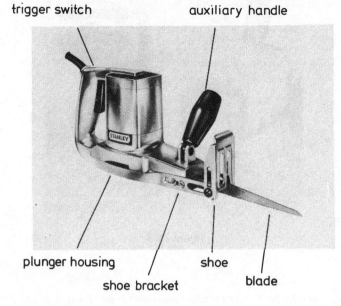

trigger switch   auxiliary handle

plunger housing   shoe

shoe bracket   blade

STANLEY ALL PURPOSE SAW

Figure 18.6

Changing blades

(1) Disconnect the plug from the power circuit.

(2) Loosen the blade clamp screw.

(3) Slide the blade out.

(4) Slide a new blade between the plunger and the blade clamp until it stops.

(5) Ensure that the pin in the clamp engages in the hole in the blade.

(6) Tighten the blade clamp screw.

Shoe

The shoe is attached to the shoe brackets and has two operating-positions. The normal position for cutting is with the shoe in the *down* position. For horizontal and flush cutting, the shoe must be in the *up* position. To change the shoe position remove the blade clamp from the plunger, loosen the two screws and slide the shoe until the screws hit the end of the slots. Tighten the two screws. Replace the blade and blade clamp in the desired position.

The shoe assembly is held on the plunger housing by four screws and as the blades become worn the shoe assembly may be relocated by loosening the four screws, sliding the shoe assembly forward, and tightening the four screws. This shifting

of the shoe enables the operator to utilise the forward or unused portion of the blade, thus gaining maximum service life from each blade.

Caution: Hold the shoe firmly against the work.

Plunge cutting

To make plunge cuts without a starting hole

(1) Make sure that the shoe is in the *down* position.

(2) Mark the line of cut clearly on the work.

(3) Grasp the auxiliary handle with one hand and the rear handle with the other.

(4) Place the tip of the blade (not running) on the line to be cut.

(5) Rest the tip of the shoe on the work and hold firmly in position.

(6) Squeeze the trigger switch, and with the saw blade in motion slowly pivot the saw downwards on the shoe until the tip of the blade starts cutting the work. (Hold the edge of the shoe firmly against the work.)

(7) After the blade penetrates the work, tilt the saw until the blade is perpendicular to the work.

Flush cutting

(1) The shoe should be adjusted to the up position for all flush cutting.

(2) To cut flush to a perpendicular surface (for example, down a wall flush to the floor), mount any blade to the left of the plunger, using the clamp with either the raised or countersunk head screw.

(3) To flush cut along a perpendicular surface, mount the flush-cutting blade, 86219, to the bottom of the plunger, using the blade clamp with the countersunk head screw. Insert the 86219 blade into the 1.6 mm deep recess in the blade clamp and place the blade clamp on the plunger with the blade. Insert and tighten the screw.

Auxiliary handle adjustment

The handle adjusts to any one of five positions for either right- or left-handed operators' comfort and ease of handling.

SABRE SAWS

The double-insulated Stanley sabre saw, shown in figure 18.7, is one of several in this range. This type of machine can be purchased as a single-speed, two-speed or a variable-speed machine.

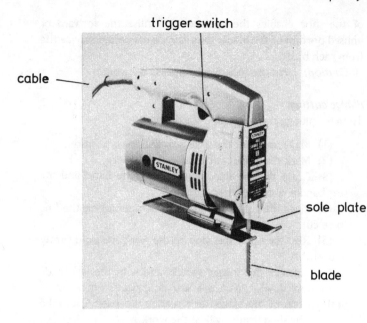

trigger switch

cable

sole plate

blade

STANLEY SABRE SAW

Figure 18.7

The first of the single-speed machines has a speed of 2800 blade strokes per minute, while the second (figure 18.7) gives 3000 strokes. The two-speed model has speeds of 1200 and 3000 strokes per minute and the variable-speed machine gives speed variation from 900 to 3000 strokes per minute.

Figure 18.8 shows a Trend sabre saw being used for cutting sheet material. The inset shows that it can be packed away in a convenient carrying-case.

Stanley sabre saw 460 series

Sole plate
The sole plate is designed so that when orientated at 180° it enables thin plastic or laminate sheets to be cut without chipping or cracking, due to the enlarged sole plate supporting-area. To orientate the sole plate remove the three fixing-screws, turn through 180° in the same plane and replace the three fixing-screws ensuring that they are tight.

Speed selection — for two-speed unit type 463

1st speed — switch trigger — position 1
2nd speed — switch trigger — position 2

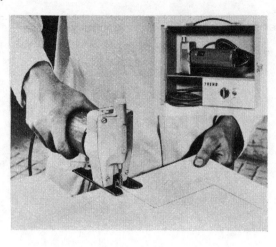

Figure 18.8

Speed selection — for variable-speed unit type 464
The speed can be changed by rotating the speed-selection dial located on the rear cover. This can be done while the motor is stationary or in motion. The dial has five different-coloured segments, the fastest being green and the slowest white. It is important that the correct speed be selected for the job, and listed are a number of materials that can be tackled and recommendations of the colours to be selected. However, in a number of cases conditions vary according to the type of material being used so that recommendations made should serve as a guide.

Colour code	Recommended cutting
Green	Soft wood up to 25 mm thick
Yellow	Aluminium up to 6 mm thick
Blue/Red	Mild steel up to 6 mm thick
White	Thermoplastics

Note: When the dial is set at the slow speed a slight 'knocking' or uneven running will be noticed when the tool is running light. This is the normal effect of the electronic speed-control unit functioning and is in no way detrimental. It will cease when load is applied.

Guide fence
Provision is made in the base of the sabre saw to accommodate guide fence 83555, which can be purchased from Stanley stockists. Used correctly this facility will provide fast straight accurate cuts of varying widths.

Blade selection

Choose the blade best suited to the work: for smoothness of cut use 75 mm blades for wood up to 25 mm thick, and 100 mm blades for wood up to 50 mm thick. High-speed blades must be used for abrasive materials such as plywood, masonite and plastics. High-speed-steel blades are recommended for hardwoods.

Attaching the blade

To change blades, loosen the screw on the blade collar, slip out the old blade and insert the new one. Ensure that hollow-ground blades are pushed in so that none of the shank is showing below the collar. Set-tooth blades should be inserted as far as possible. After the blade had been positioned, tighten the screw with a screwdriver.

Caution: If a blade breaks in use be sure to remove broken portions from the plunger before inserting the new blade.

Bevel cuts

The 462, 463 and 464 sabre saws are fitted with a tilt base for producing bevel cuts. The base angle may be adjusted from 30° tilt to the right through to a 45° tilt to the left. The base is locked in the normal cutting position of 0° tilt. The base angle can be changed by loosening the tilt cradle screw. The cradle lock is retracted by pulling it back with a screwdriver. The base can then be moved to any desired angle. Angles are indicated on the graduated scale and read at the edge of the gear housing. When the base is set to 0° tilt engage the cradle lock by pushing it forward into the groove of the cradle casting, then tighten the cradle screw.

Pocket cuts

Use only 75 mm blades for making pocket cuts. Ensure that the base plate is in its forward position. To start the cut, tilt the saw forward with both base-plate prongs on the work. switch on and slowly lower the blade into the work.

Flush cutting

When cutting flush to a wall or other obstruction, use the flush-cutting blade. To take full advantage of this blade remove the three screws holding the base plate and relocate the plate on the back position.

Operation of tool

Stanley sabre saws are designed for comfort and balance. For most sawing operations one-hand operation is easier. Grip the handle firmly without strain. Place the saw flat on the work using only a slight downward thrust. Guide the saw forward. Do not push the machine too hard because it will slow down the speed of cutting, causing blade breakage and a rough cut. When scroll cutting, always feed the saw forward as you go around corners. Avoid overloading by excessive pressure or twisting of the saw blade against the work. All forms of overloading can be avoided by exercising normal care.

Disconnect the saw from the mains supply when not in use. Disconnect the plug from the mains supply when removing or replacing the saw blade. A portable tool should always be running before being applied to the work and should not be switched on and off while under load.

DRILLS

A portable drill is probably the most widely used electric tool in existence today. It should be remembered that the cutting of holes in different materials requires different speeds — for instance, drilling holes in concrete would require a slower-rotating speed than would the drilling of a hole in timber. Most portable-tool manufacturers, especially Stanley and Wolf, provide single-speed, two-speed, four-speed and percussion drills. (Percussion drills are used for drilling holes in masonry and make for more efficient drilling.) If a drill is to be used for a variety of jobs, the choice should be between a double-speed and a four-speed machine.

Figure 18.9 shows a Stanley two-speed percussion drill which has two speeds — 11 000 and 31 500 percussions per minute. Figure 18.10 shows a two-speed drill fixed in a drilling stand and a smaller single-speed drill. The chuck, into which the bit is placed, is opened by a key which fits into a steadying hole in the chuck side; teeth on the key fit into corresponding teeth on the chuck. By turning the key the jaws of the chuck will open, allowing the bit to be fitted. The key is then turned in the opposite direction to secure the bit. The key should be clipped to the cable to avoid loss.

Figure 18.11 shows a Wolf two-speed rotary percussion drill being used for drilling into concrete, and shows a depth gauge and nose bracket being used to control the depth of the drilling. It should be noted that percussion drills can also be used for normal drilling of holes, the percussion side of the tool being quite easily isolated.

SANDING MACHINES

There are two types of sanding machine in general use by carpenters and joiners — the orbital sander, which is used more

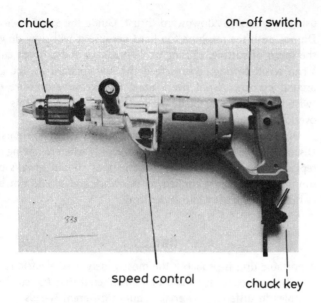

chuck

on–off switch

speed control

chuck key

STANLEY TWO SPEED PERCUSSION DRILL

Figure 18.9

Figure 18.11

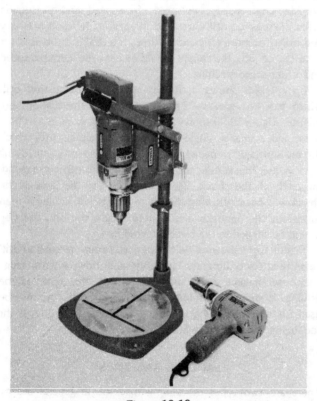

Figure 18.10

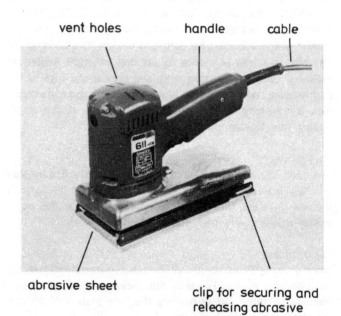

vent holes   handle   cable

abrasive sheet

clip for securing and
releasing abrasive
sheets

STANLEY ORBITAL SANDER

Figure 18.12

Figure 18.13

sanding disc

Figure 18.14

for finishing off joinery work, and the belt sander used for sanding wide surfaces, floors and for production work.

Figure 18.12 shows a Stanley Orbital Sander 611 and is a two-speed finishing sander with 5500 and 3800 orbitals per minute. It can sand flush into any corner. Figures 18.13 and 18.14 show two Elu sanders. Figure 18.14 shows something new in this type of tool — instead of having an orbital action it has a rotating disc to which can be fitted various grades of abrasive disc. With this tool rebates, bevelled edges and similar work can be sanded with extreme accuracy. The sanding disc has a diameter of 115 mm and the tool has a bevel fence that can be adjusted up to 45°. It also has a dust bag for the extraction of dust.

Stanley Orbital Sander 611

Speed switch
The switch has a locking pin to lock it in the high or low speed 'on' position. It is only necessary to depress the trigger to obtain the required speed (for example, fully depressed for high speed) and press the locking pin which is located in the handle cover. To release the switch lock squeeze the trigger lightly.

Attaching abrasive sheets
Snap spring clips are provided at each end of the sander base for replacement of abrasive sheets. Raise one clip and insert one end of the abrasive sheet under the opened clamp then lower the clamp to retain the sheet. Raise the other clip and

insert the free end of the sheet into the opened clamp, draw the sheet tight and lower the clip.

Note: Disconnect the sander from the power circuit before changing abrasive sheets.

General instructions
Switch off the sander when not in use. Never insert anything into the vent holes. Frequently blow out all dust from the motor unit to ensure adequate ventilation. A portable tool should always be running before being applied to the work and should never be switched on and off while under load.

Operation of tool
Maintaining a firm grip on the handle, switch on the sander before applying it to the work. Place the sander flat on the work and, using only light pressure, guide the machine over the surface to be sanded, using long slow forward and back strokes.

Note: Undue pressure on the sander wears out the abrasive sheet rapidly and also reduces the sanding speed. Never let the sander dwell in one spot, keep it moving evenly over the entire surface. The sander can be used vertically, horizontally or on a flat or convex surface.

Stanley Belt Sander 497

Figure 18.15 shows a Stanley Belt Sander 497. It is a two-speed machine and has a 102 mm wide sanding belt and is capable of fast removal of a surface, a fine finish, paint and

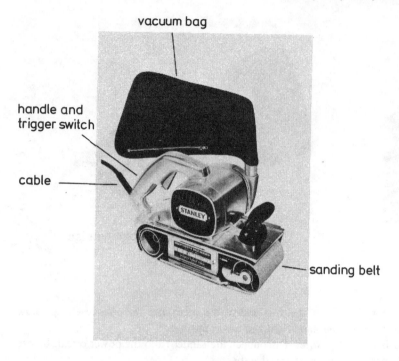

vacuum bag

handle and
trigger switch

cable

sanding belt

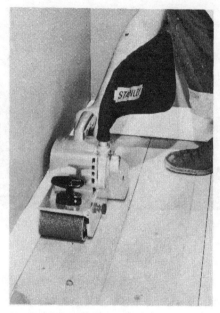

Figure 18.17

STANLEY BELT SANDER

Figure 18.15

Figure 18.16

varnish removal, etc. It has a non-slip rear roller which transmits full power to the sanding area. It also has a tracking device to allow the belt to run centrally on the rollers. Figure 18.16 shows the sander being used on a wide surface and figure 18.17 shows how it is useful for sanding up against vertical surfaces.

Operation

Hold the sander firmly. With the motor running full speed, apply the sander to the work with a forward motion. Let the back of the platen touch the work first, then bring the platen into full contact as the stroke moves forward.

The sander should be fed back and forth parallel to the grain of the wood. The sander is designed to operate under its own weight. Do not apply extra pressure on the sander because this will only reduce the speed of the sanding belt and cut down the rate of stock removal.

As the sander is fed back and forth over the surface guide the sander sideways overlapping the strokes. Work the whole surface down evenly and do not let the sander dwell or a hollow will be made. Avoid tilting the machine when feeding or the belt will make a gash in the work.

Important: A portable tool should always be running before being applied to the work and should not be switched on and off while under load.

Switches

The sander has two switches: a speed-selector switch and an 'off-on' switch that has a locking pin to lock it in the on position. It is only necessary to switch on and press the locking pin which is located in the handle cover. To release the switch lock, squeeze the trigger lightly. The speed is selected by moving the lever of the speed switch to the speed indicated on the data plate.

Warning: The 497 belt sander should not be operated unless the vacuum bag is attached. To operate it without the vacuum bag attached will cause the sanded particles and dust to be thrown from the machine at high velocity and may result in serious injury or damage.

Tracking

Turn the machine upside down and rest the front handle on the edge of a bench. Hold the switch handle in the left hand and start the motor. Adjust the tracking adjusting screw, located on the right side of the machine, by turning it in the required direction, so that the sanding belt runs flush with the outer end of the rear drive pulley. Turning the tracking adjusting screw clockwise will move the sanding belt to the outer edge of the pulleys. Turning the tracking adjusting screw anticlockwise will move the sanding belt towards the inner edge of the pulleys.

Changing abrasives

To retract and lock the front idler pulley, hold the machine by the two handles and stand it on the front pulley with the belt vertical. Push down until the front pulley is retracted and automatically locks. With the sander lying on its side, the sanding belt can be removed easily. Hold the new sanding belt so that the arrow printed on the inside points in the same direction as the arrows on the data plate. First slip the sanding belt over the front pulley then over the rear pulley. To release the front pulley, rest the heel of the right hand on the front of the platen. Extend the fingers around and up over the front pulley and pull down.

Note: Disconnect the sander from the power circuit before changing the sanding belt.

PLANING MACHINES

Portable planing machines are useful on the site as well as in the joiner's shop. They can be used for a large variety of jobs including shooting doors into frames, cleaning up large items such as laminated beams — in fact any planing work in

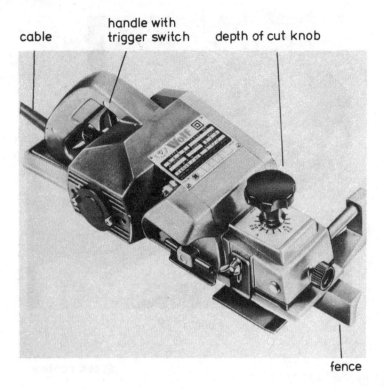

cable — handle with trigger switch — depth of cut knob — fence

WOLF ELECTRIC PLANER

Figure 18.18

situations or dimensions where it would be impossible to use an overhand or thicknesser. The planer shown in figure 18.18 is a Wolf 136 mm (width of cut) machine, one of three they produce. It has a maximum depth of cut of 3 mm and the two-cutter block revolves at 16 000 r.p.m. It weighs 7.4 kg and is 430 mm in length and 205 mm wide.

Wolf Planer 8630

Depth of cut

Adjustment is made by turning the front handle or graduated knob clockwise for increased cut. Graduations are in tenths of a millimetre.

Operating

Begin planing by placing the front or movable base plate on the edge of the timber. Hold the front handle lightly and push with the rear switch handle firmly held. Idle running should be avoided owing to the danger from the cutter block revolving at high speed.

Figure 18.19

WOLF PLANERETTE   *Figure 18.20*

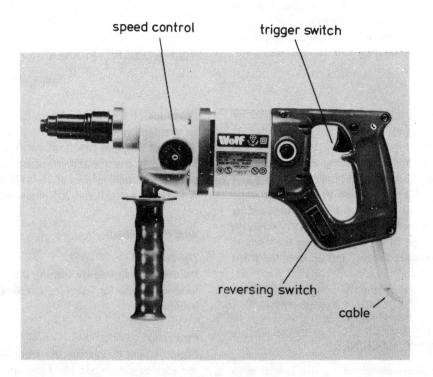

WOLF TWO SPEED SCREWDRIVER 3625

Figure 18.21

Adjustment of cutter blades
Remove the machine from the power supply before adjusting or removing blades. The cutter block can be rotated by moving the drive belt. It is important that the cutter blades are correctly adjusted in the cutter block. Check with the triangular gauge plate provided, or a straight edge, that the cutting edge of each blade is level along its length with the surface of the rear base. If the blades are not parallel with or are set above or below the level of the rear base, this will affect the cut on the work. To adjust a blade, slacken the hexagonal head-fixing screws and turn the two adjusting screws, the heads of which engage in slots in the blade so that screwing or unscrewing lowers or raises it. When tightening the hexagonal head-fixing screws, give a turn to each, first on the outer screws and then on the inner screw(s) until these are tightly secured. Finally, screw down the adjusting screws so that they do not become loose in the slots.

Blade sharpening
Cutter blades must always be kept sharp. Blunt blades will increase the loading on the motor and give a poor finish on the work. *Always replace cutter blades in pairs.* To fit a new blade with an old one will upset the balance of the cutter block assembly, cause vibration and give an inferior finish to the work.

Quality of finish
The finish obtained on the work surface depends on the depth of cut and the speed with which the planer is moved across the surface. For rough planing the maximum depth of the cut is used. When a finer surface is required, however, decrease the depth of cut and move the planer at such a speed as to prevent the accumulation of shavings at the motor cooling outlet.

Figure 18.19 shows how the planer is used to prepare the edge of a piece of material.

Figure 18.20 shows another planer in the Wolf range — the Planerette (because it is a small machine, limited in what it can do and can be operated one-handed). It can do a variety of lightweight jobs, has a width of cut of 81 mm and a maximum depth of cut of 1 mm. It weighs only 2.5 kg, so can be easily carried by the carpenter to jobs away from his works.

SCREWDRIVERS

Electric screwdrivers are probably the least-known portable tools because only a small section of the woodworking industry use them. Those factories mass-producing such items as timber buildings will, of course, use these tools and they are considered commonplace among the workmen. However, many men who work in small joiner's shops or on small sites may never use these tools because their use is limited.

A knowledge of portable screwdrivers is useful from time to time, so three of those from the Wolf range have been selected for description. Figure 18.21 shows a Wolf two-speed electric screwdriver and this, like all their other models, has a reversing switch. Figures 18.22 and 18.23 show other screwdrivers in the Wolf range. The first, type 3599, is a high-speed tool designed for dry-wall fixing and is light in weight; the second tool, type 3617, is a slow-speed model designed for general-purpose work.

Wolf Screwdrivers

On—off and changeover switch
This is used for reversing. The lever for reversing is located above the trigger and is interlocked with the trigger in the 'on' position, to ensure that the machine cannot be reversed while being switched on. To reverse the machine, switch 'off' and then move the reversing lever from one side of the trigger to the opposite side when the machine has stopped.

Warning: No attempt should be made to operate the reversing lever while the switch is in the on position.

Model 3625 — the reversing switch is fitted in the loop handle cavity, separate from the main switch. To reverse, switch off and allow the machine to stop before operating the reversing switch and restarting the machine.

Clutch mechanism
These models are fitted with a simple positive clutch, which comprises two angle face clutches in conjunction with a depth-setting device to give accurate setting of screws.

Depth-setting sleeves
These are available in various lengths, and are made of hardwearing thermoplastic material. By use of a sharp knife the end may be trimmed to suit a particular fastener. The sleeves are push fit on the 'O' ring fitted to the adjusting attachment as standard on models 3599, 3609 and 3625.

Depth-setting adjustment
This is fitted to the clutch housing on the nose of the machine. To adjust, the locking sleeve nearest the motor is pulled back against the spring, this disengages the castellations on the ends

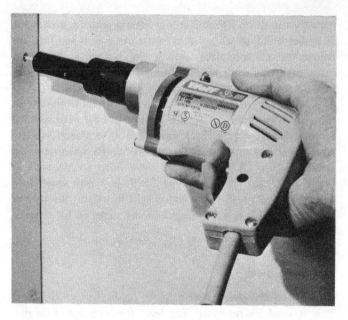

Figure 18.22

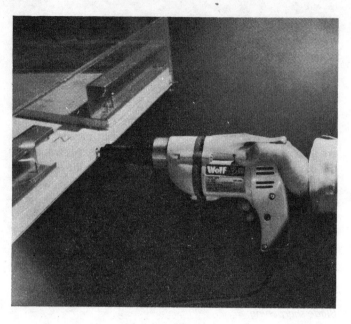

Figure 18.23

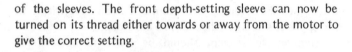

of the sleeves. The front depth-setting sleeve can now be turned on its thread either towards or away from the motor to give the correct setting.

(1) Select the correct bit and sleeve and assemble.

(2) Place a screw on the bit and push it by hand as far as it will go. Note that there are two positions, one deeper than the other. Make sure that the top position is used which means that the clutch faces are disengaged.

(3) For example, to drive a countersunk headed screw, adjust the depth sleeve until the end is level with the face of the screw. This when driven will set the head of the screw flush with the face of the work. If the head of the screw is inside the sleeve it will remain proud of the work surface. If the head of the screw is outside the sleeve it will be driven below the work surface. When driving hexagon or cheese headed screws, fasteners, etc., the underside of the head should be used for setting purposes.

(4) When the correct setting is obtained the spring-loaded section is released to lock the selected position by reengagement of the castellations.

Note: (1) The castellations allow for setting the depth of sleeve in increments of 0.13 mm. (2) If it is necessary to remove a driven screw, take off the depth-setting sleeve, switch to reverse, and unscrew from the workpiece.

Screwdriver bits, sockets, and driver assemblies
All have a common hexagonal shank for complete interchange-ability on all models.

Speed selection
Change of speed is affected by a selector mounted in the front of the gearbox. To change speed, switch off and operate the selector while the machine is running down.

ELECTRIC ROUTERS

Some craftsmen consider that the portable router is the most versatile tool in the whole range of electric tools used by woodworkers. This is, of course, a matter of opinion, but it cannot be denied that the router can do a great many jobs at an economical rate and with high quality. Many regard the router as an essential tool to the bench joiner who does not have the benefit of woodcutting machinery at his disposal. The tools can groove, rebate, mould, recess, cut mortises and tenons and other useful work that takes the person using hand tools much more time to carry out.

Figure 18.24 shows a Stanley heavy-duty router in the 264—267 range. The first of these has a 1 h.p. motor and the second 1½ h.p. Its adjustment controls are very precise and quick.

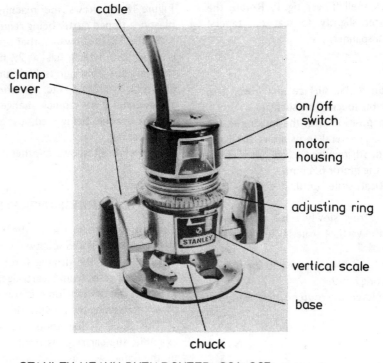

cable

clamp
lever

on/off
switch

motor
housing

adjusting ring

vertical scale

base

chuck

STANLEY HEAVY DUTY ROUTER 264-267

Figure 18.24

Stanley Routers 264–267

General instructions
Switch off the motor when not in use. Never insert anything in the vent holes. Keep the motor clean and the air holes free from dirt and sawdust. Disconnect the plug from the mains supply when changing bits or cutters. A portable tool should always be running before being applied to the work and should not be switched on and off while under load.

Handle adjustment
The handles adjust to any one of three positions for comfort and ease of handling. Handle adjustment is obtained by removing the handle fixing screw and reseating the handle to the required position, then replacing the screw and tightening firmly.

Shaft lock
Shaft lock and switch lever are combined. To lock the armature shaft, throw the switch lever to the 'off' position and push up and to the left. *Do not push up the lever until the motor stops.*

Chuck
The collet-type chuck must be fitted with bits and cutters with 6.4 mm shank only. Clean shaft, collet and chuck shell tapers frequently to maintain accuracy. The long taper on the collet fits into the motor shaft.

  Important: Stanley routers are high-speed machines, therefore it is recommended that only Stanley mounted points and cutters for use at high speeds should be used.

Base
The motor unit is locked in place by pushing down the locking lever on the side of the base. The position of the motor locking lever may be changed to suit the operator's convenience by loosening the centre screw that holds this lever.

Mounting cutters
Lock the armature shaft. The long taper of the collet fits in the motor shaft. Insert the shank of a mounted point, bit or

cutter and tighten the chuck shell 'finger tight'. Rotate the mounted point, bit or cutter slightly to seat the tapers. Tighten the chuck shell with a spanner.

Depth of cut adjustment

(1) Place the router on a flat surface and lower the motor in the base until the bit touches the surface.

(2) Lock the motor in position with the locking lever.

(3) Raise the adusting ring several turns above the base to any point beyond the depth required (each full turn of the ring will raise or lower the motor 6.4 mm).

(4) Push up the vertical scale until it touches the adjusting ring.

(5) Lower the adjusting ring slowly until the desired depth of cut appears on the vertical scale in line with the pointer.

(6) Release the locking lever, lift the base and the motor will drop to the proper cutting depth.

(7) Tighten the locking lever; the router is now ready to operate.

Precision setting

To set the depth of cut precisely, use the graduations on the adjusting ring with reference to the vertical pointer on the base. Each graduation equals about 0.1 mm of the vertical movement of the bit.

Sharpening cutters

Dull cutting-tools overload and overheat the motor and produce poor-quality work. Ordinary sharpening can be done with a fine oil-stone, but for best results a Stanley-Bridges GF.H1 grinding fixture is recommended.

Template guides

Template guides should be attached to the bottom of the base with the neck extending below the base, to permit the router to follow the contour of the template. The bit protrudes through the hole in the template guide to make the required cut.

Figure 18.25 shows a Stanley 264–267 being used for grooving, with the fence controlling the position of the cutter, while figure 18.26 shows the machine doing a similar job but in this instance the groove is dovetailed. Figure 18.27 shows the machine being used for cutting a dovetailed joint, the dovetailing accessory being necesary for this operation.

Figure 18.28 shows the machine being used for trimming plastic, a tipped cutter being required for this type of work.

Figure 18.29 shows another router in the Stanley range; this is type 290 which has a 2½ h.p. motor. It is capable of carrying out continuous high production in wood, plastics, plywood, laminates, etc. Its controls are easily and quickly adusted and it has a quick-change collet (cutter-holding sleeve) with no spanner being used, just a turn of a knob for loosening or tightening.

Figure 18.30 shows another heavy-duty Stanley router in action.

CARTRIDGE-OPERATED FIXING TOOLS

These have been in use in the United Kingdom for the past twenty years. There are two types of tool: (1) direct-acting tools in which the driving force on the pin comes form the compressed gases from a cartridge, and (2) indirect-acting tools in which the driving force is transmitted to the pin by means of an intervening piston with limited axial movement.

The direct-acting tools are always spring-operated — for example, the cartridge is fired by a spring released by a trigger in the same way as with a gun. The indirect tools may be hammer-operated — for example, the cartridge is fired by an externally applied blow with a club hammer; alternatively they may be spring-operated.

In order to penetrate a hard surface a pin must have considerable energy. (Note that the term 'pin' is used in this section to mean nail, stud, eyelet or a similar object that is driven into the working surface by means of a cartridge-operated tool.) The pin and the cartridge that supply the energy are therefore capable of causing serious injury to the workman or a bystander. To avoid this hazard, cartridge tools should incorporate certain safety devices.

(1) Spring-operated tools have an interlock provided to make it impossible to fire the tool unless it is pressed against the working surface with a specified force. This forces compresses the internal spring which either cocks the firing action, releases the safety catch or opens a shutter between the firing spring and the cartridge. BS 4078:1966 specifies that it shall be impossible to fire the tool unless it is pressed fully home against the working surface with a force of at least 5 kg and that any direct-acting tool shall not fire if dropped from a height not exceeding 3 m on to a hard surface. Some tools required a force of 13.6 kg to enable them to be fired, to stop them firing if dropped on to a hard surface.

Figure 18.25

Figure 18.27

Figure 18.26

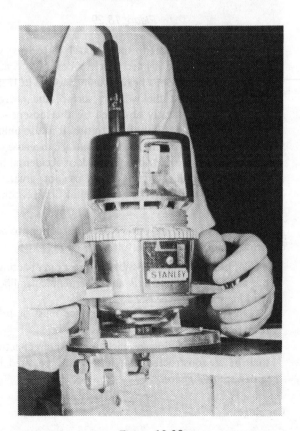

Figure 18.28

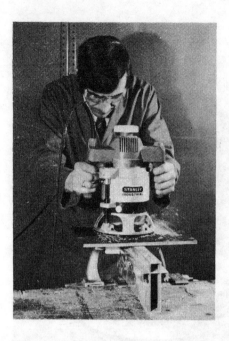

Figure 18.29

Figure 18.30

(2) Hammer-operated tools have cartridges with a relatively insensitive primer which is designed to need the energy of a blow from a heavy hammer to fire it. If the tool is not held against the working surface the energy of a hammer blow is largely absorbed by the looseness of the operator's arm and it is unlikely to fire. It is also unlikely to fire if dropped on to a hard surface because of the insensitivity of the cartridge. The risk of accidental firing of low-powered indirect-acting tools is not great, so no positive means of preventing accidental firing is considered necessary.

BS 4078 also specifies other safety precautions to be taken in the design of these tools as follows.

(1) It should be impossible to fire a direct-acting tool if the angle between its axis and a perpendicular line to the working surface exceeds 7°.

(2) A pin fired into a hard surface must be prevented from ricocheting back towards the operator.

(3) A direct-acting or high-power indirect-acting tool shall be so constructed that it can only be fired if fitted with a splinter guard.

Cartridges

Cartridges for different makes of tool are not usually interchangeable. Packages of cartridges should be labelled to show the make and model of tool for which they are to be used. Accidents can happen if cartridges made for indirect-acting tools are used with direct-acting tools.

To cope with the difference in the hardness of the working surfaces, some means is required for adjusting the energy applied to the pin. This is done by providing a range of cartridges with different charges. BS 4078 requires that the cartridge package shall show the strength of the cartridge and every cartridge shall be marked with a distinctive colour to indicate its strength. This colour coding is not universally followed so an operator changing to a different make of tool should never rely on the colour of the cartridge to indicate its strength but should refer to the label on the cartridge package. To avoid errors in identification, cartridges should always be carried in the maker's package, never loose. Some direct tools have a provision for varying the power level so that one type of cartridge can be used for all the jobs it is capable of doing.

Pins

These are intended to penetrate hard surfaces such as mild steel, concrete and timber and have different properties to the common type of nail. Each manufacturer produces a wide range of pins, threaded studs and eyelets that are intended to be used in the tools made by that firm. *Never* attempt to interchange pins between different makes of tool.

Training

It is a statutory requirement that explosives shall only be handled or used by or under the immediate control of a competent person. All operators of cartridge-operated fixing tools should be trained in their safe use. On every site where several tools are in use there should be a person who has received additional training in dismantling a tool and diagnosing faults. No other person should be allowed to do this work.

Manufacturer's instructions

There are wide variations in the mechanical details of the tools from different makers, so it is important that the maker's instructions related to a specific tool should be carefully followed for efficient fixing and safe handling. A copy of the manufacturer's instructions should be kept with every tool.

Working area

To avoid accidents due to richocheting or complete penetration of the pin through the working surface, the area around and behind the working area should be fenced off to stop others wandering into the danger area.

Operator

The operator and others in close proximity must be protected from hazards such as discharge noise, dust, splinters and fragments and it is recommended that a safety helmet and eye protection should be worn, especially when working in confined spaces.

Pin selection

The length of pin required depends on the thickness of material to be fixed, the amount of projection from the working surface required and the required depth of penetration. There may be a tendency to use too long a pin; this should be avoided and manufacturers publish guides on the selection of pin length including recommendations on the penetration required for various materials. These are only a guide and should always be verified by a test.

Cartridge selection

Manufacturers' instructions give guidance in this direction. However, they cannot cover every situation and trial fixes are therefore necessary. Trial fixes should be made with the *weakest* cartridge first, increasing the cartridge strength by one grade at a time until the required penetration and strength of pin are achieved. *Do not* begin with the strongest cartridge first — accidents may happen.

Splinter guards

These should always be in position when using a cartridge tool. Special guards can be supplied for irregular surfaces or narrow surfaces such as metal window sections.

Hard and brittle materials

Not all materials are suitable for the use of cartridge tools. A brittle material such as marble possesses very high surface-hardness. Any attempt to fire a pin into this type of material will result in a ricochet or shattering of the material. If in doubt about a material, try to drive a pin with a hammer. If the point of the pin is blunted or fails to penetrate 1.5 mm, or if the surfaces crazes, a cartridge tool should not be used.

Fixing to steel

Cartridge-operated tools should only be used on mild steel and the higher-tensile steels from which structural sections are rolled. Do not try to fix a pin into tool steel or other heat-treated alloy steels or malleable cast iron, without first referring to the manufacturer of the tool. A pin driven into steel tends to follow the line of least resistance, so if a pin is driven into mild steel near to the edge of the material it could travel to the edge and continue in free flight. No fixing should be attempted in mild steel or structural-steel sections closer then 13 mm from the edge of the material. This distance not only applies to the edges of the material but also to holes in the material. A fixing should not be attempted less than 50 mm from a weld in the material, due to a possible hardness of the material resulting from the welding process.

Fixing into thin materials

The danger in making fixings in thin materials with a cartridge gun is that the pin may completely penetrate the material and continue free flight after the penetration. The precautions on guarding working areas should be carried out in these situations. When fixing a number of thin materials together they should be securely clamped together to avoid spaces in between each layer and so eliminate the danger of ricocheting.

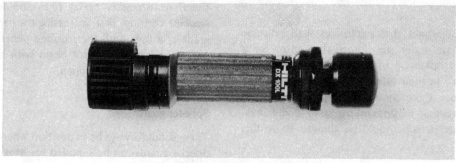

HILTI DX 100

Figure 18.31

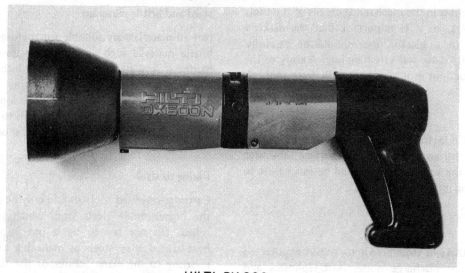

HILTI DX 600

HILTI CARTRIDGE GUNS

Figure 18.32

Fixing to brickwork and concrete

A pin driven into concrete may fail to hold; a second pin driven into the hole may ricochet; therefore the second pin should never be driven into the material less than 50 mm from the edge of the hole. There is a tendency for a pin to deflect towards the free edge of concrete or brickwork, this will cause shattering and the pin will go into free flight, against which the splinter guard gives no protection. To prevent this, pins should not be driven into concrete or brickwork nearer than 65 mm from a free edge or a joint in the materials. If the material is rendered, the distance should be 65 mm plus twice the thickness of the rendering. These notes also apply to stonework but since the characteristics of stonework can vary quite considerably they must be taken into account; if there is any doubt regarding this matter the manufacturers should be consulted.

GENERAL RULES REGARDING CARTRIDGE-OPERATED TOOLS

Cartridge guns must always be used with the utmost care. Only use a gun if you are standing on a firm flat surface — a scaffold is preferable to a ladder (the pressure to cock a spring-operated tool and the reaction to the recoil may cause you to overbalance on a ladder).

A tool should never be left unattended when loaded and should only be loaded as the last operation before firing.

Cartridge guns should never be used where there is inflammable vapour or risk of a dust explosion.

If it is found that more than light finger pressure is needed to insert a cartridge, the attempt to load should be abandoned and the tool returned to stores.

MISFIRES

The procedure to follow after a misfire is laid down in BS 4078 and should be very closely followed. When removing the misfired cartridge there should be no pressure on the rim of the cartridge — accidents have occurred through using a screwdriver or knife or prise the cartridge out of the gun.

Hilti (Great Britain) Ltd, make a wide range of cartridge guns with many accessories suited to all types of fixing. Figure 18.31 shows their DX 100 cartridge tool — an indirect-acting type. It weighs 2 kg, is 250 mm long, and the cartridge removal is semi-automatic. Figures 18.33 and 18.34 show this tool in use.

Figure 18.32 shows Hilti's DX 600 cartridge tool which is designed for medium- and heavy-duty fastenings into concrete and steel. It weighs 4 kg and is 360 mm long; it has an automatic cartridge ejection. Figure 18.35 shows this tool being used for a fixing in concrete. It is direct-acting.

Figure 18.36 shows some of the fastenings supplied by Hilti for their cartridge-operated tools.

Figure 18.37 shows a Stanley bench grinder.

ABRASIVE WHEELS

The use of abrasive wheels for the grinding of cutting tools is extensive in the woodworking trades. The danger when they are used and maintained incorrectly has made it necessary of the Government to pass legislation to ensure that accidents are reduced to a minimum. These regulations are *The Abrasive Wheels Regulations, 1970* and, as they point out, an 'abrasive wheel' means

(1) a wheel, cylinder, disc or cone which, whether or not any other material is comprised therein, consists of abrasive particles held together by mineral, metallic or organic bonds, whether natural or artificial;

(2) a mounted wheel or point and a wheel or disc having in either case separate segments of abrasive material;

(3) a wheel or disc made in either case of metal, wood, cloth, felt, rubber or paper and having any surface consisting wholly or partly of abrasive material;

(4) a wheel, disc or saw to any surface of any of which is attached a rim or segments consisting in either case of diamond abrasive particles, and which is, or is intended to be, power driven and which is for use in any grinding or cutting operation.

Below, in simple language, are the main points of the Regulations but it must be pointed out that any person who is responsible for the correct usage of abrasive wheels (and incidentally, any such person must be fully trained under the Regulations) should obtain a copy of the Regulations so that he may be satisfied that he is fully aware of his responsibilities.

Regulation 6

This states that every abrasive wheel with a diameter of more than 55 mm, or its washer, shall be marked with the maximum permissible speed, in revolutions per minute, that has been specified by the manufacturer.

Wheels of a diameter of 55 mm or less must be kept in the workshop where the grinding is to be carried out with that wheel and there should be a notice permanently fixed in the workshop clearly stating the maximum permissible speed, in revolutions per minute, specified by the manufacturer for that wheel or for abrasive wheels of the class to which that abrasive wheel belongs.

In the case of mounted wheels and points, the overhang permissible at that speed must be marked. (Overspeeding must be avoided because this is the cause of the bursting of abrasive wheels.) The maximum permissible peripheral speed (speed at the rim) is the maximum safe working speed and is stated in m/s (or ft/min) and these have been established by the manufacturers for each type of abrasive wheel. *This speed must never be exceeded.*

Regulation 7

This regulation states that every grinding machine must have a notice attached stating the working speed or speeds of the machine. This will allow the person mounting the wheel to check that the speed of the spindle does not exceed the maximum permissible speed of the wheel.

The occupier of the workshop shall provide all facilities and

Figure 18.33

Figure 18.34

Figure 18.35

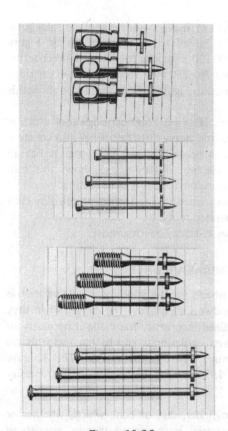

Figure 18.36

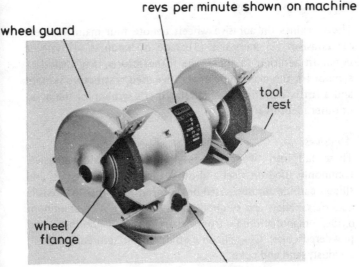

wheel guard

revs per minute shown on machine

tool rest

wheel flange

on/off switch

Note: where no eye protection is fitted goggles must be worn.

STANLEY BENCH GRINDER

Figure 18.37

information to the Factory Inspector, when requested to do so, to enable him to determine the working speed of any spindle, shaft, pulley or other appliance that is used to operate an abrasive wheel.

The speed of every air-driven machine must be adequately controlled by a governor or other device, so that the speed of the spindle does not at any time exceed the speed required for the abrasive wheel. The governor or device must be maintained in proper working order at all times.

Regulation 8

This requires that every abrasive wheel must be properly mounted.

Regulation 9

This states that each person who is required to mount abrasive wheels must be properly trained and must be competent to carry out that duty. He must be appointed by the occupier of the premises to do so. Every such appointment

shall be made by a signed and dated entry in, or signed and dated certificate attached to, a register kept for that purpose.

The particulars of the training required by Regulation 9 are given in a schedule on p. 7 of the regulations and are as follows.

Schedule

The training shall include suitable and sufficient instruction in the following matters in relation to each class or description of abrasive wheel in respect of which it is proposed to appoint the person being trained, that is to say

(1) approved advisory literature relating to the mounting of abrasive wheels;

(2) hazards arising from the use of abrasive wheels and precautions which should be observed;

(3) methods of marking abrasive wheels as to type and speed;

(4) methods of storing, handling and transporting abrasive wheels;

(5) methods of inspecting and testing abrasive wheels to check for damage;

(6) the functions of all components used with abrasive wheels, including flanges, washers, bushes and nuts used in mounting and including knowledge of the correct methods of assembling all components and correct balancing of abrasive wheels;

(7) the proper method of dressing an abrasive wheel;

(8) the adjustment of the rest of an abrasive wheel;

(9) the requirement of these regulations.

Regulation 10

This requires that a guard be provided and always kept in position at every abrasive wheel unless, due to the nature of the work, this is impracticable.

Regulation 11

(1) Every guard provided shall as far as possible be constructed so as to contain every part of the abrasive wheel in the event of a fracture of the wheel while it is in motion.

(2) Each guard must be properly maintained and secured so that it is not displaced due to a fracture of the abrasive wheel.

(3) Each guard must enclose all of the abrasive wheel except for that part which must be exposed for the purpose of the work being carried out.

Regulation 12

This deals with tapered wheels and protection flanges.

Regulation 13

This requires that all practicable steps must be taken to ensure that the abrasive wheel selected is suitable for the work for which it is to be used.

Regulation 14

This requires that any machine fitted with an abrasive wheel must have an efficient device or devices for starting and stopping the machine and the devices must be in such a position as to be operated readily and conveniently by the person operating the machine.

Regulation 15

This requires that where there is a rest for supporting the work, the rest shall at all times be properly secured and adjusted so that it as close to the exposed part of the wheel as possible. Every rest must be of substantial construction and properly maintained.

Regulation 16

This requires that the approved cautionary notice must be fixed in every room where abrasive wheels are used.

Regulation 17

This requires that floors around every fixed machine on which abrasive wheels are mounted must be maintained in good and even condition and kept clear of loose material and prevented from becoming slippery.

Regulation 18

This states that no person using an abrasive wheel shall wilfully misuse or remove any guard or wilfully misuse any protection flanges or other appliance provided by the regulations or any rest for a workpiece. Every employed person shall make full and proper use of guards, protection flanges and other appliances provided by the regulations and of rests for workpieces; if any defects are found in the foregoing, he must report the matter to the appropriate person.

The markings on abrasive wheels

The markings on abrasive wheels denote four main features: (1) abrasives (2) grain size (3) grade of hardness (4) type of bond. In addition to these, the manufacturer may include a symbol for the exact type of abrasive used, a structure symbol and a suffix denoting the manufacturer's symbol for the bond or other identification.

Abrasives

These fall into two categories — aluminium oxide abrasive, commonly used on steel and other high-tensile materials, and silicon carbide abrasive, used on cast iron and other low-tensile materials. They are symbolised as follows: 'A' — aluminum oxide, manufactured from bauxite, iron borings and powdered coke; 'C' — silicon carbide, manufactured from salt, sawdust, sand and coke.

Grain size

This is indicated by numbers and can vary from 8 (very coarse) to 600 (extremely fine). These figures indicate the number of meshes per linear inch through which the grains have passed. In cases where grain combinations have been made in the manufacture this can be denoted by a symbol after the grain-size numbers or by the use of two grain-size numbers.

Grade

For all types and bonds, the grade or hardness of the wheel is indicated by letters ranging from A (soft) to Z (hard). The main range of wheels used falls within the letters F to T.

Structure

The structure of the wheel, or the spacings of the grains, is denoted by a number. (This is optional to the use of individual manufacturers.) Numbers 1—15 cover the range generally in use. 1 is extremely dense and as the number increases the more open the wheel becomes.

Bond type

This is denoted by letters: 'V' — vitrified, 'B' — resinoid (synthetic resin), 'R' — rubber, 'E' — shellac, 'S' — silicate. As a rough guide, soft wheels should be used on hard materials and hard wheels on soft materials. If wheels of unsuitable structure are used for a job it is possible that the wheel will become clogged with particles from the material being ground. A wheel may also be too hard or too soft, resulting in glazing — which usually results in excessive pressure being applied to the wheel — with the possibility of a breakage.

Handling of wheels

(1) Care must be taken to prevent dropping or banging a wheel against a hard object.

(2) Never stack wheels on the floor; they may be damaged by impact or become contaminated with oil, etc.

(3) On receiving new wheels, they should be closely inspected for damage during transport; they should be tapped to ensure that they are sound (if sound, the wheel will give a clear metallic ring).

(4) The wheel should be given a test run for about 1—2 minutes, making sure that all guards are in position and no one is in line with the wheel.

(5) When not in use, wheels should be carefully stored in a clear area not subjected to extreme temperature changes. Small wheels can be hung on pegs or pins or stacked on their flat sides in a cupboard with corrugated paper between them. Organic bonded wheels can be laid flat on a horizontal surface in a cool place to prevent warping. Racks should be made for the larger type of wheel. Wheels of the same size and classification should be stored together in their own compartment, each compartment being marked with the details of the wheels.

The common causes of wheel breakage are as follows (1) centrifugal force (2) heat of grinding (3) mounting strain (4) work pressure (5) accidents. The last — which is the main cause of wheel breakage — includes such incidents as mechanical shock before and after mounting, unchecked traverse of the work into the side of the wheel, unchecked high rates of feed of the workpiece towards the wheel, wedging of the workpiece or other objects between the wheel and the work rest, etc.

There are two major types of grinding in general use throughout industry. These are: (1) *offhand*, which is grinding to broad tolerances by applying the grinding wheel manually to the work or applying the work offhand to the grinding wheel; (2) *precision* which is machine grinding where the tolerance limits are exceedingly small. In either type 'grinding' is the cutting action of thousands of sharp abrasive grains on the face of the grinding wheel; the grains actually cut chips out of the work. It is obvious therefore that whatever grinding is taking place particles are apt to fly and protection is necessary.

In addition, most wheels are breakable (some are very fragile) and incorrect handling and storage can lead to problems, hazards and possible injury. The following points will be of assistance if followed at all times.

(1) *Always* handle and store wheels in a careful manner.

(2) Visually inspect all wheels before mounting for possible damage in transit.

(3) Check maximum operating speed established for the wheel against machine speed.

(4) Check mounting flanges for equal and correct diameter (should be at least one-third of the diameter of the wheel and relieved around the hole).

(5) Use mounting blotters supplied with wheels.

(6) Make sure that the work rest is properly adjusted (no more than 3 mm away from wheel and centre or above).

(7) *Always* use a guard covering as much of the wheel as possible.

(8) Allow newly mounted wheels to run at operating speeds, with guard in place, for at least one minute before grinding.

(9) *Always* wear safety glasses or some form of eye protection when grinding.

(10) Turn off coolant (if used) before stopping the wheel to avoid creating an out-of-balance condition.

(11) *Never* use a wheel that has been dropped.

(12) *Never* force a wheel on to the machine or alter the size of the mounting hole.

(13) *Never* exceed the maximum operating speed established for the wheel.

(14) *Never* use mounting flanges on which the bearing surfaces are not clean and flat.

(15) *Never* tighten the mounting nut excessively.

(16) *Never* start the machine until the wheel guard is in place.

(17) *Never* grind on the side of the wheel unless the wheel is specifically designed for that purpose.

(18) *Never* jam work into the wheel.

(19) *Never* stand directly in front of a grinding wheel whenever a grinder is started.

(20) *Never* grind material for which the wheel is not designed.

(21) *Never* expose wheels to extreme changes in temperature.

The paper washers on grinding wheels display the following characteristics: (1) maximum permissible speed at which the wheel should run, (2) a code used by the manufacturer indicating details of its manufacture and (3) the diameter, thickness and size of arbor.

Regulation 6 requires that every wheel over a diameter of 55 mm should be marked with its maximum permissible speed in revolutions per minute (of course, wheels may be used on machines with a slower speed than the maximum shown but never on those with a greater speed).

The details of a wheel's manufacture are given in a code in which each letter or figure represents a characteristic. Four main features are always given but other optional ones are sometimes included. The main features are

(i) The abrasive used ('A' indicates the abrasive as being aluminum oxide and 'C' silicon carbide).

(ii) The size of grain (this is expressed as a number and indicates the size of the mesh used to give the grain; the number 46 for instance, would mean that there would be 46 holes per square inch (25 mm square) of the mesh.

(iii) The grade of hardness of the bond; the letters used for this purpose range from A, very soft, to Z, very hard.

(iv) Letters used in this section indicate the type of bond ('V' means vitrified, 'B' means resinoid, 'R' means rubber and 'E' means shellac).

For example

(Abrasive)	(Grain size)	(Bond hardness)	(Bond type)
A	46	L	V

which shows that aluminium oxide has been used as the abrasive, the grain is 46, the bond grading is L and the bond type vitrified.

(1) What is the present colour code for the wiring of electrical devices?

Live ....

Neutral ....

Earth ....

(2) What is the colour coding for the outdated system that is still often seen in industry and the home?

Live ....

Neutral ....

Earth ....

(3) What is the recommended voltage for electrical tools in the woodworking industries?

....

(4) What is the correct procedure to follow when adjustments are to be made to a portable tool that has recently been used?

....

....

(5) Why should the lower guard on a portable rip-saw never be fixed back in the open position when the tool is being used?

....

(6) What is a percussion drill?

....

(7) Why is an orbital sander so called?

....

(8) For what type of work would the following electric tools be used?

Belt sander. ....

Orbital sander ....

General-purpose saw ....

Router ....

(9) What is the difference between direct- and indirect-cartridge tools?

....

....

....

(10) Make a list of the precautions that should be taken prior to using a portable cartridge-tool

....

....

....

....

....

(11) Describe how the correct selection of a cartridge for a particular job should be carried out.

....

....

....

(12) Should the colour coding applied to cartridges be strictly adhered to? If not, why not?

....

....

....

(13) Explain what should and should not be done after a cartridge has misfired.

....

....

....

(14) What are the four main markings on an abrasive wheel and explain what they mean

(a) ....

....

(b) ....

....

(c) ....

....

(d) ....

(15) What are the common causes of breakage of abrasive wheels?

....

....

....

....

19. WOODCUTTING MACHINERY

After the text for the volume 1 of this series went to press, the Woodcutting Machinery Regulations were published in a revised form. These regulations are known as *The Woodworking Machines Regulations, 1974*; they came into operation on the 24 November 1974, except Regulation 41, which is operational from 24 May 1976.

Because the City and Guilds are preparing new syllabuses for advanced Carpentry and Joinery and Machine Woodworking certificates, it has been thought wise to print the Regulations in their entirety (except their application, interpretation and exceptions) since it is presumed that other machines in addition to those in the craft syllabuses will be included.

THE WOODWORKING MACHINES REGULATIONS, 1974

Part II All Woodworking Machines – General

Provision and construction of guards

5. – (1) Without prejudice to the other provisions of these Regulations, the cutters of every woodworking machine shall be enclosed by a guard or guards to the greatest extent that is practicable having regard to the work being done thereat, unless the cutters are in such position as to be as safe to every person employed as they would be if so enclosed.

(2) All guards provided in pursuance of the foregoing paragraph of this Regulation shall be of substantial construction.

Adustment of machines and guards

6. No person shall, while the cutters are in motion –

(*a*) make any adjustment to any guard on a woodworking machine unless means are provided whereby such an adjustment can be made without danger; or

(*b*) make any adjustment to any part of a woodworking machine, except where the adjustment can be made without danger.

Use and maintenance of guards, etc.

7. – (1) At all times while the cutters are in motion, the guards and devices required by these Regulations and all such safeguards as are mentioned in Regulation 8 shall be kept constantly in position and properly secured and adjusted except when, and to the extent to which, because of the nature of the work being done, the use of any such guard, device, or safeguard is rendered impracticable:

Provided that the said exception shall not apply to the use of any guard required by Regulations 18(1), 21(1) or (2), 22(1), 23, 28, 30 or 31.

(2) The said guards, devices, and safeguards, and all such appliances as are mentioned in Regulation 14(1)(*b*) shall be properly maintained.

Exception from obligations to provide guards, etc.

8. Regulations 5, 16, 21, 22, 26, 28, 30, 31 and 36 shall not apply to any machine in respect of which other safeguards are provided which render the machine as safe as it would be if the provisions of those Regulations were complied with.

Machine controls

9. Every woodworking machine shall be provided with an efficient device or efficient devices for starting and stopping the machine and the control or controls of the device or devices shall be in such a position and of such design and construction as to be readily and conveniently operated by the person operating the machine.

Working space

10. There shall be provided around every woodworking machine sufficient clear and unobstructed space to enable, in so far as is thereby practicable, the work being done at the machine to be done without risk of injury to persons employed.

Floors

11. The floor or surface of the ground around every woodworking machine shall be maintained in good and level condition and, as far as reasonably practicable, free from chips and other loose material and shall not be allowed to become slippery.

Temperature

12. – (1) Subject to the following provisions of this Regulation, effective provision shall be made for securing and maintaining a reasonable temperature in every room or other place (not in the open air) in which a woodworking machine is being worked.

(2) In that part of any room or other place (not in the open air) in which a woodworking machine is being worked, a temperature of less than 13 degrees Celsius shall not be deemed at any time to be a reasonable temperature except where and in so far as the necessities of the business carried on make it impracticable to maintain a temperature of at least 13 degrees Celsius.

(3) Where it is impracticable for the aforesaid reasons to maintain a temperature of at least 13 degrees Celsius in any such part of a room or place as aforesaid, there shall be provided in the said part, to the extent that is reasonably practicable, effective means of warming persons working there.

(4) There shall not be used in any such room or place as aforesaid any heating appliance other than an appliance in which the heating element or flame is so enclosed within the body of the appliance that

there is no likelihood of the accidental ignition of any material in that room or place by reason of contact with or proximity to the heating element or any flame, except where the heating appliance is so positioned or protected that there is no such likelihood.

(5) Paragraphs (2) and (3) of this Regulation shall in their application to parts of factories which are used as sawmills have effect as if for the references to 13 degrees Celsius there were substituted references to 10 degrees Celsius.

(6) No method of heating shall be employed which results in the escape into the air of any such room or place as aforesaid of any fume of such a character and to such extent as to be likely to be injurious or offensive to persons employed therein.

Training

13. — (1) No person shall be employed on any kind of work at a woodworking machine unless —

(a) he has been sufficiently trained at machines of a class to which that machine belongs in the kind of work on which he is to be employed; and

(b) he has been sufficiently instructed in accordance with paragraph (2) of this Regulation,

except where he works under the adequate supervision of a person who has a thorough knowledge and experience of the working of the machine and of the matters specified in paragraph (2) of this Regulation.

(2) Every person, while being trained to work at a woodworking machine, shall be fully and carefully instructed as to the dangers arising in connection with such machine, the precautions to be observed, the requirements of these Regulations which apply and, in the case of a person being trained to operate a woodworking machine, the method of using the guards, devices and appliances required by these Regulations.

(3) Without prejudice to the foregoing provisions of this Regulation, a person who has not attained the age of 18 years shall not operate any circular sawing machine, any sawing machine fitted with a circular blade, any planing machine for surfacing which is not mechanically fed, or any vertical spindle moulding machine, unless he has successfully completed an approved course of training in the operation of such a machine. Save that where required to do so as part of such a course of training, he may operate such a machine under the adequate supervision of a person who has a thorough knowledge and experience of the working of the machine and of the matters specified in paragraph (2) of this Regulation.

Duties of persons employed

14. — (1) Every person employed shall, while he is operating a woodworking machine —

(a) use and keep in proper adjustment the guards and devices provided in accordance with these Regulations and all such safeguards as are mentioned in Regulation 8; and

(b) use the spikes, push-sticks, push-blocks, jigs, holders and back stops provided in accordance with these Regulations,

except (in cases other than those specified in the proviso to Regulation 7(1)) when, because of the nature of the work being done, the use of the said guards, devices or other safeguards, or of the appliances mentioned in sub-paragraph (b) of this paragraph, is rendered impracticable.

(2) It shall be the duty of every person, being a person employed by the occupier of a factory and trained in accordance with Regulation 13, who discovers any defect in any woodworking machine in that factory or in any guard, device or appliance provided in accordance

with these Regulations or in any such safeguard as is mentioned in Regulation 8 (being a defect which may affect the safe working of a woodworking machine) or who discovers that the floor or surface of the ground around any woodworking machine in that factory is not in good and level condition or is slippery, to report the matter without delay to the occupier, manager or other appropriate person.

Sale or hire of machinery

15. The provisions of section 17(2) of the principal Act (which prohibits the sale or letting on hire of certain machines which do not comply with the requirements of that section) shall extend to any woodworking machine which is for use in a factory and which is not provided with such guards or devices as are necessary, and is not so designed and constructed as, to enable any requirement of the following Regulations to be complied with, that is to say, Regulations 9, 16, 17(3), 21, 22, 24, 25, 26, 27, 28, 30, 31 and 39 in so far as the requirement applies to that woodworking machine.

Part III Circular Sawing Machines

Guarding of circular sawing machines

16. — (1) The part of the saw blade of every circular sawing machine which is below the machine table shall be guarded to the greatest extent that is practicable.

(2) There shall be provided for every circular sawing machine a riving knife which shall be securely fixed by means of a suitable device situated below the machine table, be behind and in a direct line with the saw blade, have a smooth surface, be strong, rigid and easily adjustable and fulfil the following conditions:—

(a) the edge of the knife nearer the saw blade shall form an arc of a circle having a radius not exceeding the radius of the largest saw blade with which the saw bench is designed to be used;

(b) the knife shall be capable of being so adjusted and shall be kept so adjusted that it is as close as practicable to the saw blade, having regard to the nature of the work being done, and so that at the level of the machine table the distance between the edge of the knife nearer to the saw blade and the teeth of the saw blade does not exceed 12 millimetres;

(c) for a saw blade of a diameter of less than 600 millimetres, the knife shall extend upwards from the machine table to a height above the machine table which is not more than 25 millimetres below the highest point of the saw blade, and for a saw blade of a diameter of 600 millimetres or over, the knife shall extend upwards from the machine table to a height of at least 225 millimetres above the machine table; and

(d) in the case of a parallel plate saw blade the knife shall be thicker than the plate of the saw blade.

(3) Without prejudice to the requirements of Regulation 18(1), that part of the saw blade of every circular sawing machine which is above the machine table shall be guarded with a strong and easily adjustable guard, which shall be capable of being so adjusted and shall be kept so adjusted that it extends from the top of the riving knife to a point above the upper surface of the material being cut which is as close as practicable to that surface or, where squared stock is being fed to the saw blade by hand, to a point which is not more than 12 millimetres above the upper surface of the material being cut.

(4) The guard referred to in the last foregoing paragraph shall have a flange of adequate depth on each side of the saw blade and the said guard shall be kept so adjusted that the said flanges extend beyond the roots of the teeth of the saw blade. Where the guard is fitted with an adjustable front extension piece, that extension piece shall have along the whole of its length a flange of adequate depth on the side

remote from the fence and the said extension piece shall be kept so adjusted that the flange extends beyond the roots of the teeth of the saw blade:

Provided that in the case of circular sawing machines manufactured before the date of the coming into operation of this Regulation, the requirements of this paragraph shall not apply until two years after the said date and in the case of such machines, until the expiration of the said period, the said guard shall have along the whole of its length a flange of adequate depth on the side remote from the fence and shall be kept so adjusted that the said flange extends beyond the roots of the teeth of the saw blade.

Sizes of circular saw blades

17. – (1) In the case of a circular sawing machine the spindle of which is not capable of being operated at more than one working speed, no saw blade shall be used thereat for dividing material into separate parts which has a diameter of less than six-tenths of the diameter of the largest saw blade with which the saw bench is designed to be used.

(2) In the case of a circular sawing machine which has arrangements for the spindle to operate at more than one working speed, no saw blade shall be used thereat for dividing material into separate parts which has a diameter of less than six-tenths of the diameter of the largest saw blade which can properly be used at the fastest working speed of the spindle at the saw bench.

(3) There shall be securely affixed to every circular sawing machine a notice specifying the diameter of the smallest saw blade which may be used in the machine in compliance with paragraph (1) or (2) (as the case may be) of this Regulation.

Limitations on the use of circular sawing machines for certain purposes

18. – (1) No circular sawing machine shall be used for cutting any rebate, tenon, mould or groove, unless that part of the saw blade or other cutter which is above the machine table is effectively guarded.

(2) No circular sawing machine shall be used for a ripping operation (other than any such operation involved in cutting a rebate, tenon, mould or groove) unless the teeth of the saw blade project throughout the operation through the upper surface of the material being cut.

(3) No circular sawing machine shall be used for cross-cutting logs or branches unless the material being cut is firmly held by a gripping device securely fixed to a travelling table.

Provision of push-sticks

19. – (1) A suitable push-stick shall be provided and kept available for use at every circular sawing machine which is fed by hand.

(2) Except where the distance between a circular saw blade and its fence is so great or the method of feeding material to the saw blade is such that the use of a push-stick can safely be dispensed with, the push-stick so provided shall be used—

(*a*) to exert feeding pressure on the material between the saw blade and the fence throughout any cut of 300 millimetres or less in length;

(*b*) to exert feeding pressure on the material between the saw blade and the fence during the last 300 millimetres of any cut of more than 300 millimetres in length; and

(*c*) to remove from between the saw blade and the fence pieces of material which have been cut.

Removal of material cut by circular sawing machines

20. – (1) Except as provided in paragraph (3) of this Regulation, where any person (other than the operator) is employed at a circular sawing machine in removing while the saw blade is in motion material which has been cut, that person shall not for that purpose stand elsewhere than at the delivery end of the machine.

(2) Except as provided in paragraph (3) of this Regulation, where any person (other than the operator) is employed at a circular sawing machine in removing while the saw blade is in motion material which has been cut, the machine table shall be constructed or shall be extended over its whole width (by the provision of rollers or otherwise) so that the distance between the delivery end of the table or of any such extention thereof and the up-running part of the saw blade is not less than 1200 millimetres. Provided that this requirement shall not apply to moveable machines which cannot accommodate a blade having a diameter of more than 450 millimetres.

(3) The requirements of paragraphs (1) and (2) of this Regulation shall not apply to a circular sawing machine having a saw bench in the form of a roller table or a saw bench incorporating a travelling table which (in either case) is in motion during the cutting operation.

Part IV Multiple Rip Sawing Machines and Straight Line Edging Machines

Multiple rip sawing machines and straight line edging machines

21. – (1) Every multiple rip sawing machine and straight line edging machine shall be provided on the operator's side of the in-feed pressure rollers with a suitable device which shall be of such design and so constructed as to contain so far as practicable any material accidentally ejected by the machine and every such device shall extend for not less than the full width of the said pressure rollers.

(2) Every multiple rip sawing machine and straight line edging machine on which the saw spindle is mounted above the machine table shall, in addition to the device required to be provided under paragraph (1) of this Regulation, be fitted on the side remote from the fence with a suitable guard, which shall extend from the edge of the said device along a line parallel to the blade of the saw at least 300 millimetres towards the axis of the saw and shall be of such a design and so constructed as to contain as far as practicable any material accidentally ejected from the machine.

(3) In the case of multiple rip sawing machines and straight line edging machines manufactured before the date of the coming into operation of this regulation, the requirements of this Regulation shall not apply until two years after the said date.

Part V Narrow Band Sawing Machines

Narrow band sawing machines

22. – (1) The saw wheels of every narrow band sawing machine and the whole of the blade of every such machine, except that part of the blade which runs downwards between the top wheel and the machine table, shall be enclosed by a guard or guards of substantial construction.

(2) That part of the blade of every such machine as aforesaid which is above the friction disc or rollers and below the top wheel shall be guarded by a frontal plate which is as close as is practicable to the saw blade and has at least one flange at right angles to the plate and extending behind the saw blade.

(3) The friction disc or rollers of every such machine as aforesaid shall be kept so adjusted that they are as close to the surface of the machine table as is practicable having regard to the nature of the work being done.

Part VI Planing Machines

Limitation on the use of planing machines

23. No planing machine shall be used for cutting any rebate, recess, tenon or mould unless the cutter is effectively guarded.

Cutter blocks for planing machines for surfacing

24. Every planing machine for surfacing which is not mechanically fed shall be fitted with a cylindrical cutter block.

Table gap

25. — (1) Every planing machine for surfacing which is not mechanically fed shall be so designed and constructed as to be capable of adjustment so that the clearance between the cutters and the front edge of the delivery table does not exceed 6 millimetres (measured radially from the centre of the cutter block) and the gap between the feed table and the delivery table is as small as practicable having regard to the operation being performed, and no such planing machine which is not so adjusted shall be used for surfacing.

(2) In the case of planing machines manufactured before the date of the coming into operation of this Regulation, the requirements of the foregoing paragraph of this Regulation shall not apply until twelve months after the said date.

Provision of bridge guards

26. — (1) Every planing machine for surfacing which is not mechanically fed shall be provided with a bridge guard which shall be strong and rigid, have a length not less than the full length of the cutter block and a width not less than the diameter of the cutter block and be so constructed as to be capable of easy adjustment both in a vertical and horizontal direction.

(2) Every bridge guard provided in pursuance of paragraph (1) of this Regulation shall be mounted on the machine in a position which is approximately central over the axis of the cutter block and shall be so constructed as to prevent its being accidentally displaced from that position.

(3) In the case of planing machines manufactured before the date of the coming into operation of this Regulation, the requirements of this Regulation shall not apply until twelve months after the said date, and until the expiration of the said period such machines for surfacing shall be provided with a bridge guard capable of covering the full length and breadth of the cutting slot in the bench and so constructed as to be easily adjusted both in a vertical and horizontal direction.

Adjustment of bridge guards

27. — (1) While a planing machine which is not mechanically fed is being used for surfacing the bridge guard provided in pursuance of Regulation 26 shall be so adjusted as to enable, so far as is thereby practicable, the work being done at the machine to be done without risk of injury to persons employed.

(2) Except as provided in paragraph (4) of this Regulation and in Regulation 29, when a wider surface of squared stock is being planed or smoothed, the bridge guard so provided shall be adjusted so that the distance between the end of the guard so provided shall be adjusted so that the distance between the end of the guard and the fence does not exceed 10 millimetres and the underside of the guard is not more than 10 millimetres above the upper surface of the material.

(3) Except as provided in paragraph (4) of this Regulation, when a narrower surface of squared stock is being planed or smoothed, the bridge guard so provided shall be adjusted so that the end of the guard is at a point not more than 10 millimetres from the surface of the said material which is remote from the fence and the underside of the guard is not more than 10 millimetres above the surface of the feed table.

(4) When the planing or smoothing both of a wider and of a narrower surface of squared stock is being carried out, one operation immediately following the other, the bridge guard so provided shall be adjusted so that when a wider surface is being planed or smoothed the underside of the guard is not more than 10 millimetres from the surface of the said material which is remote from the fence.

(5) Except as provided in paragraph (6) of this Regulation, when the planing of squared stock of square cross section is being carried out, the bridge guard so provided shall be adjusted in a manner which complies with the requirements either of paragraph (2) or of paragraph (3) of this Regulation.

(6) When the planing of two adjoining surfaces of squared stock of square cross section is being carried out, one operation immediately following the other, the bridge guard so provided shall be adjusted so that neither the height of the underside of the guard above the feed table nor the distance between the end of the guard and the fence exceeds the width of the material by more than 10 millimetres.

(7) When the smoothing of squared stock of square cross section is being carried out, the bridge guard so provided shall be adjusted in a manner which complies with the requirements either of paragraph (2) or of paragraph (3) or of paragraph (6) of this Regulation.

Cutter block guards

28. — (1) In addition to being provided with a bridge guard as required by Regulation 26, every planing machine for surfacing which is not mechanically fed shall be provided with a strong, effective and easily adjustable guard for that part of the cutter block which is on the side of the fence remote from the bridge guard.

(2) In the case of planing machines manufactured before the date of the coming into operation of this Regulation, the requirements of the foregoing paragraph of this Regulation shall not apply until twelve months after the said date.

Provision and use of push-blocks

29. When a wider surface of squared stock is being planed or smoothed and by reason of the shortness of the material the work cannot be done with bridge guard adjusted as required by Regulation 27(2), a suitable push-block having suitable handholds which afford the operator a firm grip shall be provided and used.

Combined machines used for thicknessing

30. That part of the cutter block of a combined machine which is exposed in the table gap shall, when the said machine is used for thicknessing, be effectively guarded.

Protection against ejected material

31. — (1) Every planing machine used for thicknessing shall be provided on the operator's side of the feed roller with sectional feed rollers, or other suitable devices which shall be of such a design and so constructed as to restrain so far as practicable any workpiece ejected by the machine.

(2) Paragraph (1) of this Regulation shall not apply to any machine manufactured before the date of coming into operation of this Regulation; provided that—

(a) not more than one work piece at a time shall be fed to any such machine, and

(b) there shall be securely affixed to every such machine a notice specifying that only single pieces shall be fed.

Part VII Vertical Spindle Moulding Machines

Construction, maintenance and mounting of cutters etc.

32. Every detachable cutter for any vertical spindle moulding machine shall be of the correct thickness for the cutter block or spindle on which it is to be mounted and shall be so mounted as to prevent it, so far as practicable, from becoming accidentally detached therefrom.

Provision of false fences

33. Where straight fences are being used for the purposes of the work being done at a vertical spindle moulding machine, the gap between the fences shall be reduced as far as practicable by a false fence or otherwise.

Provision of jigs or holders

34. Where by reason of the nature of the work being done at a vertical spindle moulding machine it is impracticable to provide in pursuance of Regulation 5 a guard enclosing the cutters of the said machine to such an extent that they are effectively guarded, but it is practicable to provide, in addition to the guard required to be provided by Regulation 5, a jig or holder of such a design and so constructed as to hold firmly the material being machined and having suitable handholds which afford the operator a firm grip, the machine shall not be used unless such a jig or holder is provided.

Design and construction of guards for protection against ejected parts

35. Every guard provided in pursuance of Regulation 5 for the cutters of any vertical spindle moulding machine shall be of such a design and so constructed as to contain, so far as reasonably practicable, any part of the cutters or their fixing appliances or any part thereof in the event of their ejection.

Provision and use of back stops

36. Where the work being done at a vertical spindle moulding machine is work in which the cutting of the material being machined commences otherwise than at the end of a surface of the said material and it is impracticable to provide a jig or holder in pursuance of Regulation 34, the trailing end of the said material shall if practicable be supported by a suitable back stop where this would prevent the said material being thrown back when the cutters first make contact with it.

Limitation on the use of vertical spindle moulding machines

37. No work shall be done on a vertical spindle moulding machine being work in which the cutting of the material being machined commences otherwise than at the end of a surface of the said material and during the progress of the cutting the material is moved in the same direction as the movement of the cutters, unless a jig or holder provided in pursuance of Regulation 34 is being used.

Provision of spikes or push sticks

38. Where the nature of the work being performed at a vertical spindle moulding machine is such that the use of a suitable spike or push-stick would enable the work to be carried on without unnecessary risk, such a spike or push-stick shall be provided and kept available for use.

Machines driven by two speed motors

39. — (1) Where the motor driving a vertical spindle moulding machine (other than a high-speed routing machine) is designed to operate at two working speeds the device controlling the speed of the motor shall be so arranged that the motor cannot run at the higher of those speeds, without first running at the lower of those speeds.

(2) In the case of machines manufactured before the coming into operation of this Regulation, the requirements of the foregoing paragraph of this Regulation shall not apply until twelve months after the said date.

Part VIII   Extraction Equipment and Maintenance

Cleaning of saw blades

40. The blade of a sawing machine shall not be cleaned by hand while the blade is in motion.

Extraction of chips and other particles

41. Effective exhaust appliances shall be provided and maintained at every planing machine used for thicknessing other than a combined machine for surfacing and thicknessing, every vertical spindle moulding machine, every multi-cutter moulding machine, every tenoning machine and every automatic lathe, for collecting from a position as close to the cutters as practicable and to the extent that is practicable, the chips and other particles of material removed by the action of the cutters and for discharging them into a suitable receptacle or place:

Provided that this Regulation shall not apply to any high-speed routing machine which incorporates means for blowing away from the cutters the chips or particles as they are removed or to either of the following which is not used for more than six hours in any week, that is to say, any vertical spindle moulding machine and any tenoning machine.

Maintenance and fixing

42. — (1) Every woodworking machine and every part thereof, including cutters and cutter blocks, shall be of good construction, sound material and properly maintained.

(2) Every woodworking machine, other than a machine which is held in the hand, shall be securely fixed to a foundation, floor, or to a substantial part of the structure of the premises, save that where this is impracticable, other arrangements shall be made to ensure its stability.

Part IX   Lighting

Lighting

43. In addition to the requirements of subsections (1) and (4) of section 5 of the principal Act and the Factories (Standards of Lighting) Regulations 1941(a), the following provisions shall have effect in respect of any work done with any woodworking machine:—

   (a) the lighting, whether natural or artifical, for every wood-working machine shall be sufficient and suitable for the purpose for which the machine is used;

   (b) the means of artificial lighting for every woodworking machine shall be so placed or shaded as to prevent glare and so that direct rays of light do not impinge on the eyes of the operator while he is operating such machine.

(a) S. R. & O. 1941/94 (Rev. VII, p. III: 1941 I, p. 280).

Part X   Noise

Noise

44. Where any factory, or any part therof, is mainly used for work carried out on woodworking machines, the following provisions shall apply to that factory or part, as the case may be:—

(a) where on any day any person employed is likely to be exposed continuously for 8 hours to a sound level of 90dB(A) or is likely to be subject to an equivalent or greater exposure to sound—

   (i) such measures as are reasonably practicable shall be taken to reduce noise to the greatest extent which is reasonably practicable; and

   (ii) suitable ear protectors shall be provided and made readily available for the use of every such person;

(b) all ear protectors provided in pursuance of the foregoing paragraph shall be maintained, and shall be used by the person for whom they are provided in any of the circumstances specified in paragraph (a) of this Regulation;

(c) for the purposes of paragraph (a) of this Regulation, the level of exposure which is equivalent to or greater than continuous exposure for 8 hours to a sound level of 90 dB(A) shall be determined by an approved method.

Signed by order of the Secretary of State.

Harold Walker,
Joint Parliamentary Under Secretary of State,
23rd May 1974.　　Department of Employment.

SCHEDULE 1

Regulation 2(2)

Machines which are woodworking machines for the purposes of these Regulations

1. Any sawing machine designed to be fitted with one or more circular blades.
2. Grooving machines.
3. Any sawing machine designed to be fitted with a blade in the form of a continuous band or strip.
4. Chain sawing machines.
5. Mortising machines.
6. Planing machines.
7. Vertical spindle moulding machines (including high-speed routing machines).
8. Multi-cutter moulding machines having two or more cutter spindles.
9. Tenoning machines.
10. Trenching machines.
11. Automatic and semi-automatic lathes.
12. Boring machines.

Regulation 1(2)

SCHEDULE 2

Column 1 Regulations revoked	Column 2 References	Column 3 Extent of Revocation
1. The Woodworking Machinery Regulations 1922.	S.R. & O. 1922/1196 (Rev. VII, p. 458: 1922, p. 273).	The whole Regulations.
2. The Woodworking Machinery (Amendment) Regulations 1927.	S.R. & O. 1927/207 (Rev. VII, p. 462: 1927, p. 440).	The whole Regulations.
3. The Woodworking (Amendment of Scope) Special Regulations 1945.	S.R. & O. 1945/1227 (Rev. VII, p. 462: 1945 I, p. 380).	The whole Regulations.
4. The Railway Running Sheds (No. 2) Regulations 1961.	S.I. 1961/1768 (1961 III, p. 3410).	In the Schedule, the items numbered 2, 5 and 9.

EXPLANATORY NOTE

(This Note is not part of the Regulations.)

These Regulations impose requirements as to guards and certain other safety devices for woodworking machines used in factories and certain other places to which the Factories Act 1961 applies.

The Regulations also impose requirements as to working space, condition of floors, noise, lighting and temperature in those factories and places and as to the training of persons operating woodworking machines.

The Regulations prohibit the sale or letting on hire for use in factories and other places to which the Regulations apply of woodworking machines which do not comply with specified provisions of the Regulations as to guards and other safety devices.

As respects guards and other safeguards for woodworking machines, the provisions of the Regulations are in substitution for the provisions of section 14(1) of the Factories Act 1961 and as respects the temperature of rooms, they are in substitution for the similar provisions of section 3(1) of the said Act.

Regulation 67(2) of the Shipbuilding and Ship-repairing Regulations 1960 and Regulation 42 of the Construction (General Provisions) Regulations 1961 (which require the secure fencing of dangerous parts of machinery) are amended so that they no longer apply to the parts of woodworking machines required by these Regulations to be guarded or to have other safeguards.

The Regulations supersede the Woodworking Machinery Special Regulations 1922 to 1945 which are revoked.

LAYOUT OF MACHINE SHOP

When planning the layout of a woodcutting machinery shop, it must be kept in mind that the aim should be to keep the timber moving in one direction — from the timber store towards the joiners shop, where the assembly of the manufactured items will take place.

Where small firms have their machine section in the assembly shop, the machines should be kept well clear of the joiners' benches and in firms of moderate size that have the two sections separate, the machines involved will probably be: crosscut saw, rip saw, overhand planer, thicknesser, mortiser, tenoner (probably), bandsaw and spindle (probably). Figure 19.1 shows a suggested layout for a medium-size machine shop. As can be seen in the diagram, the timber store is to the left and the aim is to keep the timber travelling towards the right where the assembly shop is situated.

The first machine the material will go to is the crosscut saw, which will cut the timbers to the required lengths. In machine shops with limited space, the crosscut saw would probably be situated in the timber store, which would stop long lengths of timber being brought into the machine shop.

Next, the rip saw will cut the material near to size when it will pass on to the overhand planer for squaring two surfaces and then it will go to the thicknesser for bringing to the finished sizes. When the timber has reached this stage, it must

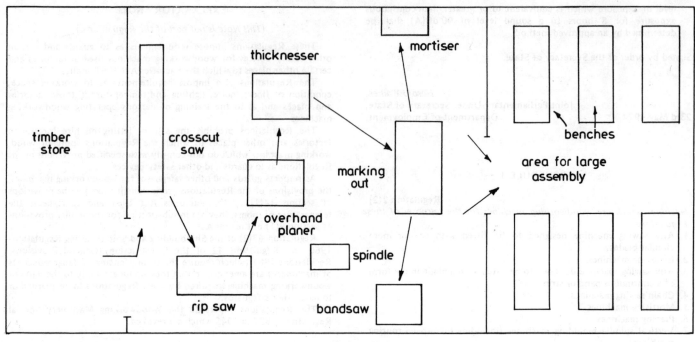

Figure 19.1

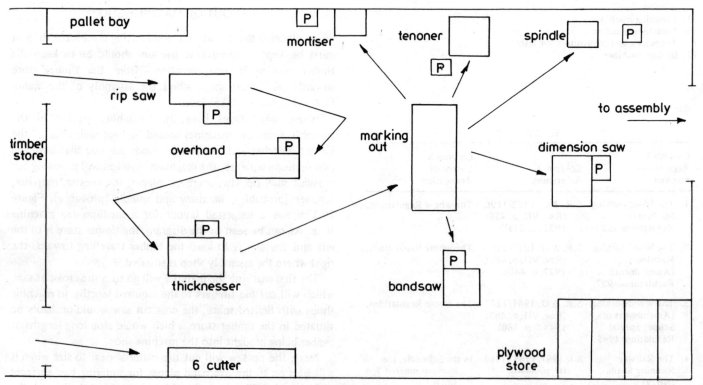

Figure 19.2

be 'marked out' by the person who is responsible for this work. It can be done in the machine shop or in a convenient place adjacent to the mill.

When the necessary marking out has been completed, the timbers will go to various machines, depending on the work needed — for example, those that are to have mortises cut into them will, naturally, go to the mortiser; those requiring tenons will go to the tenoner or, if no tenoner is available, to the spindle. Other pieces may have to go to the bandsaw or even to all the machines previously mentioned.

When all machining has been completed, the various components will pass into the assembly shop, where the joiners will finish off any work remaining to be assembled and cleaned up.

In larger mills, especially where high levels of production take place, although the aim is to keep the timber moving in one direction, much more sophisticated machinery will be involved, faster production being the criterion, so more organisation will be necessary. Figure 19.2 shows a layout for a large machine shop mass-producing items such as doors, windows, etc. Since production will be fairly rapid in such a mill, it may be an advantage to have pallets positioned near the machines, so that components can be stacked for easy removal by truck. (Space would be required for the stacking of spare pallets for use when required.)

Assuming that the crosscut saw is situated in the timber store area, the timber would be brought into the mill to the rip-saw bench then, as in the previous example, to the surfacer and thicknesser. From this machine the components will go to the marker-out and in this instance he is situated in the machine shop between the basic and more-specialised machines. The arrows in the drawing show the flow lines of the timber. The plan only shows one mortiser and one spindle; these would, of course, be increased as required, as would any other machine.

A separate plywood store has been provided and a six-cutter machine that would be capable of preparing match-boarding, tongued and grooved flooring, etc., from the sawn board. Spaces around all these machines have been provided for pallets on to which the components can be stacked as they come off the machines and then be moved easily by truck to the next stage in the production line.

(1) Make a list of some of the accessories that should be provided for woodcutting machinery to enable work to be carried out efficiently and safely.

....

....

....

....

....

(2) Woodcutting machinery must be correctly placed in a workshop if efficient handling and work progress is to be obtained. Place in the order you think the following machines should be placed in a woodcutting machine shop: mortiser, bandsaw, crosscut saw, dovetailing machine, recesser, lathe, overhand planer, rip saw, tenoner, thicknesser, six cutter, dimension saw, jig saw.

(1) ....

(2) ....

(3) ....

(4) ....

(5) ....

(6) ....

(7) ....

(8) ....

(9) ....

(10) ....

(11) ....

(12) ....

(13) ....

20. SPECIAL FIXING DEVICES

Although Rawlplug hand tools, (figure 20.1) are still used, they are becoming less popular, especially since the tipped drill (figures 20.2a and b) makes the work much easier when fitted to a portable electric drill — time is also saved, to say nothing of the greater accuracy obtained by the drill. The drill, which is tipped with tungsten carbide, is designed to fit into the chuck of a portable electric drill but it can, of course, be used in a wheel brace.

The best electric drill to use is a two-speed machine. The slow speed should be selected for drilling into masonry materials. For deep drillings, extension sleeves (figure 20.3) can be obtained; these have female threads to receive the male thread on the end of the tipped drill (figure 20.2b). The sleeves can also be inserted into each other to make up any drilling length required.

There are three common types of plug in use; these are seen in figures 20.4, 20.5 and 20.6 and are used in conjunction with the drilling accessories already mentioned.

The fibre plug (figure 20.4) is a general-purpose plug designed to be used with screws that have their size numbers the same as that of the plugs; for example, a no. 12 screw should be used with a no. 12 plug.

The white bronze plug shown in figure 20.5 — although only able to carry about 60 per cent as much weight as the same size fibre plug carry — can be used in conditions of excessive heat, damp and atmospheric pollution. Stainless steel or cadmium screws should be used with these plugs.

The Rawlplug screw anchor (figure 20.6) is used where excessively corrosive atmospheres or liquids are present. Stainless steel screws should be used.

Rawlbolts, (figures 20.7 and 20.8) are used for fixing heavy materials to walls, floors, etc., and can be obtained in two types — one with the bolt end protruding from the body (figure 20.7) on to which the washer and nut are placed and one (figure 20.8) where the bolt is threaded into the body separately. The hole is drilled in the masonry surface so that the body of the bolt will just slip in, then, when the item to be fixed is in position, the nut or bolt is turned and the result is that the body of the Rawlbolt expands to grip the sides of the hole to make a firm fixing.

TOGGLES

These are used for fixing items to hollow partitions, ceilings, etc., where there would be nothing for screws or nails to be driven into.

The gravity toggle (figure 20.9a) has a bar that is able to swivel around a nut threaded on the screw. One end of the bar is heavier than the other, so it will always hang free in the vertical direction. In use, the fixing screw must first be passed through the item being fixed and entered into the swivel nut of the toggle for a couple of turns; then the toggle is pushed through a clearance hole in the partition (figure 20.9b) and when clear of this the toggle will drop down into a verticle position. The screw is tightened to fix the item. When fixed, the toggle cannot be withdrawn. The gravity toggle is suitable only for vertical surfaces.

The spring toggle (figure 20.10a) is more suitable for horizontal surfaces such as ceilings, but of course it can also be used on surfaces suitable for the gravity toggle. The toggle on this device is made in two halves, each hinged about a swivel nut and kept in position by a spring. These halves can be folded back over the fixing screw which allows them to pass through the clearance hole in the sheet material (figure 20.10b). When they are clear of the back of the material they spring open to enable a good fixing to be made.

H toggles (figure 20.11a) are a much heavier form of gravity toggle, made of malleable iron and used for fixing heavy items to walls or breeze-block partitions. Bolts are not supplied with them, but ordinary coach bolts are all that are necessary, in addition to the toggle, to make a secure fixing after the hole through the wall has been made (see figure 20.11b).

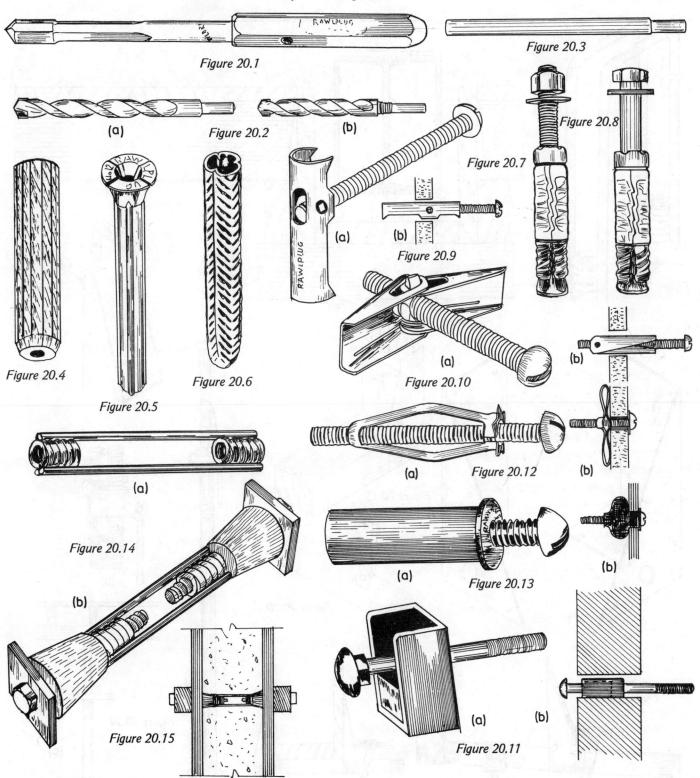

Figure 20.1

Figure 20.3

Figure 20.2 (a) (b)

Figure 20.8

Figure 20.7

Figure 20.4

Figure 20.5

Figure 20.6

(a) *Figure 20.9* (b)

(a) *Figure 20.10* (b)

(a)

(a) *Figure 20.12* (b)

Figure 20.14

(b)

(a) *Figure 20.13* (b)

(a) (b)

Figure 20.15

(a) *Figure 20.11*

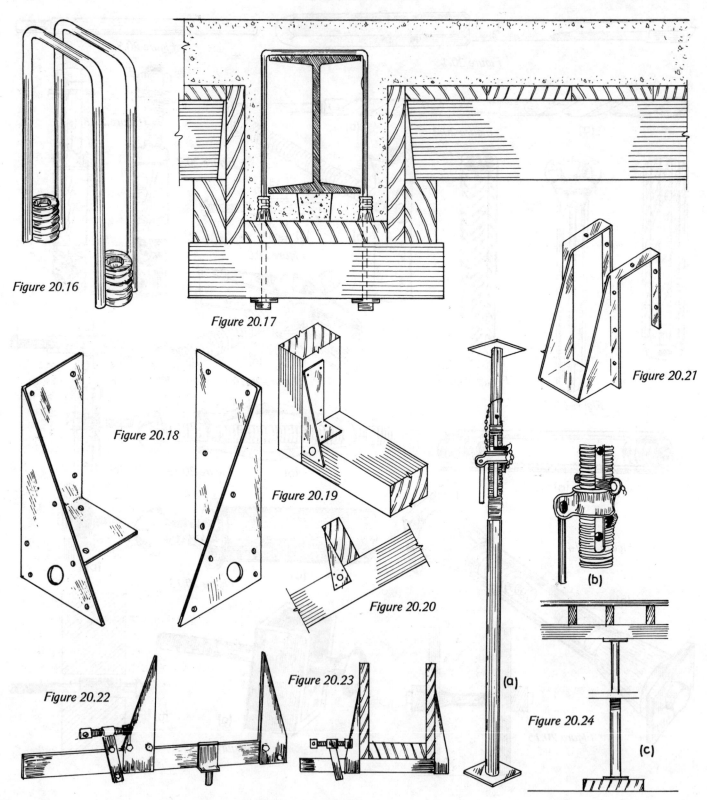

Figure 20.16

Figure 20.17

Figure 20.18

Figure 20.19

Figure 20.20

Figure 20.21

Figure 20.22

Figure 20.23

Figure 20.24

(a)

(b)

(c)

RAWLANCHORS

(Figure 20.12a) These are designed to make permanent fixings in thin sheet materials, such as plywood, asbestos, insulating board, hardboard, etc. They provide threaded holes from which the screw can be removed and replaced as often as necessary. The anchor is pushed through a pre-bored hole until the flange rests against the surface of the sheet material. The fixing screw is placed through the item to be fixed and then entered into the anchor. On turning the screw, the threaded portion of the anchor is drawn towards the back surface of the sheet material with the side arms bowing outwards to come to rest, behind the material. To tighten the fixing a few extra turns of the screw are necessary. The fixing screw can be removed and replaced as necessary.

RAWLNUTS

(Figure 20.13a) These are designed to give a secure fixing in thin, thick, solid or hollow materials. They are vibration-proof and waterproof, consisting of a tough rubber sleeve with a metal nut securely bonded in one end. At the other end is a flange which prevents the Rawlnut from being pushed through the drilled hole in the material to which the item is to be fixed.

To fix an item to, say, a sheet of plywood, drill a hole in the ply just large enough for the rubber sleeve to be pushed through up to the flange. The screw should be removed and threaded through the item to be fixed. The end of the screw is then replaced in the rubber sleeve and turned into the nut at the rear end. If turning is continued the screw will pull the moulded nut towards the flange forcing the sleeve to bulge outwards to make a tight fixing (figure 20.13b).

RAWLTIES

(Figure 20.14) These are made chiefly for use where distance pieces are required in concrete formwork, for example, where two shutters, such as the wall shuttering shown on p. 36, have to be fixed a certain distance apart. Rawlties are placed between the shutters at various points. So that the metal ties will not show on the surfaces of the concrete, wooden cones are placed immediately next to the shutters and the ties lie between the cones as shown in figure 20.15. Bolts pass through the shuttering and the cones and engage wire spirals welded to the connecting rods. The bolts and cones can be removed from the work when the shuttering is struck but the ties are embedded in the concrete. The holes made by the cones are filled in later with a cement mortar.

RAWLHANGERS

(Figure 20.16) These are made to save timber in concrete beam work. With this type of device it is possible to support the formwork to a concrete floor and beam on the beam itself (see figure 20.17). No supports from the floor below are necessary when using Rawlhangers.

TRIP-L-GRIP ANCHORS

(Figure 20.18) These are in three styles and have many applications. They can be used to connect two timbers running at right angles to one another, purlin supports in roofs, etc. Special nails have to be used; these are supplied with the anchors. Figures 20.19 and 20.20 show just two of the applications of these fixings.

JOIST HANGERS

(Figure 20.21) These are, as their name implies, used for connecting joists at right angles to one another. They save time because joints such as the tusk tenon joint and the housed joints are eliminated. This type of fixing and its application is seen in figures 10.5 and 10.13.

BEAM CRAMPS

(Figure 20.22) These are used for securing and fixing the three sides of boxes used for casting concrete beams. Figure 20.23 shows how they are applied to such work; they save much time and material that would otherwise be used for supporting the box.

METAL PROPS

Other devices designed to save time and materials are the metal props similar to that shown in figure 20.24a. These are made to be adjusted quite easily and are used for supporting heavy weights from below. Figure 20.24b shows how the prop can finally be adjusted to give support, the initial adjustment being made by sliding the inner tube upwards or downwards as the case may be near enough to the correct height. The metal dowel will secure the two tubes to this position, the final adjustment being made by turning the hand lever over the threaded portion on the large tube to adjust the over-all length. Figure 20.24c shows how a metal prop can be used for supporting concrete shuttering to a floor.

(1) What items of ironmongery would you select for the following situations?

(a) Securing a batten to a concrete wall.

(b) Drilling a hole through a 200 mm thick brick wall.

....

(c) Fixing a batten to a plasterboard ceiling.

....

(d) Supporting a shelf batten to a vertical surface of a hollow partition.

....

(e) Giving extra support to a purlin on the roof of a shed.

....

(f) Strengthening the butt joints in a stud partition.

....

(g) Supporting shuttering for concrete and obtaining a uniform distance between their inner surfaces.

....

(h) Fixing a heavy timber to a brick wall.

....

(i) Securing two timbers at a joint in a modern roof truss.

....

(2) State briefly what tools would be required and the procedure to follow in providing support for a batten using gravity toggles.

....

....

....

....

....

....

(3) How would a metal prop be adjusted to give support to the shuttering for a concrete floor with beams?

....

....

(4) What are column clamps and what are they used for?

....

....

....

(5) Make a freehand sketch of one corner of some column clamps.

(6) What are timber connectors and for what purpose are they used?

....

....

21. TECHNICAL DRAWING AND GEOMETRY

THE CIRCLE

The circle features a great deal in building, especially in carpentry and joinery. The circle was partially covered in volume 1. To revise the characteristics of the circle, figure 21.1 shows the linear characteristics (radius, chord, normal, etc.) and figure 21.2 shows the area characteristics (quadrant, segment and sector).

Figure 21.3 shows how a segmental arch can be set out, a—c being the springing line and d—b the rise. If a—b or c—b is bisected, the bisecting line will intersect with the centre line in e, the point into which the compass should be placed to construct the arch.

Figure 21.4 shows how a portion of a circle may be drawn freehand, when the compass is not large enough to draw the curve. Let O—8 be half the chord and 8—8' be the rise. Construct the rectangle with the base O—8 and the height 8—8'. Divide O—8 into eight equal parts and draw the diagonal 8'—O. Draw O—O' at right angles to the diagonal and divide O'—8' into eight equal parts. Draw the lines 1—1', 2—2', etc., and then divide O—x into eight equal parts. Draw lines from 8' to join up with all the points on O—x. These will give a number of intersections on the lines between the base and the top of the rectangle through which a freehand curve can be drawn. This curve is part of a circle. A parallel curve can be drawn by opening the compasses to the required distance and making a series of arcs above the existing curve. If the drawing is to represent the elevation of a segmental arch point 9 can be obtained by bisecting O—8' and then placing the compass point in y and, with radius y—8", mark off the point 9.

If a semi-circle or a segment of a circle is drawn and several triangles are constructed in the figures, as shown in figure 21.5, it will be found that the angles opposite the hypotenuses of the triangles are constant (in other words, exactly

the same as each other). Take the semi-circle with the diameter a—b. If the angles at c and d are measured they will both be found to be 90°, so it will be fairly simple to construct a right-angled triangle with sides of specified length. It will also be found that angles at g and h in the segment below the semi-circle are the same as each other. The smaller the segment the greater will be the angle opposite the hypotenuse.

Figure 21.6 shows how to construct a segment in which a triangle of any shape can be drawn. Let g be the centre of the circle and g—b be its radius. Draw the normal to pass through b and the tangent e—f which passes through b at right angles to the normal. Draw the chord b—d so that the angle ebd is equal to the number of degrees required at c in the triangle bcd. Measure this angle to satisfy youself that this solution is correct.

Figure 21.7 shows how to draw a tangent to a portion of a circle when the position of its centre is unknown. Let the portion of the circle's circumference be a—b with the tangent required to pass through c on the curve. With compass point in c and open to any distance, mark off points d and e on the curve. Bisect d—e to give the normal f—g which is a normal to the curve passing through c. With compass point in c and open any distance, mark off f and g on the normal. Draw tangent h-i at right angles to f-g to pass through c.

The circle is used a great deal in the construction of mouldings and such things as tracery designs. When drawing mouldings and designs with circles, it must be remembered that where curves consist of more than one radius, irregularities in the curves must be avoided. Look at figure 21.8. This is an S curve drawn with the compass open at two different distances. To avoid an irregularity at b the two curves must have a common normal. The common normal in this case is d—e, d being the centre of the larger curve and e being the

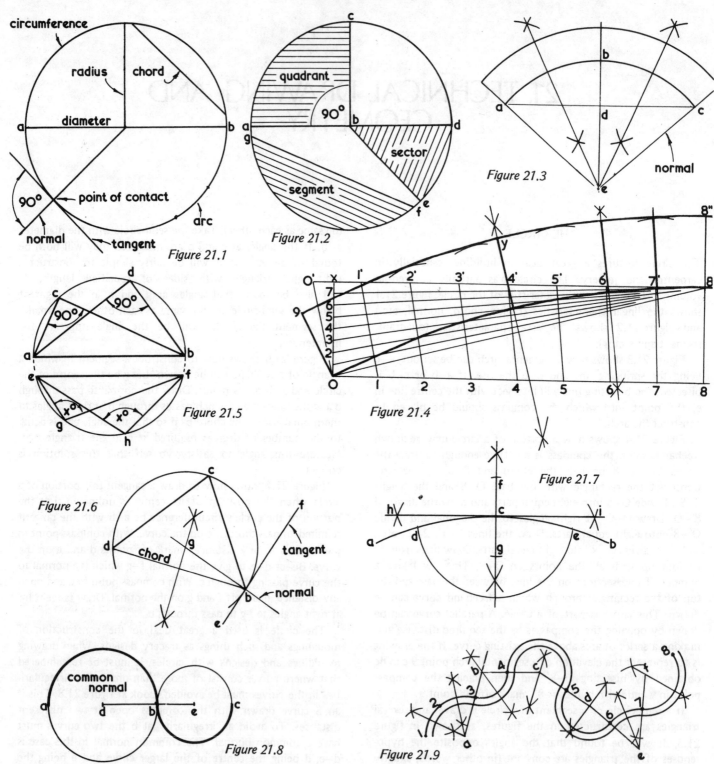

circumference

radius   chord

diameter

a   b

90°

point of contact

normal   arc

tangent

Figure 21.1

c

quadrant

90°
a   b   d

g

sector

segment

f e

Figure 21.2

b

a   d   c

normal

Figure 21.3

d

90°

c   90°

90°

a   b

e   f

x°   x°

g

h

Figure 21.5

O' x 1' 2' 3' 4' 5' 6' 7' 8"

y

7
6
5
4
3
2

O 1 2 3 4 5 6 7 8

8

Figure 21.4

f

Figure 21.7

c

Figure 21.6

d   chord   g

tangent

b   normal

e

h   c   i

a   d   e   b

g

Figure 21.7

common
normal

a   d   b   e   c

Figure 21.8

b A c

2   3

1

5 d

6 7

a   e

8

Figure 21.9

centre of the smaller one. The intersecting point between the two curves is b which is also the point through which the common normal passes.

Figure 21.9 shows a more complicated curve, but again it contains no irregularities. Place on the paper a series of points, 1, 2, 3, etc. The first part of the curve can be made to pass through the points 1, 2 and 3 by bisecting the distances between each pair of points to give the first centre a. The common normal should then be drawn from a to pass through point 3. The centre b will fall somewhere on this line, the exact point being found by bisecting the distance between points 3 and 4. The next common normal should then be drawn from b to pass through point 4 and the position of centre c found by bisecting the distances 4–5, and so on, until the complete curve has been drawn.

TRACERY

Tracery designs are often found in churches, not only in the stonework around the stained-glass windows but also in many other positions including the woodwork. Tracery consists, very often, of inscribing circles in other figures such as squares, triangles, circles, etc.

Figure 21.10 shows four circles inscribed in a square. First the diagonals of the square are drawn and then a vertical and a horizontal line drawn through the intersection of the diagonals dividing the large square into four smaller squares. The remaining diagonals of the smaller squares can then be drawn to give the centres of the inscribed circles. The tracery is completed by giving the design width, which means drawing lines on either side of the geometrical outlines as seen on the right of the figure. If horizontal and vertical lines are drawn from the centres of the four circles the amount of the design that is omitted can be determined.

Figure 21.11 also shows four circles inscribed in a square, this time in the centres of the sides of the square as opposed to the corners of the square in the previous drawing. If the diagonals of the square are drawn it will be seen that it has been divided into four triangles and a circle has to be inscribed in each of these. If one of the angles at the base of a triangle is bisected as at a, the bisecting line will give the centre of the circle at b.

Figure 21.12 shows three circles inscribed in an equilateral triangle. If each corner of the triangle is bisected it will be divided into three equal portions in which a circle is to be inscribed. If the angle at a is bisected, the centre of the circle in that portion of the triangle will be obtained at b.

In Figure 21.13 three circles have again been inscribed in an equilateral triangle, but in different positions compared with the previous drawing. First, the three corners are bisected twice as at a, giving the centre in this portion at b.

Figure 21.14 shows that six circles have been inscribed in a regular hexagon. It is quite simple to divide the figure up into six equal triangles and if one of the base angles of a triangle is bisected as at a, the centre of the circle in this triangle will be at b.

Figure 21.15 is a similar design, but in this case only semi-circles have been inscribed. After dividing the hexagon into six triangles with the centre lines drawn through each of the triangles, the angle at a is bisected to give point b on the side of the triangle. A line is then drawn from b, parallel to the base of the triangle, to give the centre of the semi-circle at c.

Figures 21.16, 21.17 and 21.18 show how to inscribe circles in larger circles.

In figure 21.16 four circles have been inscribed. Two lines are drawn at 45° through the centre of the circle dividing the figure into four equal parts. Let us take the top quarter. If a horizontal line is drawn from point a to meet with the extended 45° line at b, the angle at b can be bisected to give the centre of one of the smaller circles at c.

In Figure 21.17 three circles have been inscribed. The circle can be divided into three equal parts by drawing two lines at 30° through its centre as well as a vertical line through the centre. A horizontal line is then drawn from point a to intersect with the 30° line at b. The angle at b is bisected to give the centre at c.

Figure 21.18 shows six circles inscribed in a larger circle. Vertical, horizontal, 30° and 60° lines are first drawn through the centre of the large circle to divide the figure into six equal parts. The centres of the smaller circles can be found in a similar way to that shown in figures 21.16 and 21.17.

Use of loci in tracery

Sometimes in tracery designing circles have to be inscribed in figures such as pointed arch outlines, ellipses, quadrants, etc., and these can create problems if the method for carrying out this process is unknown.

Let us first of all take a figure that can have a circle inscribed within its boundaries by the conventional method but carry out the scribing by the method that has to be used for awkward figures. Figure 21.19 shows an equilateral triangle with an inscribed circle. Normally all we have to do is bisect two of its corners to obtain the centre of the circle. We can

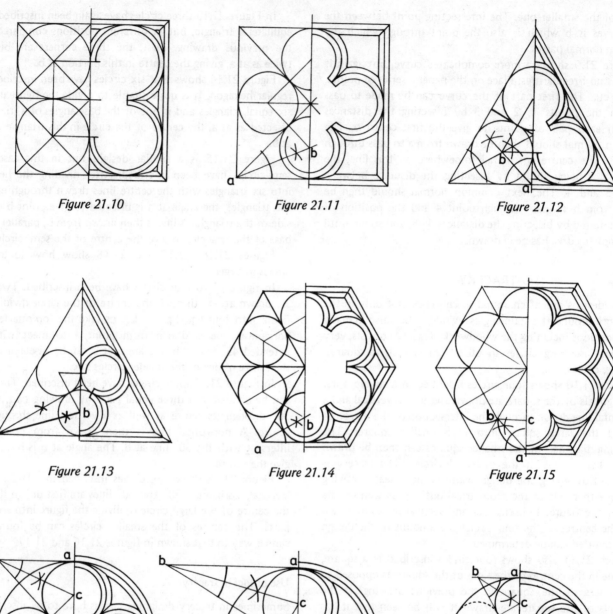

Figure 21.10   *Figure 21.11*   *Figure 21.12*

Figure 21.13   *Figure 21.14*   *Figure 21.15*

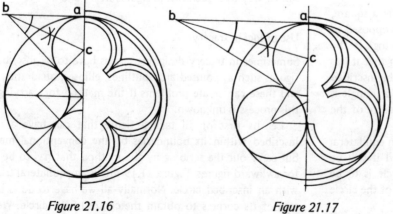

Figure 21.16   *Figure 21.17*

Figure 21.18

bisect the two corners by drawing a series of lines — all the same distance apart — parallel with the two sides that form the angles and obtain the bisectors by drawing them through the intersections of the two series of lines. For example, 1 and 1 meet at a point, 2 and 2 meet at a point, 3 and 3, and so on. A line (straight in this case) can be drawn through the intersections to give the bisecting line. If two of the corners are treated in this way, the two bisectors will meet at x which is the centre of the inscribed circle.

Figure 21.20 shows a quadrant with an inscribed circle. The 90° corner can be bisected in the normal way but the method used above for the triangle must be used for the second corner. A series of lines must be drawn parallel to the straight side and another parallel with the curved side. A line (curved in this case, so it must be drawn freehand) will pass through the intersections and it meets the bisector of the first corner in the centre of the inscribed circle.

Figure 21.21 shows a pointed arch outline inscribed with a circle and two semi-circles. The semi-circles can be drawn quite easily; the difficulty is inscribing the circle just to touch the semi-circles and the arch outline. The centre line through the drawing will bisect the top corner. To bisect the corner set up by one of the semi-circles and the arch outline, two series of lines must be drawn — the first parallel to the arch outline and the second series parallel to the semi-circle. The intersections will give the bisecting line which, being curved, will have to be drawn freehand.

Figure 21.22 shows an approximate ellipse inscribed with a circle and two semi-circles. This drawing can be completed by following the steps explained for figure 21.21.

Figure 21.23 is another pointed arch outline, with two smaller pointed arches set on the base line. The centre of the inscribed circle can be found in a similar way to that used for figures 21.21 and 21.22.

Figure 21.24 shows a tracery design in its completed form.

TANGENTS TO CIRCLES

The construction of mouldings and other items involving straight and curved lines, often requires a knowledge of how to construct tangents to curves. It may be necessary to construct a tangent to pass between two circles of unequal radii and to point out the exact positions of the points of contact between the tangent and the circles. The next five drawings show how tangents to circles and their points of contact can be drawn.

Figure 21.25 shows how to draw a tangent to a circle starting from a point p. First draw the circle, any radius, and mark point p. Draw a line from p to o (the centre of the circle). Bisect p—o in a and describe the semi-circle. Point b is the point of contact between the circle and the tangent starting from p.

Figure 21.26 shows a tangent drawn to pass between two circles of equal radii. Draw the circles any distance apart and draw a line to connect the two centres o and o'. Bisect o—o' in a. Now bisect o—a and a—o' to give points b and c. With compass point in b describe the semi-circle with radius b—a; do the same with the compass point in c. These will give the points d and e which are the points of contact between the tangent and the two circles.

Figure 21.27 shows a tangent drawn across the tops of two unequal circles that are touching. Draw the circles with different radii so that they touch at point a. Connect the two centres with the line o—o'. Bisect o—o' in b. Then with compass point in b and radius b—o, describe the semi-circle o—c—o'. Draw a line from a perpendicular to o—o' to give point c on the semi-circle. Then with compass point in c and radius c—a, draw the semi-circle d—a—e. Points d and e are the points of contact between that tangent and the two circles.

In figure 21.28 a tangent has been drawn across two unequal circles that are not in contact. Draw the two circles any distance apart. Connect the two centres o and o', bisect this line in b and draw the semi-circle with radius b—o. From a mark off the radius of the smaller circle to give point c on o—o', with centre o and radius o—c draw the arc to give point d on the semi-circle. Draw a line from o through d to give point e at the top of the circle. Draw o'f parallel to o—e. Points e and f are the points of contact between the tangent and the two circles.

Figure 21.29 shows how to draw a tangent to pass between two circles of unequal radii. First draw the circles to any size and any distance apart. Draw a line to join the two centres o and o'. Bisect o—o' in b and draw the semi-circle. From a and towards o' mark off the radius of the larger circle to give c. With centre o and radius o—c, draw the arc to give point d on the semi-circle. Draw d—o', and then o'—e at right angles to d—o'. Point e is one of the points of contact. Then draw d—o giving point f, which is the other contact point.

Figure 21.30 shows how a moulding involving one of the problems on tangents is set out, and figure 21.31 is a drawing of a section through a plywood column.

In figure 21.32 there is a problem for the student to solve. It shows the shape of a templet for a job and the student is required to set out, to scale, the templet using the methods shown in figures 21.25, 21.27 and 21.28 to obtain its correct shape.

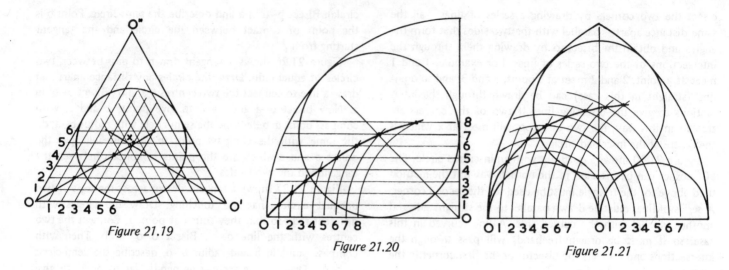

Figure 21.19

Figure 21.20

Figure 21.21

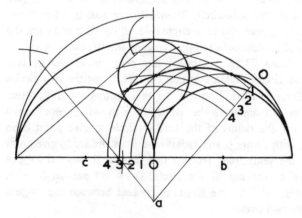

Figure 21.22

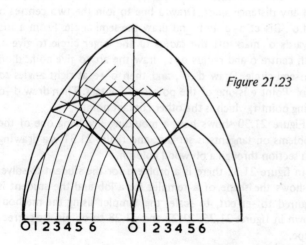

Figure 21.23

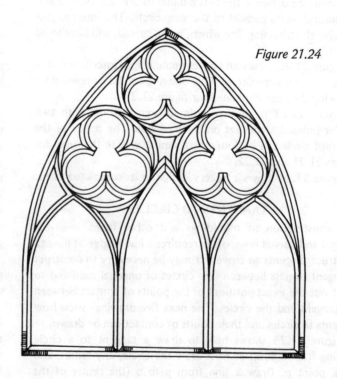

Figure 21.24

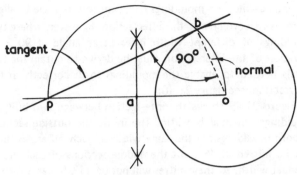

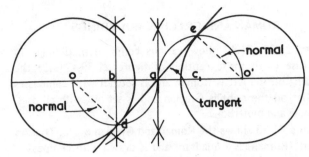

Figure 21.25

Figure 21.26

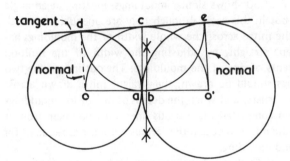

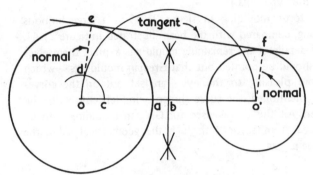

Figure 21.27

Figure 21.28

Figure 21.29

Figure 21.32

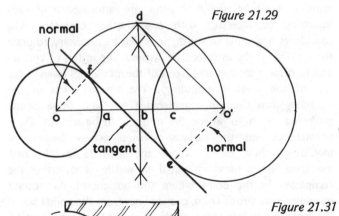

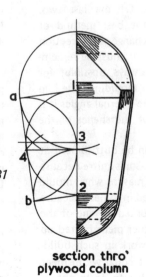

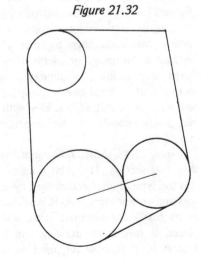

Figure 21.31

section thro' plywood column

Figure 21.30

ROMAN AND GRECIAN MOULDINGS

Figures 21.33—21.42 show various common mouldings. In each case (with the exception of figures 21.39—21.42) the moulding on the left is Roman and is set out with compasses and that on the right is Grecian and is set out with ellipses, parabolae and hyperbolae.

Figure 21.33 shows the Roman and Grecian ovolo. That on the left (Roman) is a quadrant and is drawn with compasses. The Grecian ovolo on the right is set out on a parabola.

Figure 21.34 shows the cavetto moulding, which is opposite in shape to the ovolo. (The Grecian cavetto, in this case, is set out on the hyperbola.)

The torus moulding in figure 21.35 is a large bulbous moulding, compared with the bead illustrated in figure 21.41.

The details of the remaining mouldings explain themselves but it should be pointed out that Grecian mouldings — which are more pleasing to the eye — are set out on the curves already mentioned, the curve chosen being left entirely to the designer. All the curves used for Grecian mouldings can be developed from sections through the geometrical solid, the cone, see p. 194.

INTERSECTIONS OF MOULDINGS

The drawings shown in figures 21.43—21.52, show how mouldings should correctly intersect with others. The inter-sections can be butt jointed (figure 21.43) mitred (figure 21.47) or scribed (figure 21.48). Of the last two, scribing is considered by many to be the best method of joining two mouldings together at a change of direction because of shrinkage problems. However, it must be remembered that scribing mouldings is not always possible; for example, at external angles set up by two mouldings, the join will have to be mitred, and even with some internal angles it is not always possible to scribe because of the shapes of the mouldings.

Figure 21.43 shows how mouldings can be butt jointed at their intersection. This joint is called a mason's mitre because it is the type of intersection used by stone masons when mould-ings are worked on stone. It is seldom used in joinery because of its cost — the complete mitre being worked on one of the pieces, as seen in the drawing, and the other piece butted up against it. It is, however, used on woodwork in such build-ings as churches. Where two mouldings of equal width meet at an angle of 90° (figure 21.44), all one has to do to obtain the correct mitre is to divide the 90° by two (figure 21.45),

the ends of the two mouldings being cut to this angle to allow them to fit correctly at the intersection. However, where two mouldings of different width meet at an angle of 90°, the elevation of the intersection must be drawn to obtain the two bevels needed to enable the mouldings to fit correctly at the intersection (see figure 21.46).

Figure 21.49 shows the intersection between two built-up mouldings, unequal in width. The inside and outside sections in both mouldings are the same width as each other, so these will be mitred at 45°, but the middle sections of each are of unequal width, so their mitres will not be 45°. In cases such as this the elevation of the intersection must be drawn carefully to obtain the correct mitres.

Figure 21.50 shows similar mouldings, meeting at an angle of 90°, but in this case, although they are unequal in over-all width, the mitre across the whole width of the mouldings has been kept straight, by adjusting the width of the built-up components of one of the mouldings. The outlines of the two mouldings should be drawn, the straight mitre drawn across the two corners, and when the details of one of the mouldings have been completed, the various lines must be taken from it over to the mitre to obtain the various dimensions required for the second moulding.

Figure 21.51 shows three intersections between straight and curved mouldings. At A is the mitre set up between a straight and a curved moulding. The mitre, as can be seen in the drawing, must be curved to allow the various parts of each moulding to intersect with one another correctly. The mouldings are equal in width, so it will be necessary to draw the outline of the intersection (without the mitre, of course) and to draw a section across one of the mouldings (seen at the top of the vertical moulding). The various parts of the moulding can then be numbered (1—6) and these points projected down to where the mitre is to be set out. On a normal set out the various distances across the second moulding — these being exactly the same as for the first moulding since they are equal in width — and, using the compasses in the point where the outline of the second moulding was struck from, project lines from the points across the moulding to intersect with those brought down the vertical moulding to obtain the shape of the mitre.

At B is seen the shape of the mitre when two curved mouldings meet. The radii of the curves are unequal, producing a curved mitre, but at C is seen the mitre set up between two curved mouldings of equal width, the radii of the curves are also equal; this will produce a straight mitre.

Figures 21.52 and 21.53 show the intersections between

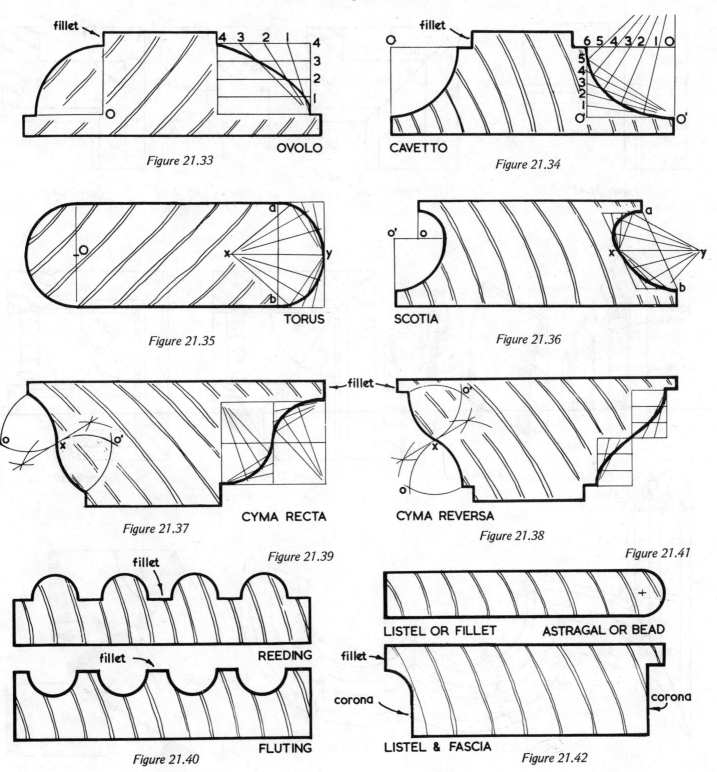

Figure 21.33 — OVOLO

Figure 21.34 — CAVETTO

Figure 21.35 — TORUS

Figure 21.36 — SCOTIA

Figure 21.37 — CYMA RECTA

Figure 21.38 — CYMA REVERSA

Figure 21.39

Figure 21.40 — REEDING / FLUTING

Figure 21.41 — LISTEL OR FILLET / ASTRAGAL OR BEAD

Figure 21.42 — LISTEL & FASCIA

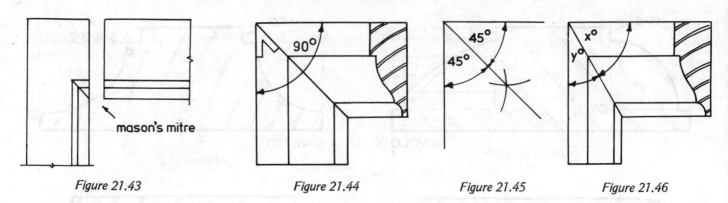

Figure 21.43   *Figure 21.44*   *Figure 21.45*   *Figure 21.46*

mason's mitre

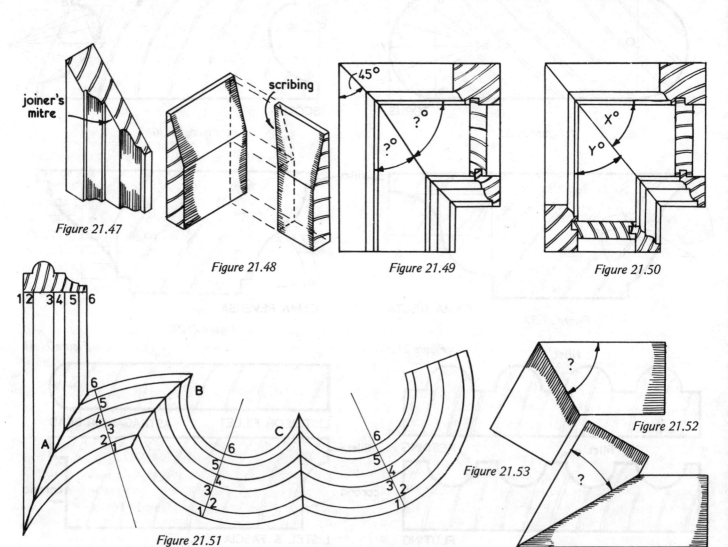

joiner's mitre   scribing

Figure 21.47   *Figure 21.48*   *Figure 21.49*   *Figure 21.50*

Figure 21.51   *Figure 21.52*   *Figure 21.53*

two straight mouldings, making an obtuse and an acute angle. Measure the mitres and insert the number of degrees in each case.

ENLARGING AND REDUCING MOULDINGS

Sometimes mouldings have to be reduced or enlarged in size, so that they can match other mouldings in the same room or building. Often these mouldings have to be reduced or enlarged in width only. In other cases their dimensions have to be changed in width and thickness or, again, they may have to be reduced proportionately in width and thickness. The common method used for these purposes is based on being able to divide a line into sections in the same proportions as another line. Take the line O—5 in figure 21.54 for instance. This line has been divided up into five parts, all unequal in length. Let us assume that the line O—5' is to be divided up into the same number of parts and each part is to be the same proportion as its opposite number in O—5. Draw O—5 and put in points 1 to 4 in any position. Then draw O—5' any length and join 5 to 5'. Then draw 4—4', 3—3', etc., all parallel to 5—5' to give the correct solution; O—5' is divided up in exactly the same way as O—5.

Now let us assume that the given moulding in figure 21.55 has to be reduced in width but the thickness is to remain the same in both mouldings. Draw the given moulding and mark off the various widths O—1—2—3, etc. Draw the back edge of the required moulding from 7 at any angle. Join O to O' and draw lines from all the other points, 1, 2, 3, etc., parallel to O—O' to give points 1', 2', 3', etc., on the back edge of the required moulding. Now draw lines downwards from various points on the given moulding to a line drawn out at right angles from 7 and with compass point in 7 project all these points round to a line brought out from 7 at right angles to O'—7. Project these points upwards, parallel to O'—7 to intersect with lines brought over at right angles to O'—7, from 1', 2', 3', etc., to give the various points on the required moulding.

Figure 21.56 shows how a moulding can be enlarged in width and thickness using the same method as in figure 21.55 but, of course, the thickness has to be treated in exactly the same way as the width. The method shown in figure 21.57 can be adopted for enlarging and reducing mouldings so that the thickness remains proportionately the same as the width.

Let abcd be a rectangle (figure 21.57) that has to be reduced so that a—d becomes a'—d' and the width a—b is reduced in size to the same proportion. Draw the rectangle abcd and, some distance away, the side a'—d' the length required. Draw a line from a to pass through a' and another line from d to pass through d', both lines meeting in o. Draw lines from c and b to meet in o. Draw a line from a' parallel to a—b to give b' on the line from b and another line from d' parallel to d—c to give point c' on the line from c. a'b'c'd' is the figure required.

Figure 21.58 shows a similar method used for reducing the figure abcde to one with a base line a—b', the other sides all being reduced in the same proportion. Figure 21.59 is another example of reducing a figure proportionately. abcde (figure 21.60) could be a simple moulding, which has to be reduced to one with a—e reduced to a'—e', all other dimensions being in the same proportion as the original. This, and the moulding in figure 21.61 can be treated in exactly the same way as the rectangle in figure 21.57. Figure 21.62 is a slight variation on that method.

SPECIAL CURVES

Although methods for setting out true and approximate ellipses were covered in volume 1, it is felt that further study should be devoted to this figure. Figure 21.63 shows a method used in the workshop and it is described, loosely, as the string-and-pin method. Once the lengths of the major and minor axes have been established, these are drawn and the positions of the focal points made on the major axis. To do this open the compass to half the length of the major axis, and from the top or bottom of the minor axis, mark off the two focal points on the major axis. If some sort of pin or nail is fixed in each of the focal points and another in the top of the minor axis (c) and a cord or thread tied firmly round these three points, as in the drawing, the pin at c removed and replaced with a pencil point, then by swinging to the left and right with the pencil point an ellipse can be drawn by keeping the thread taught.

Figure 21.64 shows how to draw parallel curves to a true ellipse. Remember that the true ellipse passes through points adbc, the other curves being lines running parallel to the ellipse — they are not ellipses.

Figure 21.65 shows a mechanical way of drawing a true ellipse. A base board, holding two grooved pieces of timber set at right angles to one another to represent the axes, should be constructed. A strip of wood, with two adjustable pins capable of running smoothly in the grooves on the base board, must also be made and the pins adjusted and secured to suit half the lengths of the major and minor axes of the ellipse

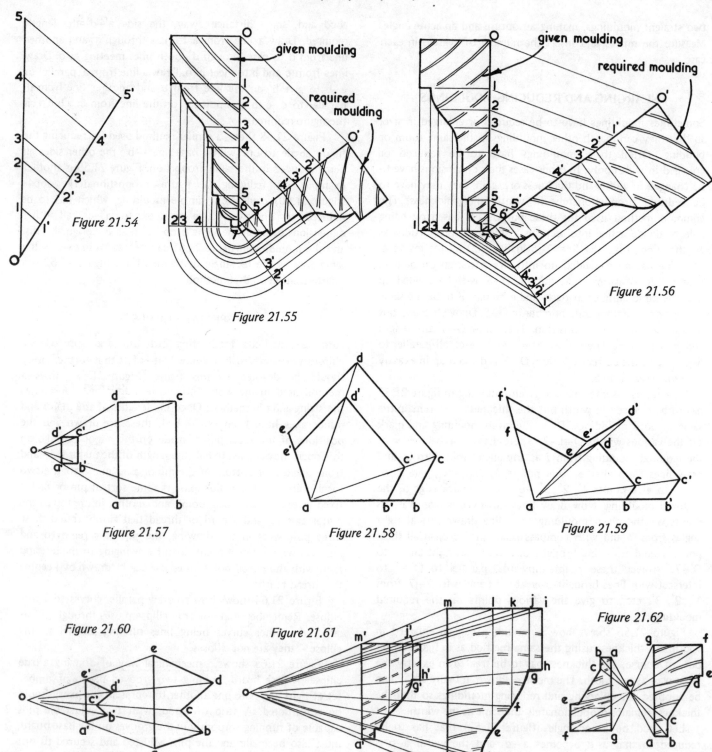

Figure 21.54

Figure 21.55

Figure 21.56

Figure 21.57

Figure 21.58

Figure 21.59

Figure 21.60

Figure 21.61

Figure 21.62

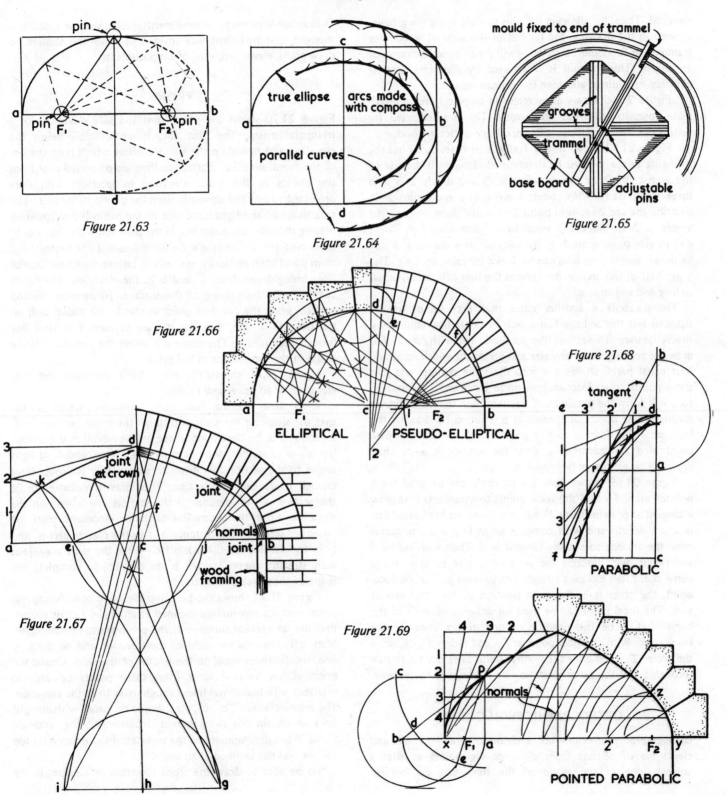

Figure 21.63

Figure 21.64

Figure 21.65

Figure 21.66

ELLIPTICAL   PSEUDO-ELLIPTICAL

Figure 21.68

Figure 21.67

PARABOLIC

Figure 21.69

POINTED PARABOLIC

required. Then, by allowing the pins to slide along the grooves as seen in the drawing, the far end of the strip of wood — or trammel, as it should be called — will pass round the curve of an ellipse. This method is often used by plasterers running elliptical mouldings, also seen in the drawing.

Figure 21.66 shows an exercise in elliptical and approximate (pseudo) elliptical arch work. The method used for setting out the true ellipse is the auxilliary-circles method.

Figure 21.67 shows how a Tudor arch is set out. First the springing line a—b must be determined along with the rise of the arch c—d. Draw the rectangle acd3 and divide a—3 into three equal parts. With compass point in a and radius a—2, describe the arc 2—e. Join point 2 to d and draw d—g at right angles to 2—d. Make d—f equal to a—e and draw e—f. Bisect e—f to give point g on d—g. By using centre e the arc a—k can be drawn and the arc k—d can be drawn by using centre g. The other half of the arch is the same as the first half, h—i is equal to h—g and c—j to c—e.

The parabola is another curve that may be of use to students but this and the Tudor arch curve are not required by the syllabuses. To set out the parabolic curve (figure 21.68) draw the rectangle cdef any size and divide the width into, say, four equal parts. Divide e—f into the same number and join these points to d. Intersections made by 1 and 1', 2 and 2', etc., will form the parabola. A freehand line should be drawn through these points. A tangent at p is found by drawing the horizontal line from p to give point a on c—d; with compass point in d and radius d—a, draw the semi-circle a—b. Then draw the tangent from b through p.

Figure 21.69 shows how the parabola can be used for a pointed arch. To find the focal points to a parabola first draw a tangent at p, as in figure 21.68; then draw the horizontal line p—c any length and with compass point in p and any radius draw the arc cde to cut the tangent in d. Then with centre d and radius d—c, describe the arc c—e to give point e on the curve cde. From e draw a straight line to meet p. F is one focal point, the other is in the same position at the other end of x—y. The focal point can be used for drawing normals to the curve. Let Z be the position of one of the joints in the stonework. With compass point in F_2 and radius F_2—z, draw the arc z—2'. Then draw the normal (joint line) from 2' to pass through z. All the other joints can be drawn in the same way.

ORTHOGRAPHIC PROJECTIONS

Orthographic projections are a means of drawing plans and elevations of objects from different viewpoints so that a correct idea of the shape of the item can be formed.

Orthographic projections were mentioned in volume 1, and it is thought that sufficient was covered to allow the student to draw plans, elevations, etc., of simple objects.

PRISMS

Figure 21.70 shows the plan, front and side elevations of a triangular prism. The plan abc, is immediately below the elevation and to obtain the side elevation, which is on the left of the front elevation, horizontal lines are projected over from the points in the front elevation to intersect with lines projected round and upwards from the points in the plan. The true shape of the right-hand side of the prism is developed by placing the compass point in c in the plan and with radius c—b, describing the arc to give x on the horizontal line brought out from c and then vertically upwards to intersect with horizontal lines brought out from c' and b in the elevation. The figure cc'b'b is the true shape of the surface. To develop the top surface, place the compass point in c and with radius c—b on the developed side, describe the arc to meet a vertical line brought up from b. The shape acb above the elevation, is the shape of the top surface of the prism.

Figure 21.71 shows the plan, front elevation and side elevation of an hexagonal prism.

After these drawings have been completed, let us assume that the shape of the section through the prism on line a"—d" is required to be developed. Place on the elevation the section line a"—d" and then draw lines from a", b", c" and d" at right angles to the section line down to where there is a space large enough to develop the section. Then draw the centre line of the section a"—d" parallel to the section line a"—d" on the elevation. From the centre line of the development, mark off on either side half the distance b—f in the plan to give b" and f" in the development. Mark off c"—e" in the same way. Join with straight lines a" to b", b" to c", etc., to complete the shape of the developed section.

Figure 21.72 shows the plan and elevation of an hexagonal prism with its top surface inclined at an angle. Let us assume that the six vertical surfaces of the prism are to be developed. Mark off, towards the right of the elevation and on the x—y line, six distances equal to the widths of the sides around the prism. Draw vertical lines from these points upwards to intersect with horizontal lines brought over from the elevation. The intersections a", b", c", etc., should be joined with straight lines to obtain the development. Incidentally, the rectangle a'a'aa is the development of the surfaces of the prism if its top surface was not inclined at an angle.

To be able to draw the front elevation of a prism, in the

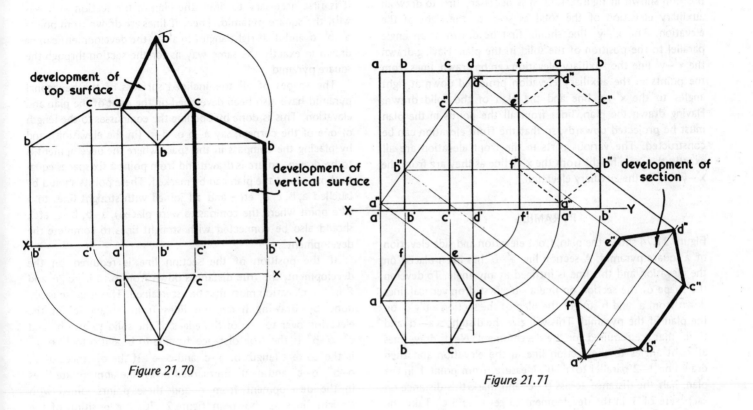

development of
top surface

development of
vertical surface

Figure 21.70

Figure 21.71

development of
section

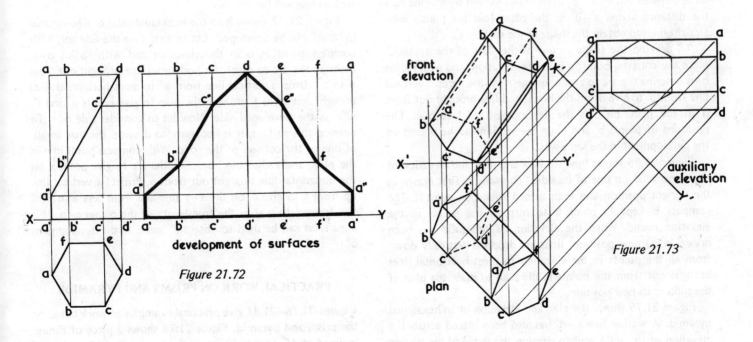

development of surfaces

Figure 21.72

front
elevation

plan

auxiliary
elevation

Figure 21.73

position shown in figure 21.73, it is necessary first to draw an auxiliary elevation of the solid as seen to the right of the elevation. The $x'-y'$ line should first be drawn at an angle parallel to the position of the solid in the plan. Having drawn the $x'-y'$ line the auxiliary elevation can be drawn, lines from the points in the auxiliary elevation projected down at right angles to the $x'-y'$ line and the plan of the solid drawn. Having drawn the plan, lines from all the points in the plan must be projected upwards, so that the front elevation can be constructed. The various parts in the front elevation are all exactly the same height from the $x-y$ line as they are from the $x'-y'$ line in the auxiliary elevation.

PYRAMIDS

Figure 21.74 shows the plan, front elevation and side elevation of a square pyramid. A section line $a'-b'$ has been placed on the elevation and this line is inclined at any angle. To develop the shape of the section on line $a'-b'$, first drop vertical lines down from a' and b' to get the plan of the section $a'b'c'd'$ on the plan of the pyramid. This will give the distances $a'-d'$ and $b'-c'$ that are required for the development. Next, draw lines at right angles to the section line in the elevation and then draw line 1–2 parallel to $a'-b'$. Measure, from point 1 in the plan, half the distance across $b'-c'$ and mark this distance on each side of 1 in the development to get b' and c'. Take the same steps to obtain $a'-d'$ in the development by making half the distance across $a'-d'$ in the plan. Join the points with straight lines to obtain the shape of the section $a'b'c'd'$.

To develop the shape of one of the sides of the pyramid, place the compass point in b in the elevation, and with radius $b-o$ describe the arc to give o' on the $x-y$ line. Drop a vertical line from o' to give o'' on the horizontal line brought out from o in the plan. $bo''c$ is the development of side boc. The positions of points b' and c' on the section can be placed on the development in the same way.

Figure 21.75 shows how to draw the plan and elevation of the same solid on one of its sides. The solid is first drawn in the upright position and then turned round on point b. The compass is kept in point b to turn all the points in the elevation round. When the elevation of the solid has been drawn in its new position, lines are dropped vertically down from all the points in the elevation to meet horizontal lines brought out from the points in the plan to draw the plan of the solid in its new position.

Figure 21.76 shows the plan and elevation of an hexagonal pyramid. A section line $a'-d'$ has also been placed across the elevation of the solid, and to develop the shape of the section

it is first necessary to draw the plan of the section as it was with the square pyramid. Then, if lines are drawn from points a', b', c' and d' at right angles to $a'-d'$ the development can be drawn in exactly the same way as for the section through the square pyramid.

The shapes of all the inclined surfaces of the hexagonal pyramid have also been developed on the right of the plan and elevation. This is done by opening the compasses to the length of one of the corners, say $a-o$ or $d-o$ (in the elevation), and by placing the compass in the space where the development is to be drawn, an arc is drawn and from point a six spaces equal to those round the plan can be marked. These points should be labelled a, b, c, d, etc., and all joined with straight lines to o (the point where the compasses were placed). a–b, b–c, etc., should also be connected with straight lines to complete the development.

If the position of the section line is required on the development, the true distances down from o to b', c', e' and f' in the elevation must first be ascertained. This is quite easily done by drawing horizontal lines from b' and c' in the elevation over to one of the edges of the solid to give b'' and c''. $o-b''$ is the true distance from o to b' and o to f'. $o-c''$ is the correct length of $o-c'$ and $o-e'$. If the distances $o-a'$, $o-b''$, $o-c''$ and $o-d'$ are marked down the appropriate lines in the development from o and these points joined with straight lines as shown in figure 21.76, the position of the section line will be obtained.

Figure 21.77 shows how the individual sides of a hexagonal pyramid can be developed. Let us first take the side aof. With compass point in o in the elevation and with radius $o-a$, describe the arc to meet the horizontal line brought out from o in a''. Drop a vertical line from a'' to meet horizontal lines brought out from f and a in the plan to give points a' and f'. $of'a'$ is the developed side. Now let us consider side ode. To develop this surface, it is necessary to develop the true length of one of the corners of the solid. With compass point in o in the plan, and radius $o-c$, describe the arc to give point x on the horizontal line brought out from o. Project a vertical line up from x to give c' on the $x-y$ line and from here a straight line from c' to o gives the true length of the corner $c-o$. This dimension can be used to obtain d' and e' in the development of $o-d-e$.

PRACTICAL WORK ON PRISMS AND PYRAMIDS

Figures 21.78–21.81 give practical examples of work based on the prism and pyramid. Figure 21.78 shows a piece of timber inclined at 45°, cut to fit round the corner of another piece of

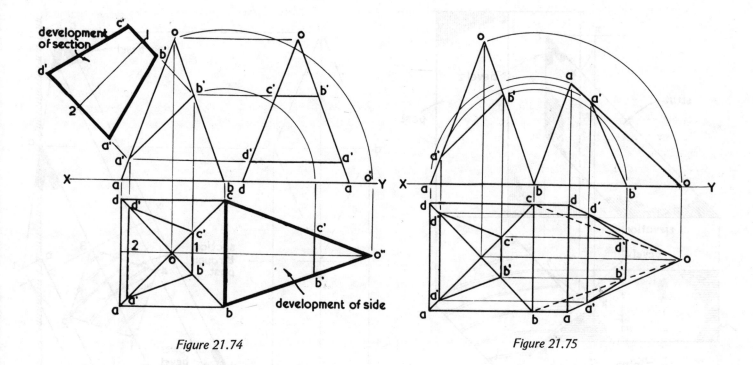

Figure 21.74

Figure 21.75

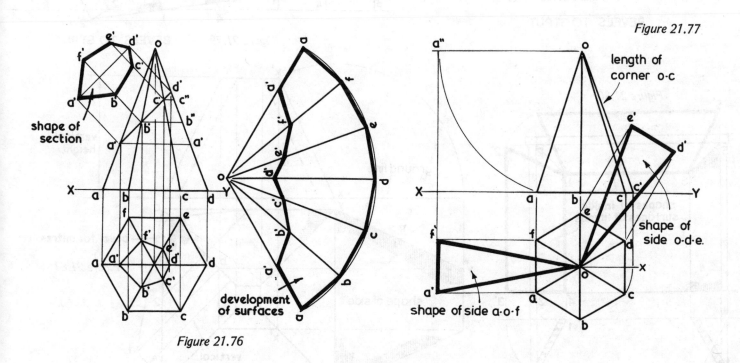

Figure 21.76

Figure 21.77

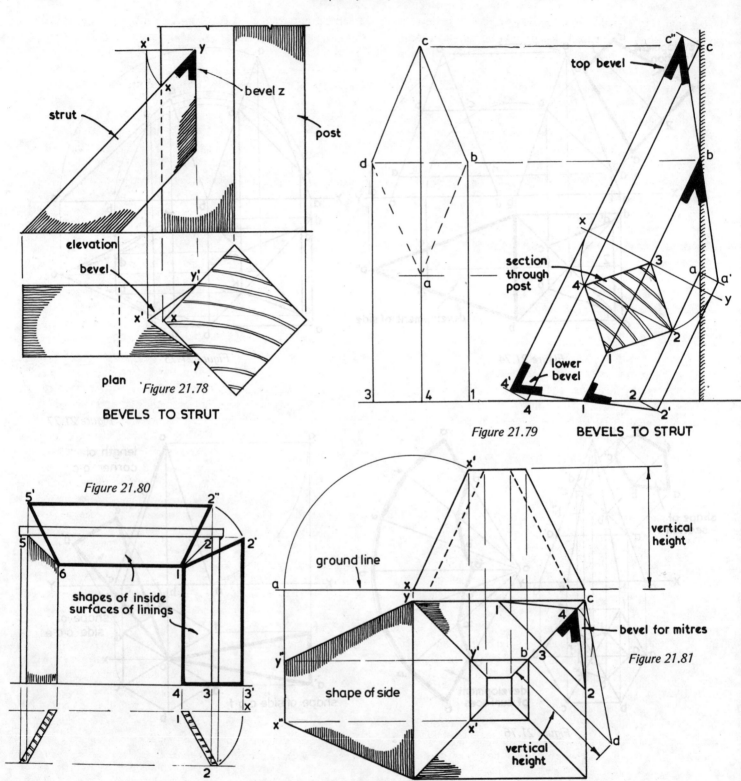

strut

bevel z

post

elevation

bevel

plan   *Figure 21.78*

BEVELS TO STRUT

top bevel

section through post

lower bevel

Figure 21.79   **BEVELS TO STRUT**

Figure 21.80

shapes of inside surfaces of linings

vertical height

ground line

shape of side

vertical height

bevel for mitres

Figure 21.81

timber that is in a vertical position. The problem is to develop the top surface of the inclined piece so that the bevels to apply to it will enable the piece to be cut to fit perfectly round the corner of the second piece.

Draw the plan and elevation and then with compass point in y in the elevation and radius y—x, describe the arc to give x′ on the horizontal line from y. Drop a vertical line from x′ to give point x′ on the horizontal line brought out from x in the plan. yx′y′ is the shape of the vee cut to be made in the top end of the inclined piece and the bevel z is the bevel to apply to the front and back surfaces of the piece after marking out the vee cut.

Figure 21.79 shows a square piece of timber cut to fit up against horizontal and vertical flat surfaces. To enable the student to picture the true position of the inclined piece accurately in his mind, a side elevation has also been included. (Ordinarily this would not be necessary for the development that has to be done.) A plan is not always necessary for these developments, since all that is required in this problem is the development of two of the surfaces of the inclined piece of timber; a section through the piece 1234 is drawn with the line 4—2 at right angles to the inclination of the piece. Project points 1, 2 and 4 up and down to the vertical and horizontal surfaces and then develop the two surfaces seen in the elevation. Draw a line through point 3 at right angles to the inclination and with compass point in 3 and open 3—4 and 3—2, describe arcs to give points x and y. Draw lines through x and y parallel to the inclination to give c″, a′, 2′ and 4′ to obtain the bevels required.

Figure 21.80 shows how the shapes of some splayed linings round a door or window opening can be developed. This problem, and that seen in Figure 21.81, is based on the pyramid. Draw the plan and elevation of the splayed linings and with compass point in 1 in the plan and radius 1—2, describe the arc to give x on the horizontal line from 1. Draw a vertical line upwards from x to give point 2′ on the horizontal line brought out from point 2. The shape 12′3′4 is the shape of the two side linings. The top lining shape can be found by placing the compass in point 1 and with radius 1—2′ describe the arc to give point 2″ on the vertical line brought up from 2. Draw a line from 2″ parallel to 2—5 to give point 5′ on the vertical line brought up from 5. 12″5′6, is the shape of the top or head lining.

Figure 21.81 is the plan and elevation of a box with its sides inclined at any angle. To develop the shape of one side, place the compass in point x in the elevation and with radius x—x′ describe the arc to give point a on the ground line. Drop

a vertical line from a to give points x″ and y″ on horizontal lines brought out from x and y. Let us assume that the corners are to be mitred. It is necessary to develop the mitre bevel in a similar way to developing the dihedral or backing bevel to a hip rafter in a roof (see chapter 8). Draw the line 1—2 across one of the corners of the plan and from b and at right angles to the corner b—c, draw the line b—d, making its length equal to the vertical height of the box. Then join c to d. With compass in point 3 and open just to touch the line c—d, describe the arc to give point 4 on c—b. Join 1 to 4 and 2 to 4. Angle 142 is the dihedral angle and the mitre bevel, 342, is half of the dihedral angle.

CYLINDERS

Figure 21.82 shows the plan and elevation of a cylinder. Since this solid has no corners, it is necessary to place vertical lines around its surface to enable us to develop its surface and sections. A section line a″—g″ has been placed across the elevation at any angle and lines are drawn from the various points on this line, a″, b″, c″, etc., at right angles to the section line, down (or up) to where the development of the section is to be drawn. The distances across the section b″—1″, c″—k″, etc., must be equal to the distances b—1, c—k, etc., in the plan. If half these distances are taken from the plan and marked on each side of the centre line in the development, the points b″, c″, d″, etc., are obtained, so that a freehand curve can be drawn giving the shape of the section. The shape is elliptical. The development of the surface of the cylinder is found by stepping off twelve distances along the x—y line equal to those around the plan and drawing the rectangle a′a′aa to obtain the development. If the section line is required on the surface development, horizontal lines from points a″, b″, etc., in the elevation to intersect with appropriate lines in the surface development will give a″, b″, c″, etc., through which a freehand curve can be drawn.

Figure 21.83 shows how to draw the plan of a cylinder that has an elevation showing it inclined at any angle.

Figure 21.84 shows how a portion of a cylinder can be drawn in plan and elevation as well as an auxiliary plan and an auxiliary elevation. The auxiliary elevation is drawn by first deciding the angle of sight of the object, drawing lines from all the points in the plan parallel to the sight line, and then drawing the x′—y′ line at right angles to the sight direction. The distances the various points are in the elevation above the x—y line are measured with compasses or dividers and these distances are transferred to the auxiliary elevation, the

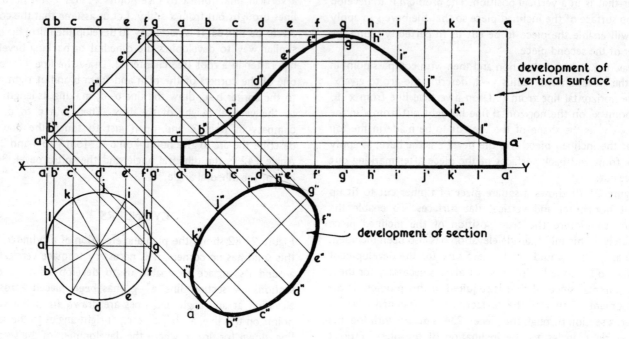

development of vertical surface

development of section

Figure 21.82

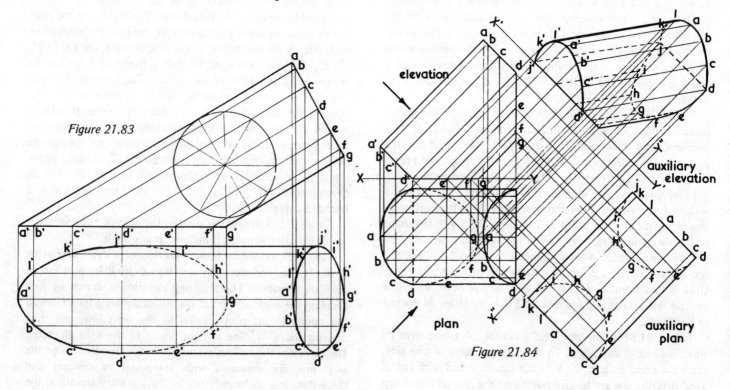

Figure 21.83

elevation

auxiliary elevation

auxiliary plan

plan

Figure 21.84

points in this drawing being exactly the same distances from the x'–y' line as they are from the x–y line in the elevation. Care must, of course, be taken to ensure that the distances are marked on the correct lines in the new drawing. The auxiliary plan is constructed in a similar manner. The angle of sight must be decided on, the lines from the points in the elevation drawn parallel to the sight direction, and the x"–y" line drawn at right angles to these lines. The points in the auxiliary plan are exactly the same distance away from the x"–y" line as they are from the x–y line in the plan.

CONES

Figure 21.85 shows the plan and elevation of a cone. In addition to the circle, there are three other important sections that can be obtained from the cone. The first of these is shown in figure 21.85 and is the ellipse. If a section line is drawn across a cone so that it cuts both sides of the figure and the section is developed, it will be found to be an ellipse. Lines, similar to the cylinder, have to be placed on the surface of the cone to assist in the developments. Draw the section line 1'7' and project the points 1', 2', 3', etc., on the plan. Now draw lines from 1', 2', 3', etc., in the elevation, at right angles to the section line and draw the centre line 1'–7' of the development. Using the centre line as for the pyramid and cylinder, make the distances 2'–12', 3'–11', etc., in the development equal to the same distances in the plan of the section. A freehand curve through these points will give the shape of the section – it is an ellipse.

Figure 21.86 shows two more sections. The section that is parallel to one of the edges of the elevation is parabolic in shape. The plan of the section is constructed in a similar way to the previous section. The distances across the development must be the same as those in the plan of the section. Half those distances must be measured from the plan and marked on each side of the centre line in the development.

The next curve to consider is the hyperbola (figure 21.86). This is a section through the cone that is parallel to its axis. The plan of the section appears as a line in the plan (d–e) and also as a line (in this case) in the elevation (d–7"). Project the points d, 5", 6", 7", 8", 9", and e, in the plan, horizontally over to where the section is to be developed. Draw d–e in the development parallel to the section line in the plan. Make d–x, d–y and d–7" equal to those distances in the elevation and draw lines through these points to give 5", 6", 8" and 9" in the development. Draw a freehand curve through these points to obtain the shape of the section.

Figure 21.87 shows how to develop the surface of a cone.

With compass point in O and radius O–1 in the elevation, (this is the length of all the lines round the surface of the solid) draw the arc and step off along the curve twelve spaces equal to those round the plan, to give points 1, 2, 3, etc. Join all these points to O to obtain the development of the cone's surface. If the section line in figure 21.85, say, is required to be placed on the surface development it is first necessary to obtain the correct distances that points 2', 3', 4', etc., on the section line, are from point O. To do this, horizontal lines must be drawn from these points across to one of the edges of the elevation to give 2", 3", 4", etc. When marking, say, the point 2' on the development measure the distance O–2" on the side of the elevation and with compass point in O, in the development, mark the point 2' on line O–2. If all the points are treated in a similar manner, the points 3', 4', 5', etc., will be obtained and a freehand curve should then be made to pass through them all.

PRACTICAL WORK ON CYLINDERS AND CONES

Figures 21.88–21.91 give practical examples of work based on the cylinder and cone. Figure 21.88 shows how to develop the soffit or lagging for a centre to an oblique semi-circular arch in a wall. The semi-circular elevation should be divided up into twelve equal parts and the points projected down to give two sets of points in the plan. A horizontal line should be drawn below the plan and from point 7 (the centre line) six distances should be marked off on each side of the centre line equal to those round the elevation. The distance 1–13 on the horizontal line is the distance round the semi-circle in the elevation. Project vertical lines upwards from these points to intersect with horizontal lines brought from the two sets of points in the plan to give 1–1', 2–2', 3–3', etc. Freehand curves are drawn through these two sets of points to give the shape of the soffit or lagging.

If an elevation of the arch, looking in the direction of the arrow, is required, project lines from all the points in the plan of the opening, parallel to the direction of the arrow and in the position required, draw the base line to the auxiliary elevation 1–13. Make the points 2, 3, 4, etc., on the auxiliary elevation exactly the same distance from the base line as they are in the elevation to obtain the drawing required.

Figure 21.89 shows a circular duct passing through a wall or partition, the problem being to develop the shape of the hole in the wall and also the surface of the section of the duct that passes through the wall. If the hole in the wall is to have a clearance between itself and the duct, this must be shown on the drawing, hence the two sections shown in the centre of the

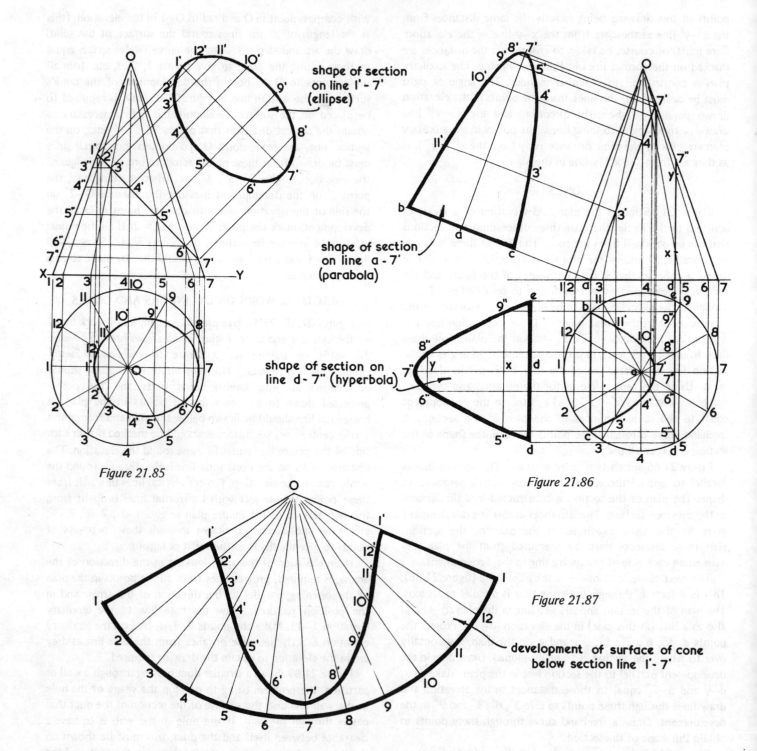

shape of section
on line 1'- 7'
(ellipse)

shape of section
on line a - 7'
(parabola)

shape of section on
line d - 7" (hyperbola)

Figure 21.85

Figure 21.86

Figure 21.87

development of surface of cone
below section line 1'- 7'

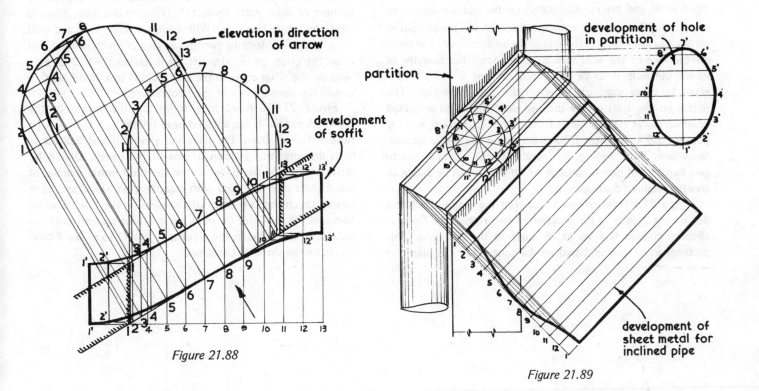

Figure 21.88

elevation in direction of arrow

development of soffit

development of hole in partition

partition

development of sheet metal for inclined pipe

Figure 21.89

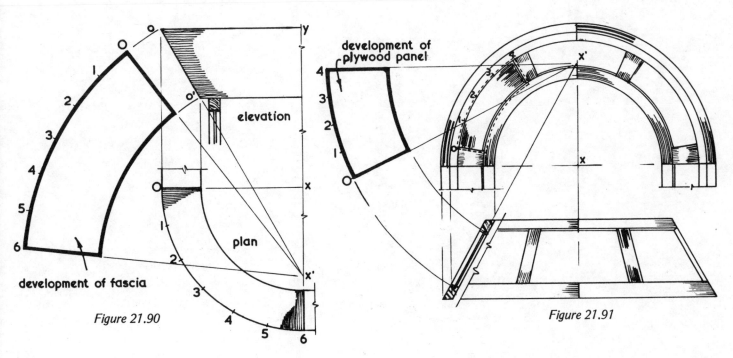

development of fascia

elevation

plan

Figure 21.90

development of plywood panel

Figure 21.91

inclined section. Divide the two sections into, say, twelve equal parts and project the points on the outside section to one of the faces of the wall, and those on the inside section through to both ends of the section to be developed. The points on the face of the wall should be projected horizontally to where the hole is to be developed, making 2'–12', 3'–11' equal to those same distances on the outside section. The points on the ends of the inclined duct should be projected downwards, at right angles to the duct's inclination, making points 1,2,3,4, etc., equal to those round the inside section. Draw lines from these points parallel to the inclined duct to give two sets of points through which curves can be drawn to give the required development.

Figure 21.90 shows how to develop the shape of a fascia board over a shop at the junction of two roads. The fascia is circular in plan and set at an angle in the elevation. This problem is, of course, based on the cone. Draw the plan and elevation and then divide the outside edge of the plan into a number of equal parts. Project O–O' in the elevation, down to meet the centre line in x'. With compass point in x' and radii x'–o' and x'–o describe two arcs as seen in the drawing. From o on the outer curve, step off the distances O–1–2–3, etc., seen on the outer curve in the plan. Join O to x' and 6 to x' to obtain the development of the fascia board.

Figure 21.91 shows how to obtain the shapes of the plywood panels in the splayed head linings to a semi-circular headed frame. Draw the plan and elevation and indicate in both drawings the position of one of the panels. Divide the outside edges of the panel in the elevation into a number of equal parts, say four, and with compass point in x' and open just to touch the two edges of the panel in the plan, describe two arcs. Then, from O, mark off the four spaces round the outside of the panel in the elevation. Join O to x' and 4 to x' to obtain the shape of the panel.